JOE KINNAIRD

SECONDARY RELIGIOUS EDUCATION IN ACTION

IN ACTION SERIES

A **WALKTHRUs** PRODUCTION

Together we unlock every learner's unique potential

At Hachette Learning (formerly Hodder Education), there's one thing we're certain about. No two students learn the same way. That's why our approach to teaching begins by recognising the needs of individuals first.

Our mission is to allow every learner to fulfil their unique potential by empowering those who teach them. From our expert teaching and learning resources to our digital educational tools that make learning easier and more accessible for all, we provide solutions designed to maximise the impact of learning for every teacher, parent and student.

Aligned to our parent company, Hachette Livre, founded in 1826, we pride ourselves on being a learning solutions provider with a global footprint.

www.hachettelearning.com

Although every effort has been made to ensure that website addresses are correct at time of going to press, Hachette Learning cannot be held responsible for the content of any website mentioned in this book. It is sometimes possible to find a relocated web page by typing in the address of the home page for a website in the URL window of your browser.

Hachette UK's policy is to use papers that are natural, renewable and recyclable products and made from wood grown in well-managed forests and other controlled sources. The logging and manufacturing processes are expected to conform to the environmental regulations of the country of origin.

To order, please visit www.HachetteLearning.com or contact Customer Service at education@hachette.co.uk / +44 (0)1235 827827.

ISBN: 978 1 9152 6191 5

© Joe Kinnaird 2026

First published in 2026 by
Hachette Learning (a trading division of Hodder & Stoughton Limited),
An Hachette UK Company
Carmelite House
50 Victoria Embankment
London EC4Y 0DZ
www.HachetteLearning.com

The authorised representative in the EEA is Hachette Ireland, 8 Castlecourt Centre, Dublin 15, D15 XTP3, Ireland (email: info@hbgi.ie)

Impression number   10 9 8 7 6 5 4 3 2 1
Year   2030 2029 2028 2027 2026

All rights reserved. Apart from any use permitted under UK copyright law, no part of this publication may be reproduced or transmitted in any form or by any means, electronic or mechanical, including photocopying and recording, or held within any information storage and retrieval system, without permission in writing from the publisher or under licence from the Copyright Licensing Agency Limited. Further details of such licences (for reprographic reproduction) may be obtained from the Copyright Licensing Agency Limited, www.cla.co.uk

Typeset in the UK.
Printed in the UK.
A catalogue record for this title is available from the British Library.
Illustrations by DC Graphic Design Limited, Hextable, Kent.

For my Mum

ABOUT THE AUTHOR

Joe Kinnaird is head of religious education at a secondary school in east London. He has a decade of experience teaching RE in the classroom and working alongside specialist teachers on curriculum, pedagogy and assessment. Beyond the classroom, he currently serves as a member of the National Association of Teachers of Religious Education (NATRE) Executive. A regular speaker at local and national RE conferences, Joe also works with ITT providers, leading training sessions to support the development of RE trainees.

ACKNOWLEDGEMENTS

I would like to thank the RE subject community for their inspiration, guidance and support in writing this book. I have learned so much from RE CPD events and conversations with so many of you about the subject, all of which have helped me develop as an RE teacher.

Thank you to my guest contributors who generously offered to share their expertise in the book: Arabella Saunders, Charlotte Newman, Nikki McGee, Alice Thomas, Karen Steele, Rachael Jackson-Royal and Zainab Ali.

I would also like to thank my school, department and colleagues for their ongoing support. In particular, thank you to Daniel and Rachel, who have encouraged me to explore professional opportunities and whose passion for RE has inspired me since I joined the school as an NQT.

Finally, thank you to my family and friends for their constant encouragement, motivation and sense of humour, which have helped me throughout the process of writing the book.

This book is a reflection of everything I have learned as an RE teacher over the past 10 years. I hope you find it a useful and enjoyable read.

CONTENTS

About the author _____ iv

Acknowledgements _____ v

Series foreword by Tom Sherrington _____ viii

Chapter 1 What is the subject about? _____ 1

Chapter 2 What are the challenges, debates and perspectives in RE? _____ 8

Chapter 3 What does the research tell us about teaching RE? _____ 19

Chapter 4 What are the different types of knowledge and concepts in RE? _____ 36

Chapter 5 How can you structure an RE curriculum? _____ 53

Chapter 6 How can I explain and model in RE? _____ 83

Chapter 7 What does questioning look like in RE? _____ 97

Chapter 8 What does writing look like in RE? _____ 110

Chapter 9 What does assessment look like in RE? _____ 124

Chapter 10 What does feedback look like in RE? _____ 150

Chapter 11 How can I use texts and scholarship in RE? _____ 164

Chapter 12 How can I teach controversial topics and sensitive topics in RE? _____ 185

Chapter 13 How can I promote RE beyond the classroom? _____ 199

Bibliography _____ 218

Supplementary resources for this title can be accessed here:
www.hachettelearning.com/john-catt-archive/john-catt-extras

SERIES FOREWORD

This series of books was commissioned as a WalkThrus Production to complement two of our other series: The *Teaching Walkthrus*, Volumes 1, 2 and 3, and the *In Action* series. We believe that, together, they represent a powerful resource for teachers in schools and colleges in multiple subject settings.

The *In Action* series has proven to be very popular with busy teachers, enabling them to engage with a range of important ideas from cognitive science and from education research more generally. In each book, the authors explore the key ideas from a specific researcher, translating them into practical approaches that teachers can adopt in their practice. So far, the series includes:

- Rosenshine's Principles of Instruction
- Collins et al's Cognitive Apprenticeship
- Fiorella & Mayer's Generative Learning
- Shimamura's MARGE Model of Learning
- Sweller's Cognitive Load Theory
- Wiliam & Leahy's Five Formative Assessment Strategies
- Annie Murphy Paul's The Extended Mind
- Dunlosky's Strengthening the Student Toolbox
- Berger's An Ethic of Excellence
- Bjork & Bjork's Desirable Difficulties
- Ausubel's Meaningful Learning
- Nuthall's Hidden Lives of Learners
- Bandura's Self-Efficacy Theory

Each of these books is a guide to interpreting the research in ways that can be applied in real-world classrooms. We have been delighted by the response to the series, with teachers telling us they value the brevity and clarity and the examples of theory in practice. It's so important for teachers to have a good grounding in cognitive science so that they have not only a clear model of how learning happens but also an understanding of all the potential barriers or difficulties that students experience.

Bridging the gap between research and practice is a significant challenge because real-world classrooms are so much more complicated than the controlled conditions usually set up to investigate specific concepts in trials. The authors of the *In Action* books are all serving teachers or have taught in schools for many years, so their take on the theories and concepts that their books focus on is important and incredibly useful, grounded in the reality of teaching whole, complex classes.

It's by no means a comprehensive list – not yet – and we recognise that many other aspects of research would benefit from the same treatment. A book on Engelmann's ideas on direct instruction is in the pipeline. We would also encourage every teacher to engage with Dan Willingham's *Why Don't Students Like School?*

Released in parallel with the research-informed *In Action* series, our *Teaching WalkThrus* have also been popular with over 350,000 copies distributed across the three volumes. The idea of breaking ideas down into five-step visual guides, with short punchy descriptions, has proven very successful, allowing teachers to engage with a broad range of ideas in a very accessible format that informs their training, coaching or personal reflection. Significantly, *Teaching WalkThrus* were written in a style that is context free. They are generic in style so that teachers of all subjects in any setting can engage with them, transposing the ideas into their real-world contexts. The 150+ WalkThrus are organised into six main series, each of which represents an important area for professional learning:

Behaviour and relationships
- Lesson management
- Planning for good behaviour
- Positive correction
- Relationships and mindsets

Curriculum planning
- Assessment issues
- Broad design concepts
- Challenge, inclusion, diversity
- Detailed planning

Explaining and modelling
- Giving explanations and modelling
- Reading and writing
- Standards, expectations and scaffolding
- Types of explanations

Questioning and feedback
- Assessment
- Core questioning techniques
- Deeper questioning techniques
- Feedback

Practice and retrieval
- Guided to independent practice
- Reading
- Building fluency
- Retrieval practice
- Support and challenge

Mode B teaching
- Choices and creativity
- Making it real
- Oracy
- Student directed activities

With over 4000 schools having engaged with our online WalkThrus toolkit, we know that a great deal of valuable professional learning can be supported with our generic guides as a starting point. However, throughout each book we are at pains to stress the crucial need to adapt the ideas for specific circumstances. A five-step visual WalkThrus guide is not a set of rigid rules – it is a framework for thinking through an idea, deconstructing it so that teachers can then reconstruct it themselves, forming their own mental models for enacting powerful techniques in their own classrooms. That's the spirit.

Now, having explored research ideas in the *In Action* series and general pedagogical ideas in WalkThrus, we felt that the logical next step was to bring in subject-specific books in this new series, completing the third pillar of the trio: research, pedagogy, curriculum. Each book in the *In Action* subject series has been written by practising teachers who were tasked with presenting a summary of important ideas and debates from their subject to support busy teachers in their work. We have not imposed a rigid common format and our authors were encouraged to share their own perspectives with our readers. There is no definitive book on teaching science or history or maths or physical education – so these books are explicitly written with that in mind. The books represent the authors' personal perspective on how the ideas that circulate within each subject community can translate into great practice in the classroom. Once again, we invite readers to then adapt and adopt the ideas that make sense in their context.

I have to congratulate each author on their excellent work. It's daunting to summarise and capture the spirit of a subject, balancing depth of detail with sufficient breadth of coverage of content and related debates and implementation issues – all in what is meant to be a short book. If there is one thing that characterises all our books it is that they are accessible to teachers who are time poor. Each book in this series achieves that goal – they have an energy to them and a brilliant balance of rigour, steeped in experience with teaching the subject, alongside tons of examples to bring things to life.

We hope you find this book interesting and useful, adding an important dimension to your wider reading as a teacher doing the most important work there is: developing young people so that they have the knowledge, experience, confidence and wisdom they need to make sense of their world and play their part in the communities they belong to.

CHAPTER 1
WHAT IS THE SUBJECT ABOUT?

Introduction

This book is aimed at all RE teachers in all RE contexts. It provides an overview of the religious education landscape and the latest curriculum developments, with evidence-informed practice and practical strategies for use in the RE classroom. I hope it will appeal to those who are new to the profession as well as those who have been in the RE classroom for some time but would like to keep developing their practice and stay informed about current changes in the subject. I also want the book to be helpful to those teachers who are not subject specialists but have been given an allocation of RE on their timetable.

Why does the subject matter?

The academic study of religion is an essential part of every child's education. Religion has been one of the central tenets of the human experience. All societies, past and present, have shared a set of beliefs and assumptions – a faith, a religion, a worldview – that provides a framework of how to understand and interact with the world. Religion provides the human being with a sense of meaning, purpose and value in the world. To study religion is to study what it means to be human.

Great RE is academically rigorous. The subject provides students with a critical lens to understand what it means to be human. RE gives a framework for helping students to unpick the core beliefs and practices involved in a religious life. It provides students with the opportunity to grapple with the ultimate questions of life and death: How did the universe begin? What is right and wrong? Why do evil and suffering exist? Our answers to these questions shape the way in which we see the world. The RE classroom enables students to examine how people of the past addressed these questions and how those alive today continue to wrestle with them. Great RE not only encourages intellectual curiosity but also develops critical thinking and respectful dialogue skills. It challenges students to analyse diverse perspectives thoughtfully and engage constructively with complex and sometimes conflicting beliefs.

In a broader sense, RE allows students to explore the existence of religion alongside economic, political and social institutions, and the impact of religion on history, arts, language and literature. The study of religion allows us to see life through a richer, more nuanced and wider lens. In addition, studying religion illuminates its role in contemporary global issues, from debates on social justice and environmental ethics to the interaction between science and belief systems. This real-world relevance helps students connect classroom learning to the challenges and conversations shaping our world today.

RE is personally significant, as students learn more about themselves through the study of the subject. As they study RE, they form and build their 'personal knowledge', which is their perspective of the world. This personal knowledge is influenced by many things, such as their own sense of identity, values and prior experiences. RE allows students to become more aware of the assumptions they hold and bring to discussions on religious and non-religious traditions.

RE allows students to enter the conversation about the religious and non-religious traditions that have shaped this country, the world and the human experience. It is an intellectually stimulating and personally enriching subject that offers students the opportunity to see religion and non-religion in the world, and make sense of their own place within it. In summary, RE prepares students to be thoughtful, compassionate citizens in a diverse world.

A brief history of the subject

Every student, parent, teacher and school leader makes assumptions about the nature, purpose and value of RE. An overview of the history of the subject is vital to help all understand why the subject is where it is today and how it got there.

Below is a brief history of developments in RE.

1944–c.1960   The subject, then known as *religious instruction* (RI), was closely linked to collective worship and rooted in Christian values. All pupils were required to receive RI according to a locally agreed syllabus, overseen by the local authority and supported by Standing Advisory Councils for Religious Education (SACREs). Parents had the right to withdraw their children, and teachers could refuse to teach the subject.

c.1960–c.1970 ↓	As society became increasingly secular and pluralist, concerns grew about the relevance of religious instruction. Research suggested pupils struggled with religious concepts and showed limited engagement, leading agreed syllabuses to focus more on relevance and shared experience, although content remained predominantly Christian.
c.1970–1988 ↓	RE expanded to include world religions and humanism, with phenomenology shaping teaching approaches. Religions were studied as lived traditions rather than confessional truths, reflecting Britain's multicultural context and promoting understanding and respect for others' beliefs.
1988–2004 ↓	The Education Reform Act 1988 formally renamed the subject *religious education* (RE) and placed it within the basic curriculum of all maintained schools. RE was required to reflect the mainly Christian traditions of the UK while also including other principal religions. Each school followed its locally agreed syllabus, determined by the local education authority working alongside the SACRE. Parents retained the right to withdraw their children from religious education, and faith schools retained their right to faith-based teaching.
2004–2015 ↓	The Non-Statutory National Framework for RE (2004) ensured that every pupil in a maintained school had a statutory entitlement to religious education and supported those responsible for its provision. Academies and free schools were not required to follow their locally agreed syllabus but still had to meet their statutory duty to provide RE.
2015–present ↓	The last few years have seen the publication of a number of reports and books concerning the current state of RE. Every facet of RE has been brought under scrutiny – its name, purpose and subject content, to name but three areas of debate. In 2018 the Commission on Religious Education (CoRE) published *Religion and Worldviews: The Way Forward. A National Plan for RE*. The report put forward 11 recommendations, and called on the government to consider and adopt them. In 2025, the Department for Education's Curriculum and Assessment Review recommended that RE become part of a new national framework from 2028.

Where is RE right now?

The legal requirements for RE in the UK run as follows.

The national curriculum states the legal requirement that:

> Every state-funded school must offer a curriculum which is balanced and broadly based, and which:
>
> - Promotes the spiritual, moral, cultural, mental and physical development of pupils; and
> - Prepares pupils at the school for the opportunities, responsibilities and experiences of later life.
>
> Source: DfE (2013a)

All state schools must teach religious education to students at every key stage.

Although there is no single national curriculum for RE, all maintained schools are required to follow the national curriculum guidelines to deliver a broad and balanced education, which must include RE. As a result, maintained schools have a statutory obligation to teach RE. Academies and free schools, meanwhile, are contractually obliged under their funding agreements to provide RE.

In 2023, the National Content Standard was produced to provide a benchmark for the minimum standard of RE that all parents can expect in a state-funded school. Schools that design their own RE curriculum are expected to make sure it matches the National Content Standard in breadth, depth and ambition.

The table shows how this standard would be applied in different types of school.

Type of school	Legal requirements for RE	National Content Standard for RE
Community, foundation and voluntary aided (VA) or voluntary controlled (VC) schools without a religious character that follow an agreed syllabus	Statutory	Recommended to the Agreed Syllabus Conference as a benchmark for high-quality RE
Academies and free schools without a religious character	Statutory	Comparable in breadth, depth and ambition to the NCS
Academies that are former VC or foundation schools with a religious character that followed an agreed syllabus	Statutory	Comparable in breadth, depth and ambition to the NCS
Academies with a religious character, current and former VA schools with a religious character	Statutory	Comparable in breadth, depth and ambition to the NCS
Foundation and VC schools with a religious character that follow an agreed syllabus	Statutory	Recommended to the Agreed Syllabus Conference as a benchmark for high-quality RE

Chapters 3 and 5 will further discuss the National Content Standard and its use within curriculum design.

All state-funded schools in England (maintained schools, academies and free schools) have a statutory duty to teach RE. This applies to all registered pupils, including those in sixth form (ages 16–19) but not to students in nursery classes.

Parents may withdraw their children from RE lessons or any part of the RE curriculum, and the school has a duty to supervise them, though not to provide additional teaching or to incur extra cost.

The pedagogy of RE

Pedagogy can be defined as the method of teaching used. Over the last 40 years, a range of pedagogical approaches have been developed and used in RE. In reality, most RE teachers will adopt a mixture of pedagogical approaches. This will be a result of reflecting on the topic being taught, their students and school context.

Here is a summary of the main pedagogies in RE:

- **Phenomenology:** Established by Ninian Smart (e.g. Smart, 1984), this approach seeks to understand religion through Smart's seven dimensions: narrative, doctrinal, ritual, practice, social, ethical and material. Phenomenologists argue that religion should be studied as a series of phenomena, with the goal of enabling the learner to develop understanding of religions.
- **Interpretive:** Most often linked to Robert Jackson (e.g. Jackson, 1997), this approach argues that we need to study the life experiences of individuals. The interpretive approach challenges the idea that religion is merely an academic construct. By looking at lives different to their own, students are able to make sense of the lived experience of religion and how religion shapes personal identity.
- **Human development:** Michael Grimmitt's work (e.g. Grimmitt, 2020) recognises the role RE plays in human and spiritual development. Grimmitt draws attention to the fact that RE is grounded in questions of 'making meaning', with a focus on ethics and morality. The RE classroom should be a space where students are allowed to reflect on how these ideas relate to their own lives.
- **Critical realism:** Angela and Andrew Wright (e.g. Wright, 1993) focus on the role of RE to guide students in discovering and assessing the truth claims made by religious groups. Students should assess the evidence presented by statements of belief, and make judgements about competing truth claims offered by different religions. This approach challenges the relativist view that all beliefs are valid, and encourages students to critically assess whether any of the truth claims presented can be accepted.
- **Concept cracking:** Based on the work of Trevor Cooling, this approach presents the idea that RE should enable students to 'crack the concepts' that underpin the phenomena of religion. This approach enables students to explore universal concepts such as justice, general concepts across religion, such as worship, and distinctive concepts within a religion such as the Trinity. The exploration of these concepts allows students to explore truth claims and the personal experience of believers.

- **Deconstructionism:** Clive Erricker's pedagogical approach (e.g. Erricker and Erricker, 2000) focuses on giving students the tools to deconstruct religious narratives and, in turn, allows them to construct their own worldview. For Erricker, the role of RE is to allow an individual to form their own meaning about themselves and the world in which they reside.
- **Experiential:** The work of John Hammond and David Hay (e.g. Hammond and Hay, 1990) draws attention to the need for RE to focus on nurturing of the emotions, identity and spiritual development of the student. Through experiential activities such as meditation or drama, students move beyond the academic study of religion and begin to experience the traditions of the religion itself.

Which pedagogy is best?

All visions of RE are valid and many RE teachers will use a range of pedagogical approaches in the classroom. A host of factors – such as your curriculum, the nature of your school, the needs of your students and your own personal belief – can shape your position on which pedagogical approach to adopt. Nonetheless, an awareness of the debates in RE pedagogy can give you a better understanding of what the subject is for.

If you wish to learn more about pedagogies in RE, visit the Methods of Teaching Religious Education page of the NATRE website: https://natre.org.uk/methods-of-teaching-religious-education/

CHAPTER 2
WHAT ARE THE CHALLENGES, DEBATES AND PERSPECTIVES IN RE?

Challenges in RE

All subjects have challenges, but some are unique to the subject and RE is no different. At the time of writing, some of the challenges RE is facing are as follows:

- **No national curriculum:** Instead, locally agreed syllabuses exist across England and Wales. These outline different content, aims and ways of teaching RE. Students are therefore receiving widely different RE curriculum provisions. A later section of this chapter discusses the arguments put forward for a national curriculum of RE and what this may look like.

- **Many schools not meeting legal obligations to teach RE:** The 2023 NATRE Secondary Survey revealed concerning trends regarding schools' compliance with their legal obligations to teach RE. While 91% of schools reported offering discrete RE lessons at key stage 3, only 61% met the legal requirements for RE at key stage 4. This indicates that nearly 40% of schools are not fulfilling their statutory duty to teach RE to all pupils, as mandated by law; 64% of students in Year 11 and 59% of students in Year 10 receive no religious education at KS4, where RE is an optional subject, even though it is a legal requirement.

- **Amount of teaching time:** There are huge inconsistencies within the RE provision students receive in the UK, with 13% of schools delivering less than the Ofqual recommended teaching time of 120–140 learning hours for the full course religious studies GCSE examination. Instead, some schools may opt for the short course GCSE entry. Others may offer KS4 core RE if any form of GCSE study is not provided, or deliver RE as 'drop-down' days throughout the school year. Some schools may deliver RE as part of a carousel alongside other humanities subjects, while others look to provide their RE provision through personal, social, health and economic (PSHE) education or citizenship.

- **Parental right to withdraw:** Parents have the right to withdraw their children from any or all religious education.
- **Recruitment of teachers:** The Religious Education Policy Unit (2023) highlights that the Department for Education (DfE) has failed to meet its RE teacher recruitment targets for the past 10 years. In 2023/24, only 285 trainees enrolled – just 44% of the goal. Additionally, enrolment in RE initial teacher training programmes dropped by 73% between 2019 and 2024, leading to a 150% increase in RE job vacancies.
- **RE taught by subject specialists:** The 2023 NATRE Secondary Survey reported that, in 79% of schools, some RE was taught by teachers who spent most of their timetable teaching another subject. In the DfE's own School Workforce Survey, which found that three times as many lessons of RE as history are taught by those with no post A-level qualification in the subject, 36% of respondents reported they had received no subject-specific training out of school in the last academic year. In addition, 55% reported they had attended no training in school.

Debates in RE

Some of the challenges facing RE are linked to current debates within the subject community. This section will look to explore what those debates are and the conversations around the subject that are currently taking place.

The name of the subject

The debates surrounding the name of the subject continue. To begin with, the two key names for the subject are:

1 **Religious education:** the most traditional, internationally recognised name for the subject and the legal name for what schools are required to teach all students in full-time education
2 **Religious studies:** the name of the GCSE and A-level examinations.

While these terms are recognised by all, the subject can go by many names in schools across the country. The list of all possible names is endless: divinity, theology, philosophy and ethics, religion, to name but a few. Since the publication of the CoRE report in 2018, the name 'religion and worldviews' has become more commonly used.

Throughout this book, I have chosen to use 'religious education' (RE) to refer to the subject and the teaching of it. With regards to the subject's name, I consider it to be a red herring. What matters more is to consider the aims of the subject, curriculum design, and what you want students to be doing and thinking about in the classroom. By directing our attention to the teaching and learning, we can see greater change in the perception of RE.

The case for a national curriculum for RE

Arguments for a national curriculum for RE remain at the forefront of debate in the subject community. As it currently exists, the RE provision across schools is a postcode lottery. In some cases the provision is undervalued, and in others it is an afterthought, meaning that children across England and Wales are experiencing very different RE during their time in school. RE is the only school subject that has a curriculum designed by committee, which will vary greatly according to borough or county. Locally agreed syllabuses (LASs), developed independently by more than a hundred SACREs, differ greatly in both depth and quality. A huge amount of work goes into these LASs, by many people who are passionate about RE, but the depth and quality of this varies. Many SACREs face funding shortages that hinder their ability to meet statutory responsibilities. Moreover, some LASs struggle to provide a balanced perspective, as religious representation on SACREs can result in vested interests.

All students deserve high-quality RE. Sadly, many are not receiving it with the current status quo. As a result, a national curriculum for the subject could help in many ways. For example:

- **Ensure equity and consistency:** A national curriculum would help to ensure that all students receive consistent and high-quality RE teaching. Many in the RE community argue that the National Content Standard for RE, developed by the Religious Education Council of England and Wales (2023a), can serve as a strong starting point for what academically rigorous RE for all can look like. Moreover, a national curriculum can serve as a benchmark to hold schools accountable for the provision they currently are providing.

- **Help the subject achieve its aims:** Chine McDonald (2024) views RE as the 'superpower' that opens our eyes to the variety of beliefs and worldviews that exist in the world. High-quality RE provides students with the tools to understand the cultural, spiritual and economic factors that influence what a person believes. A world with more empathy, dialogue and understanding is possible, and high-quality RE grounded in a national curriculum would help contribute towards this.

- **Provide clarity for RE teachers:** For some RE teachers, confidence in the material they are planning, delivering and assessing may be limited. Without a clear, consistent framework outlining essential content and learning objectives, teaching can become superficial, and students may develop misconceptions. A national curriculum would help teachers plan lessons more efficiently, and ensure that all students receive balanced and comprehensive RE provision regardless of their school's location. It would also offer professional guidance and resources aligned with national standards, reducing uncertainty and workload. Additionally, a national curriculum could promote higher-quality teaching by setting clear expectations for assessment and progression in the subject.
- **Allow for more ambitious RE:** Christine Counsell (2025) highlights how the current status of RE curriculum provision wastes years of classroom time. A national curriculum would allow for knowledge to build cumulatively, systematically and coherently across key stages. The excessive demands of content at GCSE could be dealt with by a rich national framework of common knowledge to ensure GCSE basics have been made secure in primary. This would provide RE teachers at GCSE with the space to deepen and complicate an existing body of knowledge.
- **Help schools support their staff:** If a national curriculum were to be introduced, funds and time could be reallocated to best support RE departments. For example, SACREs would no longer have to create locally agreed syllabuses. Instead, they could focus on how to provide schools with guidance on how to implement the national curriculum, and provide guidance on how to adapt for their context or how to incorporate local case studies within the national curriculum framework.

Although I strongly believe that a national curriculum would greatly increase the quality and equity of RE provision, there are many concerns raised by those in the RE community. These include:

- **Loss of local flexibility:** A locally agreed syllabus can reflect the demographics, faith traditions and community needs of an area. A single national framework could be seen as too rigid, ignoring regional diversity.
- **Risk of political or ideological influence:** If the curriculum content of RE were to be centrally controlled, the government of the day could reshape the content to suit its political priorities. Some argue this

could lead to bias or a narrowing of perspectives if certain voices dominate curriculum design.
- **Complexity of defining the content:** Religious and non-religious traditions are complex, diverse and evolving. The process of deciding the content to allow for an academically robust and accepted body of knowledge to be studied could prove contentious.
- **Diluting diversity:** Locally agreed syllabuses can incorporate smaller faith groups that might not get space in a national curriculum. A national curriculum might focus on the 'big six' world religions and marginalise others.

The Curriculum and Assessment Review Final Report is the independent, comprehensive review of England's curriculum, assessment and qualifications system. It was commissioned by the UK government and published in November 2025. It sets out detailed conclusions and recommendations on how to improve the national curriculum, assessment methods (like exams), and wider qualifications framework for learners from key stage 1 through post-16 education.

With regards to RE, the findings were:

- strong stakeholder consensus that RE is essential within the school curriculum
- RE is vital to pupils' intellectual, personal, spiritual, moral, social and cultural development
- provides a space for children and young people to encounter different beliefs, often for the first time
- helps students understand the core beliefs and practices of major faiths
- encourages pupils to reason, reflect and engage with existential questions
- vital given the influence of religion, beliefs and values in local, national and global events
- access to high-quality RE remains essential for all children and young people
- despite pockets of excellence, RE provision is inconsistent across schools
- evidence suggests many schools' RE does not adequately prepare pupils for life beyond school
- some SACREs support high-quality practice, but many lack resources and capacity

- financial pressures have reduced support, leading to fragmentation
- new syllabuses are often produced on very tight budgets, increasingly reliant on voluntary support
- RE's importance is not currently reflected in its standing in the curriculum.

The report recommends that RE is included in the national curriculum to improve access to high-quality provision and prevent further marginalisation of the subject.

The report put forward a staged approach.

Stage 1
- Led by Dr Vanessa Ogden, the sector should form a task and finish group to build on the collaborative work done so far. This task and finish group would consist of representatives from faith groups, secular groups, and the wider teaching and educator sector.
- Building on the National Content Standard, the group should engage external stakeholders, schools, RE organisations and faith communities to develop a draft RE curriculum.
- Alongside this, the DfE should consider the statutory arrangements for RE, including the potential impact of any change in curricular status on the functions of SACREs.
- As part of this review, the DfE should consider removing the statutory requirement for learners in school sixth forms to study RE.
- In parallel, the DfE should review the non-statutory guidance for RE, which has not been updated since 2010, to assess whether short-term improvements to subject content could be made without pre-empting the wider reforms recommended by the review.

Stage 2
- Subject to agreement on a draft RE curriculum, the DfE should undertake a formal consultation on its detailed content.
- At the same time, the DfE should consult on proposed changes to the legislative framework, including any proposal to remove the statutory requirement to teach RE in school sixth forms.

Where can I read it?
If you would like to read the full findings and recommendations for RE, they can be found on pp. 107–11 of the *Curriculum and*

Assessment Review Final Report: Building a World-Class Curriculum for All, or by visiting this page: https://assets.publishing.service.gov.uk/media/690b96bbc22e4ed8b051854d/Curriculum_and_Assessment_Review_final_report_-_Building_a_world-class_curriculum_for_all.pdf.

To read a NATRE summary report of the Curriculum and Assessment Review, visit the NATRE website and navigate to the relevant page of the Resources section: https://natre.org.uk/resources/the-curriculum-assessment-review-a-summary-report-by-natre/.

If you would like to read more about the debate on a national curriculum for RE, Culham St Gabriel's Focus Week in January 2025 explored the government's review of the curriculum in schools in England. They produced a range of resources examining RE's status in schools, offering solutions for achieving high-quality provision for all, and outlining the changes needed to improve the current settlement for RE in England. You can access the resources here: www.reonline.org.uk/focus-week-the-government-curriculum-and-assessment-review.

What is a worldview?

Since the CoRE report proposed a name change for the subject in 2018, the term 'worldview' has become more common in discussions regarding RE. A worldview can be defined as a person's way of understanding, experiencing and responding to the world around them. A worldview encompasses everything from the way an individual leads their life through to their answers about the ultimate questions of existence. The CoRE report makes a distinction between:

- **Institutional worldviews:** organised worldviews shared among particular groups or embedded within an institution; these include what we describe as religion, and non-religious worldviews such as humanism or atheism.
- **Personal worldview:** an individual's way of perceiving and living in the world. This may be influenced by their beliefs, values, behaviours, experiences and commitments.

The animated film *Nobody Stands Nowhere*, by Theos Think Tank, created in partnership with Culham St Gabriel's Trust and Canterbury Christ Church University, unpacks the idea of worldviews and invites the viewer to consider how their own unique view of the world might co-exist with other, sometimes quite different, vantage points held by those around them. You can watch the film here: www.youtube.com/watch?v=AFRxKF-Jdos.

Some within the subject community have raised concerns regarding the concept of worldviews. A report by the Independent Schools Religious Studies Association (2022) identifies the various difficulties with the concept. These include:

- Does a worldview mean the way the world looks to you or the way your world looks to outsiders?
- Is it the way you see yourself in relation to others or the way you see yourself in relation to everything about reality?
- Is a worldview about ethos and morality or your style of life?
- Is it a negative term used to reinforce the otherness of other people and their identities?

The Worldview Project: Discussion Papers (Tharani, 2020) seeks to answer some of these questions by exploring the concept of a worldview, how it allows for academic rigour and its implications for the classroom. In the next section, I will focus on how these discussion papers address a growing desire to shift towards a worldviews approach.

A worldviews approach

The shift towards a worldviews approach to RE by some in the subject community has been born out of the recognition that students should be exposed to a wider range of religious and non-religious worldviews. More work needs to be done to ensure that institutional worldviews of eastern religions such as Hinduism, Buddhism and Sikhism are taught thoroughly and not neglected. Similarly, non-religious worldviews have increased significantly in Britain and Western Europe. According to the 2021 census in England and Wales, 37% of the population identify themselves as having 'No religion'. This number has jumped by more than 8 million from the previous census in 2011. In contrast, the share of the population ticking 'Christian' fell from 59% to 49%.

Although the majority of the population identify as non-religious, what their worldview may be is less clear-cut. An individual who identifies as non-religious may not necessarily adhere to an institutional worldview such as humanism. An individual's personal worldview may draw upon both religious and non-religious ideas.

As a result, some in the subject community argue that there needs to be a shift away from what is termed the 'world religions paradigm'. Amira Tharani (2020) observes that the issue with the world religions paradigm is that it tends to interpret religions within a specific model – for example, founders, sacred texts, places of worship and systems of doctrine. This paradigm has been the predominant way in which religion has been taught in both schools and universities. However, the world religions paradigm has several issues, such as:

- **An implied hierarchy of 'religions':** Christianity comes to be seen as the archetypal religion, the one most worthy of study, and other religions are studied through the lens of how similar they are to Christianity.
- **Assumption of similar features:** The world religions paradigm has led to the curriculum being constructed around features such as the study of founders, key beliefs, practices and sacred texts. As a result, each organised worldview is not understood on its own terms.
- **Ignores internal diversity:** The world religions paradigm may lead some students to perceive religions as historical, monolithic and unchanging. The current approach to teaching religion does not draw students' attention to the historical development of beliefs within a religion.
- **Less focus on lived experience:** The emphasis on ideas such as sacred texts, founders and authority means that students have less understanding of how believers lead their lives. The concepts of belief, belonging and the diversity among believers are not explored sufficiently in the world religions paradigm.
- **The nature of the subject does not reflect new social realities:** As mentioned earlier, at the time of the Education Act 1944, the subject was known as religious instruction, with Christianity being the only religion taught. By the time of the Education Reform Act 1988, subject experts had recognised the need for pupils to understand both a wide range of religious and non-religious worldviews, but moreover the diversity within those worldviews.

How does a worldviews approach solve these problems?

As a result of these challenges, some have come to see the 'worldviews' approach as a tool to open up and explore more fruitful and diverse questions about religion. Tharani (2020) notes how a worldviews approach helps to:

- **Open up boundaries between religion and non-religion:** The distinction between 'religious' and 'non-religious' may not be as clear-cut as we think. An individual may draw upon aspects of both religious and non-religious worldviews in their own personal worldview. Within the classroom, it can sometimes be difficult to do justice to the diversity and complexity of the personal worldview an individual may inhabit. However, a worldviews approach may allow teachers to include groups such as 'Christian atheists' or 'ex-Muslims' within their curriculums. The benefit of this approach is that questions exploring the relationship between religion and culture can be discussed.

- **Allow for exploration of continuity and change:** The CoRE report calls for a 'national entitlement' in which pupils are taught about historical change, interactions between worldviews and how people may draw upon more than one tradition. A worldviews approach allows the teacher to explore questions relating to continuity and change. For instance, a class may study a text and the teacher may ask whether the text would have been understood in the same way in earlier times and different places. The worldviews approach allows for more space to explore the social, cultural, historical and intellectual factors that have shaped religious traditions.

- **Show the interplay between organised and personal worldviews:** All humans were born into and inhabit a range of worldviews. Some of these may overlap, and some may be formally articulated and may include being part of an organised community, religious or non-religious. All of these worldviews combine to shape the way we see the world. Integral to a national entitlement is for pupils to understand their own worldviews and those of others. A worldviews approach would enable pupils to explore how individuals relate to a range of overlapping worldviews. For example, a worldviews approach might help explain why some humanists turn to Buddhist traditions to explain spiritual practices they may partake in, such as yoga or meditation. Linking to exploration of continuity and change, a worldviews approach seeks to explore how the changes within institutional worldviews may be the result of key individuals changing their views in light of the time or place they find themselves in. For example, Tharani (2020) gives the example of the Church of England's official view on women priests. By adopting a worldviews approach, students might begin to explore how key individuals began to explore Biblical and theological sources differently. Alongside the political and cultural context, students might be able to appreciate how and why the Church of England's official position changed.

- **Encourage real conversations and real debates:** One issue within the world religions paradigm, as presented in public examinations, is that false debates and conversations are constructed. For instance, a GCSE examination may ask a student to evaluate the statement 'Hajj is the most important pillar for Muslims.' The assumption of 'X is more important than Y' debates does not correlate with historical or contemporary debates within the Muslim tradition. It is not the sort of debate that Muslim scholars would occupy themselves with. Instead, a worldviews approach shifts the focus towards authentic debates and conversations within religious communities.

CHAPTER 3
WHAT DOES THE RESEARCH TELL US ABOUT TEACHING RE?

This book is informed by contemporary research about the teaching of secondary RE. In this chapter, you will find brief summaries of key research for RE teachers, along with explanations of how this research can support teaching the subject. Many of the ideas referenced here will be explored elsewhere in the book.

Commission on Religious Education: *Religion and Worldviews: The Way Forward. A National Plan for RE* (2018)

What kind of research is it?
The Commission on Religious Education (CoRE) was established to review the legal, education and policy frameworks for RE. The aim of the review was to improve the quality and academic rigour of the subject, as well as the subject's ability to prepare pupils for life in 21st-century Britain. In 2018, CoRE published its final report, which set out a national plan for RE consisting of 11 recommendations that the government should consider and adopt.

What does it say?
The report's 11 recommendations were as follows:

1 **Rename the subject:** CoRE recommended changing the subject's name from 'religious education' to 'religion and worldviews', to better reflect the diverse religious and non-religious perspectives studied.

2 **Establish a statutory National Entitlement:** Introduce a statutory National Entitlement outlining what all pupils should learn about religion and worldviews, to ensure consistent and high-quality education across all schools.

3 **Develop national programmes of study:** Create national programmes of study to support the National Entitlement, providing a framework

for curriculum development while allowing flexibility for local adaptations.

4 **Reform local syllabus development:** Suspend the requirements for local authorities to develop agreed syllabuses, shifting towards nationally developed programmes to ensure consistency and reduce variations in content quality across schools.

5 **Revise exam qualification frameworks:** Review and revise GCSE and A-level qualifications in light of the National Entitlement to ensure alignment with the updated vision for the subject.

6 **Reform teacher education:** Among other proposals, ensure newly qualified teachers are better prepared and confident in teaching religion and worldviews by mandating a minimum of 12 hours of training on religion and worldviews in all forms of primary ITE, and bursaries for ITE in religion and worldviews, to achieve parity with other shortage subjects.

7 **Provide adequate funding:** Allocate sufficient funding to support the implementation of the National Entitlement, including resources for teacher training and curriculum development.

8 **Establish local advisory networks:** Replace Standing Advisory Councils on Religious Education (SACREs) with local advisory networks for religion and worldviews to provide support, resources and guidance to schools.

9 **Enhance inspection and accountability:** Ensure that Ofsted and other relevant bodies inspect and report on the quality of religion and worldviews education, holding schools accountable for delivering the National Entitlement.

10 **Review impact of performance measures:** The DfE should assess how current school performance measures affect the quality and provision of religion and worldviews education, specifically the consequences of excluding religious studies GCSE from the English Baccalaureate (EBacc) and omitting short course GCSEs from performance metrics.

11 **Clarify the right to withdraw:** Review the right of parents to withdraw their children from religion and worldviews education to ensure it aligns with the updated, inclusive vision of the subject.

How can it help me in my own teaching?

The report provides teachers with an insight into a bold vision for the future of the subject, which could mark the most significant developments in RE for decades. It is an attempt to reimagine and modernise the subject for the 21st century by improving the quality, consistency and relevance of what is taught in schools. By reading the report, teachers will gain insight into a bold vision of the subject that reimagines its aims, curriculum design and place within education in schools. The report provides a comprehensive explanation for why pupils in all schools deserve a high-quality and rigorous education on a range of religious and non-religious worldviews. The report argues for a curriculum created by a national body of 'professionals' that is multidisciplinary in nature.

Where can I read it?
You can find the link to the full report in the 'Our work' section of the Commission on Religious Education website: https://religiouseducationcouncil.org.uk/rec/wp-content/uploads/2017/05/Final-Report-of-the-Commission-on-RE.pdf.

Religious Education Council of England and Wales: National Content Standard for Religious Education in England (2023)

What kind of research is it?
The Religious Education Council (REC) of England and Wales introduced a National Content Standard for religious education in England to address long-standing inconsistencies in RE provision across schools. The National Content Standard offers principles for selecting content rather than prescribing specific topics. It seeks to provide a benchmark for high-quality RE, and to guide curriculum developers, syllabus writers and schools.

What does it say?
The National Content Standard outlines the purpose of study, principles for selecting study and standards for progression in the subject.

Purpose of study
The purpose of education in religion and worldviews is to:

- introduce the diversity of religious and non-religious worldviews locally and globally as essential to understanding human life and society
- spark pupil curiosity about religious and non-religious worldviews
- explore how worldviews function and influence individuals, communities and cultures

- foster interpretive skills for understanding the meaning and significance of religions and worldviews
- cultivate sensitivity to the complexity of belief systems and the challenges of religious language and experience
- teach scholarly methods for studying religion and worldviews
- help students identify academic assumptions and how they shape understanding
- connect religion and worldviews to broader human experiences, such as literature, culture and the arts
- encourage personal reflection, allowing pupils to explore and critically engage with their own developing worldviews
- support informed, personal responses based on studied content and self-reflection.

Subject content

The exemplar content in the REC's National Content Standard outlines the expected quality and scope of a strong curriculum. While not legally required, it serves as a benchmark to ensure pupils receive a high-quality understanding of key religious and non-religious worldviews.

There are three parts to the National Content Standard:

1 **Content:** The realm of religion and worldviews to explore.

2 **Engagement:** Choosing the right tools and route to undertake your exploration.

3 **Position:** Awareness of how your own worldview affects your exploration and how your exploration affects your worldview.

How can it help me in my own teaching?

The National Content Standard provides clarification about excellence of approach to RE. Due to a lack of agreement as to what constitutes high-quality RE, the National Content Standard aims to provide a benchmark for RE in all types of state-funded schools in England to meet the REC's vision for all pupils in all schools. It is not recommending a particular approach to the subject, but provides an exemplar of the breadth, depth and ambition of a high-quality RE curriculum.

Guidance on how to implement the National Content Standard will be outlined in chapter 5.

Where can I read it?

Find the link to the full report in the 'Our work' section of the Commission on Religious Education website: https://religiouseducationcouncil.org.uk/rec/wp-content/uploads/2023/09/RE-Council-National-Content-Standard-for-Religious-Education-for-England-July23.pdf.

Ofsted: *Research Review Series: Religious Education* (2021)

What kind of research is it?

Published by Ofsted, this is a literature review of the research underpinning effective RE teaching. Among other things, the review covers the literature on curriculum design, types of knowledge and assessment.

What does it say?

This is a very detailed literature review, including 246 footnotes that provide an overview of the research in the subject.

Let's look at some of the key takeaways in action ...

Curriculum planning

The curriculum is the progression model – this means it should set out what it means to 'get better at RE' as pupils journey through the curriculum. Teachers must consider the knowledge that pupils build through the RE curriculum, as accurate knowledge of religion and non-religion allows for the different aims and purposes of the subject to be achieved.

Teachers must be aware of the different types of knowledge in RE and have high expectations about scholarship in the curriculum, to ensure that pupil misconceptions do not occur.

There are three types of knowledge in RE which are central to curriculum planning:

1 **Substantive knowledge:** knowledge about religious and non-religious traditions

2 **Disciplinary knowledge:** knowledge of 'how to know' about religion and non-religion

3 **Personal knowledge:** pupils' knowledge of their own presuppositions, ideas and values about religious and non-religious traditions they study.

These three types of knowledge are to be taught alongside one another.

Substantive knowledge and concepts in RE

Substantive knowledge is the 'substance' of religious and non-religious traditions. This includes:

- the different ways that people express religion and non-religion in their lives
- knowledge about artefacts and texts associated with different religious and non-religious traditions
- concepts that relate to religious and non-religious traditions.

As not everything can be taught, teachers must make careful decisions about which content to select. It is essential that they choose the most accurate representations possible to ensure pupils do not learn misconceptions. The goal is to provide 'collectively enough' substantive content to foster deep understanding of religious and non-religious traditions.

Ensuring accurate and meaningful representations

The content of the curriculum should be based on what teachers want pupils to understand about religion and non-religion, rather than using fixed percentages per tradition. This can lead to superficial learning and prevent more complex discussions about religion and non-religion.

As the curriculum is the progression model, teachers need to sequence for complexity. Curriculum content should be sequenced so that pupils can build understanding and make sense of the complexity in religious and non-religious traditions. To allow for this, teachers should ensure that content builds towards understanding big ideas, or 'conceptual pegs'. Examples of big ideas may include the pursuit of a good life, the divine or the afterlife.

Disciplinary knowledge in RE

This form of knowledge includes knowledge of the well-established methods and processes of learning, the scholarship of RE, and the types of conversation that academics have about religion and non-religion. This form of knowledge helps pupils learn about the construction of substantive knowledge, its accuracy, its reliability and how provisional that knowledge is.

The curriculum should be explicit about teaching 'ways of knowing'. Teachers should think carefully about which 'ways of knowing' pupils need to learn, and specify this to the content pupils are learning.

'Ways of knowing' is important, as pupils will gain an appreciation of the different types of knowledge in the world and how the knowledge in the RE curriculum differs from other types of knowledge.

Some approaches to RE curriculum design may formalise 'ways of knowing' into simplified disciplines such as theology, philosophy and social sciences. This is helpful as it provides different ways of approaching similar topics.

The table presents some examples based on different substantive concepts.

Concept	Theology	Philosophy	Social sciences
God	How is Allah described in the Qur'an?	Can the Muslim concept of God be defended in light of evil and suffering?	How do Muslim beliefs about Allah shape daily practices?
Revelation	How is the Bible understood as a source of divine revelation in Christian theology?	Can the Bible be considered a reliable source of divine revelation?	How does a belief in the Bible affect the daily lives and moral decisions of Christians?
Dukkha	What does the First Noble Truth teach about the nature and cause of suffering?	Can life without suffering be achieved?	How do Buddhist responses to suffering affect wellbeing and mental health today?

Personal knowledge in RE

This form of knowledge refers to the awareness and understanding pupils develop about their own perspectives, and how these relate to the religious and non-religious content they study. It recognises that students do not enter the RE classroom as neutral observers; instead, they engage with content from their own standpoint, shaped by their values, identity and life experiences.

To support the development of personal knowledge, RE subject leaders must think carefully about choosing content that encourages meaningful reflection. Effective content for this aim is anything that connects with pupils' developing sense of self. Themes or substantive concepts that may help with this include meaning and purpose, justice and community.

An example of this working well is the Christian concept of forgiveness. Through encountering the Lord's Prayer or parables such as that of the Prodigal Son, pupils can explore how forgiveness is an expression of divine grace and a model for human relationships.

When it comes to personal knowledge, pupils may reflect on their own views about forgiveness – for example, have they ever struggled to forgive someone? They may consider whether forgiveness is a strength, a duty or a challenge. By comparing Christian ideas of forgiveness with their own, pupils clarify their own position while understanding others.

Chapter 4 will further explore the different types of knowledge in RE and their implications for the classroom.

Interplay, end goals and competences

It is essential for RE subject leaders to plan an integrated approach for substantive knowledge, disciplinary knowledge and personal knowledge. This involves teaching substantive content and establishing connections with other types of knowledge.

The substantive content serves as the foundation for pupils to learn 'ways of knowing'. For example, a statement such as 'rituals help religious communities mark significant moments in life' depends on specific substantive content such as baptism in Christianity, bar/bat mitzvah in Judaism, or funeral rites in Islam and Hinduism. Without knowing the details, such as the symbolism, timing and community involvement in these rituals, pupils cannot evaluate how significant the rituals are in religious life.

In turn, a high-quality RE curriculum would develop a pupil's personal knowledge through the substantive knowledge they have encountered. In reference to studying how religious rituals might help individuals and communities mark significant moments in life, pupils may be invited to consider how they mark important life events such as births, coming of age or grief. They may reflect on questions such as 'What events in my life have been marked with special traditions?' or 'Why do people seek meaning during times of change?'

Subject leaders must focus on their curriculum end goals; this can be done by thinking about the components and competences. The components are the language, vocabulary and concepts that pupils explore in the curriculum. The subject composites build over time. The end goal is to support deep learning. By prioritising this, pupils can work towards an understanding of religious diversity within Britain and globally, as well as engaging with the 'ways of knowing' about religion. By focusing on these end goals, superficial coverage of religious and non-religious traditions can be avoided.

Teaching the curriculum

Subject leaders and teachers have more chance of reaching curriculum end goals by carefully selecting classroom activities that enable pupils to remember the curriculum in the long term. Teachers need to be clear about what the 'object' of the curriculum is, to ensure that pupils know and remember more. By having clarity, teachers can focus their subject expertise on the best classroom activities.

Teacher judgement about best classroom activities should be informed by their subject expertise on the nature of the content that is being learned and the insights from cognitive science about learning.

For example, teaching activities should be well matched to pupils' prior knowledge. This allows for pupils to integrate new learning into their pre-existing schema. If prior knowledge is insecure, then the success of new learning will be mixed. To increase the chances of success, pupils need to have recurrent opportunities to encounter concepts that develop their schema over time. To help with the retention of substantive knowledge, such as concepts and vocabulary, retrieval practice in many forms is very effective.

Teaching activities that continue to draw on and remind pupils of parts of the RE curriculum that they have covered will help them learn the RE curriculum in the long term.

Examples of how this can be done will be found in later chapters.

Assessment

Subject leaders and teachers need to carefully consider the appropriate use of different types of assessment.

Formative assessments allow the teacher to identify misconceptions and gaps in pupils' knowledge, and what these are. This gives teachers an insight into common issues, which allows them to review and adapt lessons and/or the curriculum appropriately. This provides a really helpful feedback loop from student to teacher.

Summative assessments are useful for making judgements about how much of the curriculum has been learned and remembered. School and subject leaders must think carefully about where these are spaced in the curriculum, to ensure enough time is dedicated to the curriculum being taught and remembered.

When designing assessments, subject leaders need to focus on what is being assessed and why. The assessment must relate to the curriculum being taught, which sets out what it means to get better at RE. The purpose of the test should inform the type of assessment. As the curriculum is the progression model, curriculum and assessment should not be considered as separate entities.

For guidance on how to implement effective assessments, read chapter 9.

Systems, culture and policies

The way in which school leaders structure and plan ways to fulfil their legal obligation to provide RE as part of their curriculum is a key indicator of the quality of education in RE within a school. RE must be treated as a discrete subject, and secondary school leaders must consider whether their current RE provision is enough to deliver an ambitious curriculum.

Alongside the amount of RE provision, subject specialist RE teachers also contribute to high-quality RE. A Religious Education Council report published in 2017 found that:

- in schools of religious character, 77% of RE lessons were taught by a qualified subject specialist
- in schools where the locally agreed syllabus applied, this figure was 58%
- in academies, this figure was 47%.

Pupils should be taught by teachers who have excellent subject knowledge, can foster subject curiosity in pupils, and deal with the subject-specific misconceptions and sensitivities that arise from teaching RE.

Teacher education and CPD

It would be beneficial for RE teachers at primary and secondary to develop in four key areas:

1. **RE policy:** Teachers need to understand the policy and legal requirements surrounding the subject, such as the locally agreed syllabus. This knowledge helps teachers to adapt their teaching to different school contexts. Professional development should also include learning about the history of, current status and recent changes in RE.

2. **RE content knowledge:** Teachers need strong content knowledge, ideally grounded in relevant academic disciplines, which is relevant and sufficient for the school curriculum. In addition, it is important for teachers to continue developing the depth and breadth of their knowledge, and to understand the nature, perspective and status of what is being taught.
3. **RE pedagogical content knowledge:** Teachers need to continually develop their ability to effectively teach specific RE topics. This involves applying current insights into human learning, and using subject-specific strategies for teaching, learning and assessment. In addition, teachers need to maintain impartiality in their teaching.
4. **Research in RE:** Due to ongoing disagreements about the aims and purposes of RE, there is uncertainty around how it should be taught. Therefore, RE teachers need support to engage with educational theory and research, to inform their practice.

How can it help me in my own teaching?

The subsequent chapters in this book will address how many of the ideas in the Ofsted research review can be implemented.

In this section, I will focus on how RE teachers can look to develop their subject knowledge.

As shown in the table, there are many valuable opportunities for RE teachers to further engage with their subject. These opportunities can serve to develop your subject knowledge, deepen your passion for the subject, and connect you with other RE teachers locally and nationally.

What can I do?	What is it?	How can I find out more?
Attend a SACRE meeting	The aim of SACRE meetings is to advise the local authority on what needs to be done to support and improve religious education and collective worship for schools in its area.	Identify your local authority, find the contact details of the SACRE officer and request to attend a meeting.

What can I do?	What is it?	How can I find out more?
Attend a NATRE-affiliated local group meeting	NATRE-affiliated local groups provide lesson ideas and solutions, help the RE network to grow, share familiarity of the RE resources in the local area, and provide opportunities to understand what is happening in the region and across England and Wales.	Find out more on the 'Local groups' page of the NATRE website: www.natre.org.uk/about-natre/re-in-your-region
Join in with #REchatUK	#REchatUK is a monthly X (formerly Twitter) chat hosted by NATRE executives to build a supportive online community for teachers. It is a chance to share ideas, exchange resources and engage with other RE teachers.	Find out more on the 'Live courses & events' page of the NATRE website: www.natre.org.uk/courses-and-events/rechatuk
Engage with research on RE:ONLINE	RE:ONLINE provides recordings, case studies and resources to help teachers engage with research in the subject.	Find out more on the 'Research' page of the RE:ONLINE website: www.reonline.org.uk/research/engaging-in-and-with-research
Complete a Culham St Gabriel's e-learning course	The Culham St Gabriel's e-learning site provides free professional development for RE teachers. These courses can expand your knowledge, understanding and skills in areas such as research, curriculum and subject knowledge.	Find out more on the 'Courses' page of the Culham St Gabriel's website: https://courses.cstg.org.uk

What can I do?	What is it?	How can I find out more?
Attend NATRE's StrictlyRE Conference	NATRE hosts the UK's biggest RE conference, where delegates can attend seminars that provide valuable insights, practical strategies and inspiration to further enhance their teaching practice.	Find out more on the 'StrictlyRE' page of the NATRE website: www.natre.org.uk/events-courses/strictly-re
Explore and connect with RE Hubs	RE Hubs is a UK-based project that supports RE teachers by connecting them with resources, professional development and research. It fosters collaboration and communication within the RE community.	Find out more on the RE Hubs website: www.re-hubs.uk
Apply for the RE Quality Mark	The RE Quality Mark is a national accreditation system that recognises and celebrates high-quality religious education in schools across England, Wales and Northern Ireland. It is designed to promote good RE practices and support schools in enhancing their RE provision.	Find out more on the 'Our work' page of the Commission on Religious Education website: https://religiouseducationcouncil.org.uk/our-work/reqm/about/
Undertake a Farmington Scholarship	The Farmington Institute supports teachers working in RE or associated subjects (e.g. philosophy or moral and ethical education, SEND) to have up to 30 days out of the classroom to pursue a research project of their own.	Find out more on the 'Scholarships' page of the Farmington Institute website: https://farmington.ac.uk/farmington-institute-scholarship/

What can I do?	What is it?	How can I find out more?
Complete the Culham St Gabriel's Leadership Scholarship Programme	The Leadership Scholarship Programme supports emerging RE leaders in developing their understanding of educational leadership in the subject. It offers mentoring, structured challenges, research insights, networking events and experience in delivering professional development.	Find out more on the 'Scholarships' page of the Culham St Gabriel's website: www.cstg.org.uk/scholarship-programmes/leadership

Podcasts also offer an excellent way for teachers to develop their subject knowledge and engage with research. Here are a few:

- The RE Podcast explores a wide range of religions and worldviews, blending interviews, personal stories and expert analysis from RE teachers, academics and other voices: www.therepodcast.co.uk.
- The Religious Studies Project (RSP) produces podcasts and articles aimed at advancing the social-scientific and critical study of religion. It aims to bring contemporary issues in religious studies to a wider audience, and to provide resources for students, teachers and the public: www.religiousstudiesproject.com.
- The BibleProject podcast series offers in-depth conversations about the biblical theology explored in its animated videos. It delves into the literary structure, themes and historical context of individual books, as well as key biblical concepts and themes: https://bibleproject.com/podcasts/the-bible-project-podcast.
- The Panpsycast is a podcast that explores big philosophical questions and key thinkers, and conducts interviews with academics in a range of RE-related disciplines: https://www.thepanpsycast.com/panpsycast.
- In Our Time is a BBC Radio 4 discussion programme and podcast exploring a wide range of historical, scientific, cultural, religious and philosophical topics. The programme features expert guests who delve into the ideas, people and events that have shaped our world: www.bbc.co.uk/programmes/b006qykl.

Where can I read it?

You can find the link to the full report by searching 'Research Review Series: Religious Education' on the gov.uk homepage: www.gov.uk/government/publications/research-review-series-religious-education.

Ofsted: *Deep and Meaningful? The Religious Education Subject Report* (2024)

What kind of research is it?

Published by Ofsted, this report looks to evaluate the quality of religious education in English schools. Drawing on evidence from visits to 50 schools across England, the report identifies common strengths and weaknesses in RE provision. The evidence collated, together with the Ofsted concept of quality in the 2021 RE Research Review, provides the basis for this subject report. It focuses on curriculum, pedagogy and assessment, as well as school-level systems and their impact on RE.

What does it say?

While the report also offers an evaluation of primary RE, here I will focus only on the findings given for secondary RE.

The main findings from the report are as follows:

- Many RE curriculums lack the depth and coherence necessary to prepare pupils for life in a diverse, multi-religious and multi-secular society.
- Deeper study of fewer topics results in better learning outcomes; trying to cover many religions equally often leads to a shallow understanding and poor retention of knowledge.
- Many RE curriculums do not enable pupils to build disciplinary and personal knowledge in a structured way.
- Some RE curriculums are often driven by exam requirements, with a premature focus on exam skills that limits the range and scope of high-quality RE.
- Most non-examined RE is inadequate, and many schools are failing to meet their statutory requirements to teach RE at all key stages.
- When the quality of RE provision is weak, religious traditions are taught in overly simplistic and compartmentalised ways.

- Many school curriculums do not provide a suitable mix of content that allows students to make sense of how religious and non-religious traditions appear globally.
- Many subject leaders and teachers deem 'teaching from a neutral stance' as akin to teaching a non-religious worldview.
- While many schools have systems of assessment in place, they often fail to track whether pupils are retaining and building complex knowledge over time.
- Pupil recall of knowledge is impacted by long gaps between RE lessons.
- Few teachers have received subject-specific professional development in RE, raising concerns given the complexity and importance of the subject.

Based on these findings, the reports offers the following recommendations to further improve the quality of RE provision.

Curriculum

- **Distinct design:** Schools should establish a distinct, rigorous RE curriculum that builds progressively on pupils' prior knowledge.
- **Careful content selection:** Subject leaders must carefully choose and sequence important knowledge and concepts, avoiding oversimplified portrayals of religious and non-religious traditions.
- **Breadth and depth:** The curriculum should balance broad coverage with in-depth study to ensure pupils have an understanding of a modern, complex and diverse world.
- **Knowledge development:** All pupils should have opportunities to develop their knowledge over time. The RE curriculum can be informed by exam board specifications but should not be driven by them.
- **Types of knowledge:** Subject leaders should plan, identify and know where pupils will develop both disciplinary and personal knowledge through teaching of substantive content.

Teaching and assessment

- **Ambitious with high expectations:** Subject leaders should have high expectations for what pupils can understand and retain. The aim is to develop the substantive, disciplinary and personal knowledge of all students.
- **Knowledge progression:** Pupils should be given regular opportunities to revisit and build on key knowledge. They should use the knowledge

acquired in previous years as the curriculum becomes more challenging over time.

- **Complexity of traditions:** Teachers should help pupils to understand the rich complexity of both religious and non-religious traditions, avoiding oversimplification or simplistic representations.
- **Assessment practices:** Assessment should go beyond memorisation, focusing on pupils' long-term understanding of the curriculum over time.

Systems at subject and school level

- **Teacher knowledge:** Schools should ensure that all RE teachers have strong subject knowledge and the pedagogical skills needed to teach it effectively.
- **Timetable allocation and planning:** It should be ensured that RE teaching time is used well, to develop a curriculum that is both comprehensive and in-depth. In addition, RE timetable planning should be scheduled so that gaps between teaching are minimised.
- **Non-examined key stages 4 and 5:** The non-examined RE curriculum at key stages 4 and 5 should be ambitious and well structured, and should build on learning from key stage 3.

Where can I read it?

You can find the link to the full report by searching 'Deep and Meaningful?' on the gov.uk homepage: www.gov.uk/government/publications/subject-report-series-religious-education/deep-and-meaningful-the-religious-education-subject-report.

CHAPTER 4
WHAT ARE THE DIFFERENT TYPES OF KNOWLEDGE AND CONCEPTS IN RE?

As students progress through their RE curriculum, they will acquire and build upon different types of knowledge. In RE, we want the curriculum to be knowledge-rich. We want students to acquire knowledge that takes them beyond their own experiences and opens up new ways of thinking about the world around them.

It is vital for RE teachers to consider the types of knowledge that students will gain in the RE classroom, as this can lead to misconceptions about what is being taught and the nature of the subject itself, such as 'RE is just your own opinion.' Similarly, it is important for RE teachers to be aware of what knowledge in RE consists of as this helps clarify what makes the subject distinctive.

In recent years, conversations surrounding the types of knowledge in RE have become more commonplace and fruitful. All RE teachers want our subject to be recognised as one that provides real challenge and results in academically rigorous work. High-quality RE allows pupils to engage with and understand a complex multi-religious and multi-secular world. For all students to reach this goal, consideration of the types of knowledge in RE is essential.

Substantive knowledge

The substantive knowledge of RE is the subject content that we teach in RE – the 'substance' of religious and non-religious traditions that students study in the curriculum. Substantive content includes:

- key beliefs of religious and non-religious traditions
- sacred texts
- holy buildings
- founders and key figures
- artefacts
- concepts that relate to religious and non-religious traditions, such as ritual, sacrifice, moksha, prayer, dharma.

In RE, concepts are divided into three categories, as shown in the table.

Category A – concepts that are universal and common to all humans	Category B – concepts that are common across religions and beliefs	Category C – concepts that are specific to a religious tradition
Justice	Stewardship	Incarnation
Compassion	Worship	Moksha
Meaning	Festivals	Anatta
Identity	Sacred texts	Five Pillars of Islam
Morality	Pilgrimage	Shabbat

Pupils cannot learn all substantive content in RE – teachers need to be selective and strategically decide what substantive knowledge to teach. At key stage 3, the locally agreed syllabus may guide what you teach by providing broad headings. However, careful curriculum design is needed to navigate the what, why and when of how this substantive knowledge is taught. At key stages 4 and 5, teachers will follow GCSE and A-level specifications, which provide an outline of what needs to be taught. Yet this still needs to be translated into a well-sequenced curriculum, with additional contextual knowledge needed to provide greater meaning to the exam specification.

What strategies work well to teach substantive knowledge?

When teaching substantive knowledge, teachers need to recognise that knowledge builds through schemas. New learning is integrated into existing mental structures (schemas) in long-term memory, linking facts and concepts to create meaning.

The schemas pupils develop in RE will influence how they think, speak and act in society about matters of religion, so the knowledge taught through the curriculum should prepare them for real-world engagement with these topics.

New knowledge must be explicitly taught by the teacher, giving students the facts, ideas and explanations they need to build their knowledge. Chapter 6 will provide various strategies on how to do this to ensure that misconceptions do not occur and students build strong conceptual mental models about religion.

Retrieval practice low-stakes testing

After it has been taught, substantive knowledge should be securely embedded in the student's long-term memory, and clearly connected to what they have learned before and what they will learn in the future.

Evidence demonstrates that teachers can use retrieval practice and low-stakes testing to help with this. At the start of a lesson, retrieval practice can help to reactivate knowledge that will be relevant to the lesson. The questions set will ask students to recall specific prior knowledge that underpins the new learning about to take place.

A KS3 lesson about the Eightfold Path in Buddhism may begin with a short, low-stakes quiz asking students to recall key ideas from a previous lesson about the Four Noble Truths. An understanding of these truths would be necessary before learning about the Eightfold Path. For example:

1. What is the first of the Four Noble Truths?
2. According to Buddhism, what causes suffering?
3. What does the third Noble Truth say is possible?
4. Which Noble Truth introduces the Eightfold Path?
5. What is the Pali word often used for 'suffering' in the Four Noble Truths?

At a later point in the lesson, more low-stakes testing can be used. This low-stakes testing may be based on the new knowledge that has been taught in the lesson. For example:

1. What is the first step of the Eightfold Path called?
2. Which part of the Path involves speaking truthfully and kindly?
3. Which part of the Path focuses on meditation and mindfulness skills?
4. In which Noble Truth is the Eightfold Path introduced?
5. What part of the Eightfold Path relates to how a person earns a living?

Chapters 6, 11 and 12 will further explore strategies for teaching substantive knowledge.

What factors should be considered when selecting and teaching substantive knowledge?

When selecting and sequencing the substantive knowledge pupils encounter in the curriculum, there are many factors to consider. For example:

- **Too little breadth:** If pupils acquire substantive knowledge of only a limited range of religious or non-religious traditions, they are prevented from exploring connections between traditions. For instance, in-depth study of solely the Abrahamic religions (Judaism, Christianity and Islam) does not recognise the diversity of religious belief that exists locally, nationally or globally. This can leave pupils with a mental model of religion that is skewed and flawed.
- **Too much breadth:** At the same time, teaching a great range of religious and non-religious traditions can overload the curriculum, leading to shallow understanding and superficial impressions of the religious and non-religious traditions that have been studied in the classroom. There is a fine balancing act between depth and breadth in the substantive knowledge that is taught. It is essential to get this right to do justice to the fluidity and complexity of the religious and non-religious traditions of the world.
- **Relevancy:** There is a concern with selecting substantive knowledge based on what might be engaging, interesting or relevant to the lives of our pupils. The issue with this is that pupils do not know what they don't know. To make choices based on pupil interest will rob them of powerful knowledge. Our job as RE teachers and curriculum designers is to take pupils beyond their own world and teach them about the best that has been thought and said in the world.
- **Accuracy:** When considering substantive knowledge, accuracy is essential to avoid misconceptions. For example, learning about humanism only in relation to atheism presents humanism as merely the rejection of God, and does not provide pupils with the opportunity to recognise that humanism is a way of life with a set of beliefs, traditions and values.
- **Generalisations:** Substantive knowledge can fall victim to generalisation if beliefs are taught as fixed and stable, and do not demonstrate the fluidity of lived experience. The use of phrases such as 'Buddhists believe ...' or 'Sikhs practise ...' can lead to stereotypes if these generalisations bear no resemblance to the lived reality of the believer. Generalisation can sometimes be appropriate, for example in the primary phase or lower key stage 3, to avoid unnecessary complexity and ensure pupils gain a basic understanding of the tradition they are studying. To aid with these necessary moments of generalisation, the use of words and phrases such as 'some', 'many' and 'the majority of' can give clarity and precision, and hint at the diversity that will be studied later.

Disciplinary knowledge

The role of disciplinary knowledge in RE is an ongoing area of debate and development within the subject community. Richard Kueh describes disciplinary knowledge as the 'ways of knowing' and 'how to know' about religious and non-religious traditions. These can be collectively described as 'the sum total of the tools, norms, methods and modus operandi of the way in which humans go about exploring a field of human knowledge that has its own set of conventions' (Ofsted, 2021). It is the way that substantive knowledge is structured to form a discipline.

The importance of disciplinary knowledge is that it helps to frame pupil thinking. If we reduce RE to merely the substantive knowledge, pupils are robbed of the opportunity to think about the status of the substantive content. Disciplinary knowledge can help deal with stereotyping or oversimplifying religious traditions. The recognition that there are different 'ways of knowing' allows students to think in more informed, intelligent and reflective ways, which broadens and deepens their understanding of the religious and non-religious traditions they encounter.

For pupils to navigate the complexity of religious and non-religious traditions, a multi-disciplinary approach is needed. The CoRE report (*Religion and Worldviews: The Way Forward*, 2018) advocates for three disciplines:

1 **Theology:** This discipline explores the nature of belief – the origin of beliefs, how they have changed, their authority and consistency. Moreover, it seeks to understand the ways in which beliefs have been challenged and interpreted over time.

2 **Philosophy:** This discipline focuses on thinking – the process of reasoning by which questions of existence, meaning and knowledge are assessed. Philosophy allows pupils to reflect on the nature of reality, the way we think about ourselves, and the nature of good and evil.

3 **Human and social sciences:** This discipline explores the lived experience of belief – the multitude of ways in which beliefs impact the individual, communities and wider society. The human and social sciences allow pupils to see how religious and non-religious traditions shape the world around them.

In *Reforming RE* (Chater, 2020), Gillian Georgiou and Kathryn Wright present a range of questions that each discipline allows pupils to consider, ask and explore:

Theology	Philosophy	Human and social sciences
Can we establish the origin of this belief?	How do we know what we know?	What do we mean by the term 'religion'?
How has this belief been interpreted throughout history?	Does this belief or argument make sense?	How do people in the same religion practise their beliefs differently?
Are there diverse ways this is understood today?	How do people decide what is right or wrong?	What impact do geography and culture have on the way in which people practise their beliefs?
Who authored this key text?	What happens when different interpretations of good and evil come into conflict with one another?	How might belonging to a particular religion impact on individual identity?
What does it mean for something to have 'authority'?	Are some types of evidence more convincing than others?	What is the relationship between religious/non-religious identity and other forms of identity, e.g. nationality, gender, sexuality?

Source: Based on Georgiou and Wright (2020)

In 2024, on the Meols Cop RE YouTube channel, Natalie Ford conducted a series of 'RE disciplinary conversations' with academics, teachers and RE advisers, to get a better understanding of what is meant by each discipline. The conversations can be accessed on the following links:

- David Lundie (philosophy) – www.youtube.com/watch?v=i5bmV7j5ChE
- David Robertson (religious studies) – www.youtube.com/watch?v=U8Fc7Xakhh4
- Gareth Evans-Jones (philosophy) – www.youtube.com/watch?v=WskVLaUM48o
- Gillian Georgiou (theology) – www.youtube.com/watch?v=TeA93FIvQpk

What strategies work well to teach disciplinary knowledge?

It can be sensible to deliberately plan for both substantive and disciplinary knowledge to be taught, and for students to knowingly use the disciplines in their learning. We want students to be able to use the disciplines, ask questions from using that disciplinary framework and apply their methodologies.

Here are some examples for the disciplines of theology, philosophy and social sciences:

Theology

In the example shown in Figure 4.1, students have already studied the Genesis story. I get them to use a theological approach and to consider the theological questions related to the text. They read through the text and, as noted in the instructions on the worksheet itself, having studied it, annotate all the things they notice. They should then draw lines to connect the tools on the right to the appropriate parts of the text, adding a comment explaining what each of the tools reveals about the text. Finally, they should summarise the message of the text with reference to the theological tools.

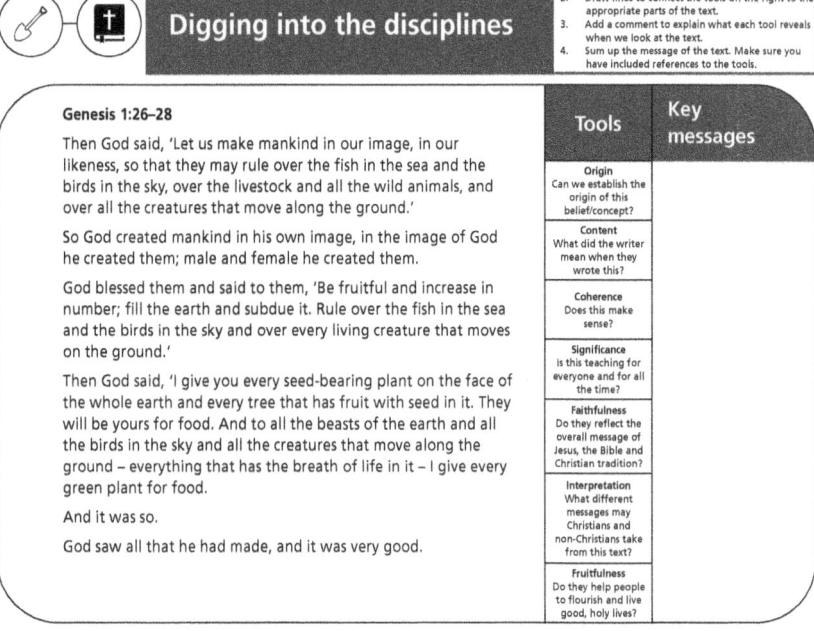

▲ Figure 4.1 'Digging into the disciplines' example 1: theology

Philosophy

In the example in Figure 4.2, students are looking at an argument presented by Karl Marx critiquing religion. They read through the argument and, as noted in the instructions on the worksheet itself, having studied it, annotate all the things they notice. They should then draw lines to connect the tools on the right to the appropriate parts of the extract, adding a comment explaining what each of the philosophical tools reveals about the extract. Finally, they should summarise the message of the argument, with reference to the philosophical tools.

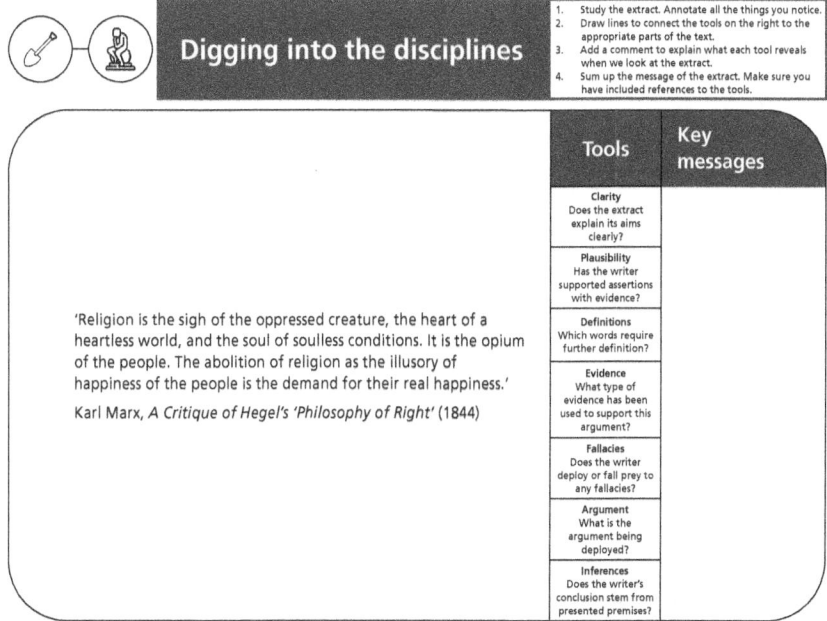

▲ Figure 4.2 'Digging into the disciplines' example 2: philosophy

Social sciences

In Figure 4.3, students are looking at some social science data relating to religion and belief in the UK. They look at the data and, as noted in the instructions on the worksheet itself, having studied it, annotate all the things they notice. They should then draw lines to connect the tools on the right to the appropriate parts of the data, adding a comment explaining what each of the social science tools reveals about the data. Finally, they should summarise the message of the data, with reference to the social science tools.

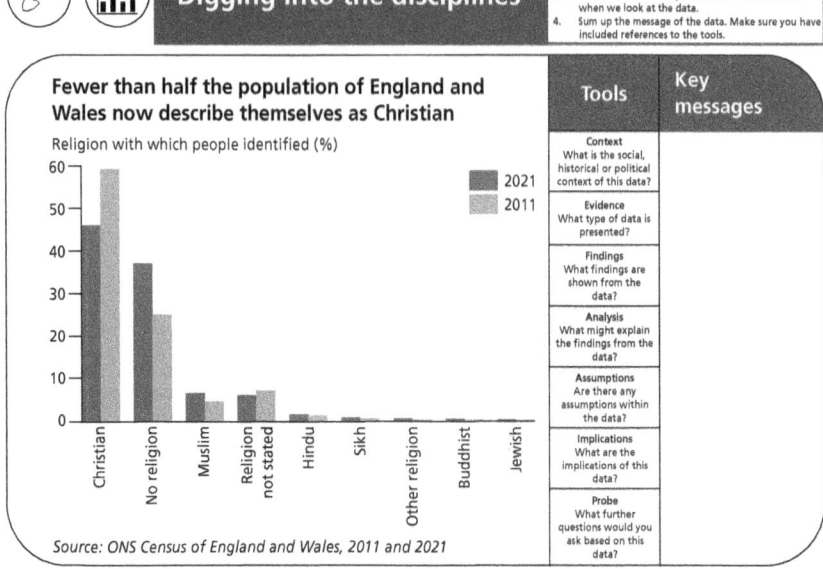

▲ Figure 4.3 Digging into the disciplines' example 3: social sciences

There are other ways in which we can incorporate disciplinary knowledge into our teaching. These will be illustrated in chapters 6, 7 and 11.

What are the pitfalls to avoid when teaching disciplinary knowledge?

As a fairly new area of discussion and practice among RE teachers, pitfalls will become more common as we trial things in the classroom. From my own experience so far, some pitfalls to be aware of are:

- **Blurring boundaries:** Mixing up substantive knowledge with disciplinary knowledge so that students can't tell the difference. Students need to know how knowledge is constructed in RE, not just what is known. In the classroom, we can combat this by being explicit when referencing disciplinary approaches, e.g. 'From a theological perspective …'.
- **Treating all disciplines as the same:** It is essential that students know that each discipline has its own methods, questions and criteria for truth. If these are blurred, students will fail to see what makes each way of knowing unique.

- **Oversimplification:** Giving an opinion is not thinking like a philosopher, and quoting a sacred text is not acting like a theologian. As RE teachers, we have to model authentic methods for ways of knowing – for example, teach the discipline of philosophy by showing what logical chains of reasoning within an argument look like.
- **Impact on time teaching substantive knowledge:** A key concern is how much time is spent teaching what disciplines are and how they work. This may lead to a reduction in the amount of substantive knowledge taught. The best way to combat this is by careful curriculum planning and sequencing, so that the precise knowledge to be taught is clearly mapped out within a lesson, scheme of work, etc. Chapter 5 on curriculum design will look at this in more detail.
- **Lack of awareness of power and perspective:** When we teach disciplinary knowledge, there is a risk of presenting disciplines as if they're timeless, objective and free from cultural influence. But, in reality, disciplines are products of particular times, places and power structures. If we don't make this explicit, students may assume these ways of knowing are 'the' way to study religion, rather than 'a' way. This can be addressed by including diverse scholarly voices and acknowledging the cultural background of methods.

To further address these pitfalls and others, the balanced RE self-audit tool on the Diocese of Lincoln Diocesan Board of Education website offers an excellent way of thinking about how you may or may not be using the disciplines within your classroom. You can find it by searching for 'A religion and worldviews approach' on the 'Religious education' page of its website: www.lincolndiocesaneducation.com/_site/data/files/key_documents/973D5723CF92948006C2B072520177BE.pdf.

Case study on personal knowledge
Arabella Saunders, Derby High School

What is personal knowledge?
RE has traditionally focused on substantive (content) and disciplinary (methods of knowing) knowledge. However, personal knowledge is just as essential. It is this third strand that allows students to truly grasp the complexity and diversity of religious and non-religious worldviews.

Personal knowledge describes the way in which 'a person encounters, interprets, understands and engages with the world' (Pett, 2024). Since each student brings a unique worldview into the classroom, a key element of high-quality RE is helping students navigate and reflect on their positionality. This means explicitly teaching them (a) to recognise that they inhabit a personal lens through which they see and interpret the world, and (b) to articulate the importance of understanding the fact that everyone inhabits a worldview.

Personal knowledge and cognitive science
When we encounter a concept in our environment and pay attention to it, it enters our working memory from our storage centre. However, when a concept is encountered it is not an isolated event but an interconnected one. It brings with it a plethora of ideas, assumptions, opinions, feelings, and so on. This happens because learning is rooted in the formation of schemas: interconnected webs of information that help us recall and apply knowledge.

As we learn we arrange information into schemas, and this helps us make sense of the world. It makes future recall easier because whole sets of information are remembered together. However, each schema is unique to the individual, shaped by experiences, perceptions and autobiography. So, in a typical classroom of KS3 students there will be 30 or more different schemas and the same number of unique worldviews.

When those students pay attention to something, they are not passive receivers but what they encounter is coloured by themselves. Take the idea 'international travel', for example. For some, this concept will evoke feelings of excitement, thrill, fond memories of adventure; for a few, dread and fear; for others, it is a luxury unavailable to them. It is not the idea 'international travel' itself that contains these ideas within, but it acts as a catalyst for a personal reaction. So, as teachers in the RE classroom it is important to bear in mind that every religious and non-religious concept encountered will, at first, be understood in 30 or so slightly different ways.

One way of understanding personal knowledge, then, is through its alignment with schemas. Personal knowledge is our own unique network of ideas that helps us understand the world.

Why is teaching personal knowledge important?

Explicitly teaching personal knowledge is important not only because it reveals a fundamental aspect of what it means to be human but also because it helps students better understand themselves and amplify their own voices.

Teaching pupils that we all inhabit a worldview unlocks an important element of what it is to be human

Michael Polanyi, the British-Hungarian philosopher, challenged the idea of objectivity, arguing that all knowledge is personal and tacit. In the RE world, he is often quoted as stating that 'nobody stands nowhere'. In his books *Personal Knowledge* (1958) and *The Tacit Dimension* (1966), he explores how nothing is objective since we all inhabit a worldview and have our own unique lens. This is true even in science, where personal biases and worldviews influence what is studied and how. Polanyi also writes about the 'self-ignorance' that we all share. He notes the phenomenon that there are many tasks we perform intuitively while being unable to verbalise the rules or procedures involved. There is a certain automacy with complex everyday activities such as navigating a traffic jam, using a knife and fork, reading the room, 'hearing' body language, knowing that your partner is upset with you from a simple text message, and so on. These examples of what Polanyi calls 'tacit knowledge' seem to apply to our worldview, and align with the way we recall concepts through schemas. Just as we recall concepts in a complex web of interconnectedness, similarly we automatically bring our worldview – our subjective, biased perspective – to every encounter we have.

But it is not the case that having a worldview is a negative thing. It is simply what it is to be human. Inhabiting a position, or a perspective, is the way we, as individual human beings, understand the world. Personal knowledge is, in fact, most often unconscious and unconsidered. For students in our classroom, it is often a completely surprising and powerful thing to begin to recognise that the way they see things and the things they might consider to be 'true' or 'factual' are only apparent truths, born out of their own autobiography, and influenced by their unique geography, religious (or non-religious) position, culture, era, experiences, upbringing, and so on.

Allowing children a window into their own worldview in this way is an entitlement

Our young people should be given access to grow self-awareness of their own positionality and how it shapes their encounters (Pett, 2024). The RE classroom is the ideal place to encounter themselves and to develop a reflexive criticality.

For example, Joseph Henrich's concept of WEIRD people (Henrich, 2020) highlights how certain perspectives dominate global discourse without acknowledgement. Many students in your classroom, and colleagues in your staffroom, will be from Western, Educated, Industrialised, Rich and Democratic (WEIRD) societies. This is one example of a common worldview that often leads students to label unfamiliar practices or beliefs as 'weird', reflecting their subconscious biases rooted in their cultural context. Teaching personal knowledge therefore allows students to become aware of their position, and enables better empathy, respect and understanding for those who are different to themselves.

Studying personal knowledge is truly inclusive

As students become more aware that they inhabit a worldview and encounter the world through a unique lens, the relevance of RE lessons becomes much more profound. The demographic data from the 2021 census in England and Wales signpost that most pupils are not part of organised religious traditions. Teaching students about their own positionality not only gives all students a sense of belonging and an amplified voice but also vastly increases the relevance of RE for students of all beliefs and none.

How might we teach personal knowledge?

I stated earlier that teaching personal knowledge can be split into two main areas:

1. recognising inhabitancy of a personal lens, and
2. articulating the importance of understanding the fact that everyone inhabits a unique worldview.

These two areas are drawn from recommendations J and K in the Religious Education Council of England and Wales' *Handbook for Curriculum Writers* (Pett, 2024). These recommendations outline how an education in religion and worldviews will help learners to explore 'how their own personal worldview shapes their encounters with and responses to the world, and how their context, experience and study can shape their personal worldview' (Pett, 2024).

Two questions that might be helpful when planning curriculums are:

1 What is my worldview?
2 Why is it important to understand that everyone has a worldview?

What is my worldview? Unpacking positionality (J. Personal worldviews: reflexivity)
1a. Y7 lesson resource: What factors shape a worldview?

In 2022, at the NATRE StrictlyRE online conference, Zameer Hussain spoke about how his Year 7 curriculum is front-loaded with a unit titled 'What is a worldview?' (Hussain, 2022). He suggests that beginning with lessons that allow students to unpack their own autobiography is an important foundation for personal knowledge education. The resources below are developed from his ideas.

In the example in Figure 4.4, students are required to write about each of the five factors in turn, reflecting carefully on their own lives. It is important to provide students with model paragraphs to ensure a higher level of reflection and detail in their answers.

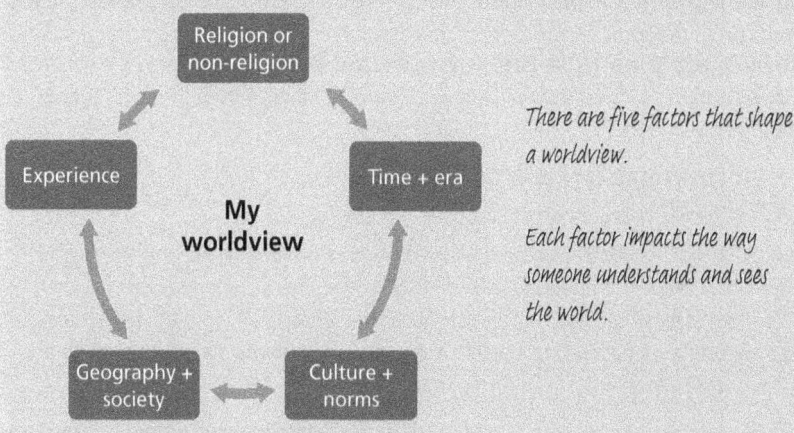

There are five factors that shape a worldview.

Each factor impacts the way someone understands and sees the world.

▲ **Figure 4.4 The five factors that shape a worldview**

Figure 4.5 shows an example model answer for the 'geography and society' factor. As shown here, students can include photos or sketches to illustrate their answers.

Geography/society influences your worldview

Where are you live influences your view on the world. The people you meet, the places you see and the society around you impact your perspective on the world in different ways. For example, you might live in a multicultural city, or in an area where most people have the same culture, religion or ethnicity.

I live in Repton, which is in south Derbyshire. My geography influences my worldview. For example, I am used to living in a boarding school and it seems normal for me to live in a house next to students and eat evening meals with the students and wider community. I've also lived around the world, including Brunei, which is a Muslim country, so I'm used to different cultures.

▲ Figure 4.5 Example worldviews activity focusing on geography and society

1b. Y13 lesson resource: What is 'WEIRD' and how might it shape my worldview?

In the OCR A-level specification, there are several topics very well suited to exploring personal knowledge. This resource is the introductory lesson to 'Gender and Society'. We begin with an examination of Ephesians 5:21–33 (NIV). I ask students to read the passage and annotate it with their ideas about what is being taught here:

Instructions for Christian Households

21*Submit to one another out of reverence for Christ.*

22*Wives, submit yourselves to your own husbands as you do to the Lord.* 23*For the husband is the head of the wife as Christ is the head of the church, his body, of which he is the Saviour.* 24*Now as the church submits to Christ, so also wives should submit to their husbands in everything.*

Of course, they arrive at all sorts of ideas that are the result of their automated worldview. This usually includes righteous indignation about the outdated gender roles and feelings of sexism within the text.

So then we stop, we talk about where our ideas come from, and consider our bias as WEIRD people (Henrich, 2020). We expand on the worldview of Paul, the writer, and we learn about the hinterland, or context, of the text. This activity therefore allows for a powerful moment where students unearth their WEIRD worldview and unpack their positionality.

Then we repeat the activity together, and this time students are much more alert and question their assumptions. We finish with another annotation of the text and draw out the key substantive knowledge. For example, the support for monogamy, the recognition that women were in a disadvantaged position in society at that time, and the command for husbands to show self-sacrificing love for their wives.

Students, now alert to their worldview and their hermeneutic, will now be much better theologians when they move on to the next Biblical text.

Why is it important to understand that everyone has a worldview? The impact of positionality (K. Personal worldviews: impact)
2a. Y7 lesson resource: The blind men and the elephant

This tale is helpful when unpacking worldviews. In it, six blind men encounter an elephant for the first time and argue over what it is. Each of them happens to hold a different part of the whole, leading to strife between them. It is useful for any secondary year group, but may require students to already understand Polanyi's idea that objectivity is impossible.

After reading a version of this story and unpacking the events, the first question asked is: 'If this story is intended to teach us about life, what do you think the elephant might represent?'

Some responses Year 7 students have given include:

- The elephant might represent the different meanings of life. This is because different people have different worldviews based on their time, era, culture, experiences, etc. So, these blind men show how they interpret the elephant (life) as different things (meanings).

- The blindness could represent people's inability to admit they are wrong. It could also show how people can be stubborn and ignorant towards each other.

The follow-up question is: 'Why is it important for us to understand that we all have a unique perspective on the world?'

Some responses from Year 7 students are:

- It helps us understand that religions are diverse. Two people who follow the same religion might have very different opinions about different issues.

- It helps you acknowledge why you might never understand why it is that people think the things they think or do the things that they do.

2b. Siddhartha's worldview

When studying the ideas of a scholar, religious founder, or any figure in the RE classroom, taking time to unpack their personal knowledge provides a powerful opportunity to deepen students' understanding of their beliefs and actions. Cooling et al (2020) emphasise that, 'in order to understand the worldviews being taught, the focus should not be so much on the institutional version as on the lived experience of adherents'.

For example, when teaching about Siddhartha Gautama's journey to becoming the Buddha, it is crucial that students grasp the worldview he held as a sheltered prince before encountering the Four Sights. Understanding the hinterland and context of Siddhartha's early life, his father's attempt to shield him from suffering and the luxury of palace life, helps students fully appreciate the profound shift in perspective that followed these encounters. A worldviews approach allows the spiritual and philosophical depth of Siddhartha's renunciation of material attachment and search for enlightenment to resonate far more deeply. So, when teaching the early life of the Buddha topic, pausing throughout to ask questions is paramount:

1 Consider Prince Siddhartha's worldview. What would he have felt in the palace? What questions might he have had?

2 Consider Siddhartha's worldview again. After the first three sights, how would he have felt? What questions might he have had?

3 Consider Siddhartha's worldview further. After the fourth sight, how would he have felt? What questions might he have had?

Conclusion: What are the benefits of teaching personal knowledge?

Overall, if the worldviews approach to RE can give a means for unpacking positionality then students will be at an advantage when encountering religious and non-religious beliefs. By explicitly teaching personal knowledge, RE teachers can anticipate misconceptions, cultivate reflexivity and support deeper, more meaningful learning.

Ultimately, developing students' awareness of their own lenses equips them to better understand not just religion but the complexity of human experience. Personal knowledge is not a distraction from RE's academic rigour: it is central to it.

CHAPTER 5
HOW CAN YOU STRUCTURE AN RE CURRICULUM?

Getting the RE curriculum right is perhaps the most important job of the RE teacher. Curriculum design needs to consider the substance of what we teach, how we teach it and how this links with the various disciplines found in the subject.

A well-sequenced RE curriculum communicates a rich narrative to our students, with each lesson carefully building upon learning from previous lessons to create accurate representations about religion and non-religion. Moreover, this supports staff, including new RE teachers and non-specialists, to develop their expertise in the subject. The curriculum is a living, breathing document, which requires constant revisiting and intellectual query to further support all involved in our subject.

While GCSE and A-level specifications set out in great detail what should be taught, there is no national curriculum for RE, which can lead to variations in the quality and approach of provision at key stage 3. Schools may turn to locally agreed syllabuses as a starting point for curriculum design. However, other factors need to be considered too, such as the balance between depth and breadth, disciplinary approaches and the aims of the subject.

The previous chapters have explored current debates and research surrounding knowledge and curriculum design in RE. In this chapter, the focus will be on showcasing the latest literature to support curriculum design, and case studies of how teachers have developed their own curriculum based on current thinking.

Context of the RE Council of England and Wales Religion and Worldviews Project

The *Developing a Religion and Worldviews Approach in Religious Education* handbook (Pett, 2024) is a major outcome of a three-year project commissioned by the Religious Education Council of England and Wales (REC). It builds on the vision set out in the 2018 Commission on Religious

Education (CoRE) report, which advocated a shift towards a more inclusive and academically grounded understanding of religious education, framed as 'religion and worldviews'. The handbook responds to ongoing concerns about the coherence, relevance and quality of RE across England, offering a national reference point for designing robust and inclusive curriculums that reflect the diversity of beliefs in modern Britain.

Aimed at a wide range of stakeholders – including curriculum developers, SACREs, multi-academy trusts (MATs), diocesan advisers and school RE leaders – the handbook provides both strategic and practical guidance for implementing a religion and worldviews approach. It is structured to support curriculum development that meets statutory requirements while aligning with educational best practices. Released alongside the National Statement of Entitlement (NSE) and a new National Content Standard, it forms part of a comprehensive toolkit intended to support curriculum reform, improve coherence and raise the profile of RE in schools across England.

As outlined in chapter 3, 11 recommendations were put forward in the 2018 CoRE report, and the handbook was heavily influenced by the following two:

1. A religion and worldviews approach. This looks at worldviews as:
   a) Objects of study
   b) Part of how we study them
   c) Part of the experience of those doing the studying

2. National Statement of Entitlement: All students in state-maintained schools are entitled to experience a high quality education in religion and worldviews.

The handbook is split into four sections:

- Section A: Overview of the religion and worldviews approach and information about the National Statement of Entitlement
- Section B: Toolkit for putting the religion and worldviews approach into practice
- Section C: Rationale and explanations for a religion and worldviews approach
- Section D: Overview of three exemplar frameworks.

Where can I read it?
You can find the link to the full handbook in the 'Our work' section of the Commission on Religious Education website: https://religiouseducationcouncil.org.uk/rec/wp-content/uploads/2024/04/24-25698-REC-Handbook-A4-DIGITAL-PAGES.pdf.

This chapter will focus on key ideas from the toolkit in section B.

Toolkit for developing a religion and worldview approach to RE

This sets out the purposes of RE, explores the NSE in more detail, and provides guidance about how to select content.

The handbook sets out clear purposes for the subject in a religion and worldviews approach. These are:

- Introduce students to the rich variety of religious and non-religious worldviews, locally and globally, as a way of understanding humanity and the world.
- Spark curiosity and interest in this diversity to encourage respectful engagement.
- Explore how worldviews influence individuals, communities and societies.
- Help students understand that studying worldviews involves interpreting meaning, not just learning facts.
- Foster appreciation of the complexity and nuance in worldviews, including sensitivity to religious language and experience.
- Teach students how religion and worldviews can be studied using academic disciplines and methods.
- By the end of their studies, enable them to recognise how different academic lenses affect understanding.
- Provide opportunities to explore connections between worldviews and literature, culture and the arts.
- Encourage students to examine their own emerging worldviews and how these relate to the broader religious and philosophical heritage.
- Support students in reflecting on how their learning influences their views on the world and their role in shaping its future.

- Promote thoughtful, informed personal responses to the content studied.
- Equip students with the skills and understanding needed to make thoughtful, critical and respectful judgements about religion and worldviews.
- Prepare them for life in a diverse society where such understanding is essential for responsible citizenship.

The National Statement of Entitlement is the tool for achieving these proposed purposes. It serves to provide a benchmark for standards in the curriculum and a pedagogical tool for the selection of content and of appropriate teaching and learning approaches to develop pupil understanding.

Content	
Core statement	**Expanded statement**
a. **Nature/formation/expression** – *What is meant by worldview and how people's worldviews are formed and expressed through a complex mix of influences and experiences.*	Worldviews develop through varied influences like rituals, texts, arts, culture, personal experiences and interactions. These elements are also ways people express and communicate their worldviews.
b. **Organised/individual** – *How people's individual worldviews relate to wider, organised or institutional worldviews.*	Individual worldviews may be conscious or unconscious and are shaped through interaction with organised traditions. Both are dynamic and influence each other over time.
c. **Contexts** – *How worldviews have contexts, reflecting time and place, are highly diverse, and feature continuity and change.*	Individual worldviews may be conscious or unconscious and are shaped through interaction with organised traditions. Both are dynamic and influence each other over time.
d. **Meaning and purpose** – *How worldviews may offer responses to fundamental questions raised by human experience.*	Worldviews help people address existential and philosophical questions about meaning, purpose, identity and truth. They offer ways of interpreting life, including space for ambiguity and paradox.

Content	
Core statement	**Expanded statement**
e. Values, commitments and morality – *How worldviews may provide guidance on how to live a good life.*	They offer ethical frameworks – defining good, justice, truth, beauty – and guide personal and communal commitments that express these values.
f. Influence and power – *How worldviews influence, and are influenced by, people and societies.*	Worldviews can shape societal norms and politics, provide narratives that guide identity and purpose, and be shaped in turn by social change, conflict or peace-making.

Engagement	
Core statement	**Expanded statement**
g. Ways of knowing – *The field of study of worldviews is to be explored using diverse ways of knowing.*	Understanding worldviews requires multiple approaches, acknowledging that concepts of truth, reliability and knowledge vary across traditions and disciplines.
h. Lived experience – *The field of study of worldviews is to include a focus on the lived experience of people.*	Study should include how real individuals live, practise and express worldviews – recognising their fluid, material, embodied and diverse nature across global/local settings.
i. Dialogue/interpretation – *The field of study of worldviews is to be shown as a dynamic area of debate.*	Worldviews are explored through ongoing dialogue and interpretation. Students engage critically with ideas and perspectives, learning to debate and evaluate.

Position	
Core statement	**Expanded statement**
j. **Personal worldviews: reflexivity** – *Students will reflect on and potentially develop their personal worldviews in the light of their study.*	Students become more aware of their own worldview and how it relates to others', equipping them to navigate and make reasoned judgements in a diverse society.
k. **Personal worldviews: impact** – *Students will reflect on how their worldviews affect their learning.*	Students learn to recognise how their own perspectives shape their engagement with RE content and how this learning, in turn, may influence their worldview.

Although set out like a list, the three elements of the NSE are integrated. The analogy of a journey is helpful to understand the relationship between content, engagement and position:

- **Destination:** Content strands a–f provide a realm of religion and worldviews to explore.
- **Preparation:** Engagement strands g–i provide the tools and route for the journey.
- **Position:** Position strands j–k allow us to recognise that the journey is being carried out from our own position. Awareness of how this affects your journey is an integral part of the exploration and should be recognised throughout.

In the religion and worldviews approach, the three elements – content, engagement and position – do not need to receive equal time in every unit. Instead, they should be integrated flexibly to best meet the learning aims. Typically:

- most time is spent on content
- engagement time varies depending on students' familiarity with the method
- position is addressed as appropriate, encouraging self-reflection at different points.

Teachers aren't expected to cover all 11 strands in each unit.

The NSE includes 11 interconnected strands, which should be seen as working in relationship rather than isolation. In any given unit, teachers may focus on one content strand, one engagement method and one position element, but this does not exclude the influence of the others.

As illustrated in Figure 5.1, the process may be compared to using a mixing desk in music: a teacher may 'fade up' certain strands for emphasis while others remain present in the background, ready to take focus in future units. For example, a unit might highlight values, commitments and morality (NSE e) and individual vs organised worldviews (NSE b), while also incorporating aspects of context (NSE f) without making it the main focus.

Similarly, teachers might prioritise the lived experience of people (NSE h) but include a disciplinary approach (NSE g).

With position, both strands often feature, but the unit may foreground one more than the other.

This flexible integration allows for depth and balance over time, not necessarily within every single unit.

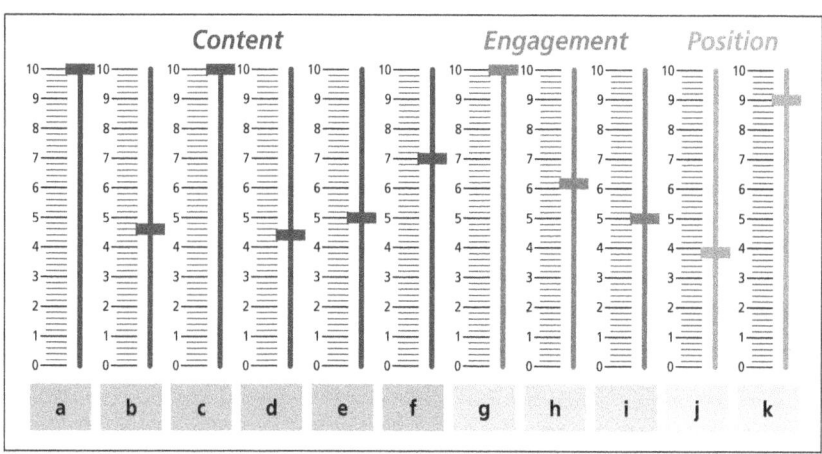

Source: Based on Pett (2024, p. 34)

▲ Figure 5.1 The process of covering the three elements may be compared to using a mixing desk

In her Coventry and Warwickshire SACRE/Diocese-led Framework, Jen Jenkins continues the mixing desk analogy by explaining how, just like a recurring melody in music or a TV theme tune, different NSE elements may come to the foreground or fade into the background depending on the focus of a unit (Coventry & Warwickshire Local Authorities, 2024). While some statements may be less prominent in certain units, they are rarely absent entirely and often re-emerge as central in others.

What does the handbook say about how to select content?

As curriculum time is limited, curriculum developers must select content carefully. Content should be based on the following criteria.

1 **Intention:** Content must align with the aims of the NSE and support students' progression through its elements and their interconnections.
2 **Legal framework:** RE must reflect that Christianity is the main tradition in Great Britain, while also covering other principal religions. For schools with a religious character, RE follows the trust deed or equivalent.
3 **Inclusivity:** In schools without a religious character, RE must be inclusive of both religious and non-religious worldviews, such as humanism, and taught in a critical, objective and pluralistic way. All traditions must be represented fairly, respecting diversity without implying equal time.
4 **Contextual relevance:** Curriculum choices should reflect the local context, including the character of the school, local communities, students' and teachers' experiences, and regional history.
5 **'Collectively enough' principle:** Students need to gain cumulatively sufficient knowledge over time (not full coverage), in relation to the NSE's three elements: content, engagement and position.

The NSE engagement element

The NSE engagement element points out that content should be studied in a variety of ways.

Ways of knowing

Understanding and applying ways of knowing is crucial because it allows students to engage with religion and worldviews through diverse disciplinary lenses such as theology, philosophy, sociology and anthropology. These methods:

- encourage asking different types of questions about the same content
- require different approaches to answer those questions

- lead to various interpretations and require appropriate tools for evaluation
- are influenced by the learner's or researcher's context and worldview.

Introducing younger students to a range of methods helps them grasp that content can be explored differently. As students progress, they should learn that different disciplines produce different types of knowledge based on their assumptions and how these affect the way the scholar will practise the discipline.

This approach should allow students to develop critical and reflective skills that help them understand the complexity and diversity of religious traditions and perspectives. Specifically, they should:

- recognise that sacred texts hold different levels of authority for insiders and outsiders to a tradition
- explore how and why these texts are interpreted and applied in varied ways across contexts
- question common categories within religion, such as the centrality of texts in all traditions
- understand that no single voice speaks for an entire tradition and consider the challenges of representation
- acknowledge the diversity of religious expression, from expert to lay perspectives
- reflect on whose voices are included in lessons and the implications of those choices
- critically assess data sources (e.g. surveys), questioning their reliability and validity
- apply appropriate methods to evaluate arguments, interpretations, truth claims and the evidential basis of theories.

Lived experience

In a religion and worldviews approach, learning about official religious beliefs, texts and rituals is balanced with exploring how people experience and practise religion in their daily lives. While traditional RE has focused on theological orthodoxy and correct practice, the religion and worldviews approach includes how non-experts engage with religion in personal, often inconsistent ways. Religion is seen as fluid and varied at the individual level, requiring exploration of real-life experiences that go beyond institutional definitions. These lived experiences also help reveal insights into the nature, influence and power of religious institutions.

Within a religion and worldviews approach, students should develop the ability to:

- understand that a worldview is more than just a set of beliefs – it includes actions, daily practices and ways of living
- recognise how people express what matters to them through their bodies, rituals, objects, buildings and art
- explore how worldviews are lived and experienced in everyday life, not just understood intellectually
- engage thoughtfully with people from different worldviews through direct encounters
- reflect on how representative an individual's perspective is of a wider community
- consider how a person's worldview influences their thoughts, choices and way of being
- develop awareness of the limits of generalisations and the importance of context in understanding lived religion.

Dialogue/interpretation

This strand shows that religion and worldviews are always changing, not fixed. Even in traditions that see their holy texts as coming from God, there are ongoing discussions about what those texts mean, where they came from and how to apply them today. These debates have often been going on for centuries, showing that religious ideas develop over time.

The strand also uses a hermeneutical approach, which means focusing on interpretation. It teaches that to understand religious texts, actions and symbols, we need to think about both their original context and our own. This process, called the meeting of two horizons, helps students connect what they are learning with their own views and experiences. It encourages them to think carefully, ask questions and make thoughtful, informed judgements about what they study.

This strand should enable students to:

- understand and explore key debates within different religious and non-religious worldviews, both past and present – for example, historical debates about the nature of the Trinity in Christianity,

or modern discussions about technology and ethics within various faith communities
- recognise that disagreement is a normal part of religious and worldviews discussion, and learn how to engage in respectful, reasoned dialogue
- develop interpretive skills to analyse texts, art, rituals and other expressions of beliefs or values
- ask thoughtful questions about texts
- reflect on how their own worldview shapes how they understand and respond to what they study
- identify and question generalisations about organised worldviews, using appropriate evidence to test or support claims.

The NSE position element: developing personal worldviews

The position element of the NSE highlights the pupil's active role in learning, and stresses that developing their personal worldview is an essential part of a thoughtful religion and worldviews approach.

This involves:

- helping students reflect on and explain their own worldviews and where these come from, so they can have thoughtful discussions about religion and worldviews (and other subjects too)
- encouraging students to recognise their own worldviews and engage in informed dialogue with others' worldviews
- developing students' self-awareness and reflection about how they learn
- supporting students in using this self-awareness to see how their personal worldviews influence their understanding of religious content and how learning about others can shape their own views
- helping students recognise that other people's responses are shaped by their own personal worldviews
- developing students' understanding of how interpretation plays a part in their learning and knowledge
- encouraging students to use art and creativity to express their ideas, and to better understand both their own and others' perspectives
- developing skills in different ways of learning, including using disciplines, dialogue and interpretation

- encouraging pupils to create their own understanding by engaging thoughtfully with religion and worldviews
- fostering academic virtues like curiosity, humility, openness to others and careful listening before forming opinions.

It is important to stress that not all of this can be fully known or measured, and in some schools – especially those with a religious background – curriculum designers may focus more specifically on moral and spiritual development.

How can the NSE be used to develop a curriculum?

The toolkit offers some principles and guidelines to consider when looking to develop a curriculum. These are:

Guidelines for using the NSE	Guidelines for curriculum content	Guidelines for questions and context
• The NSE outlines the knowledge pupils need to understand how worldviews function in human life. • The NSE is a pedagogical tool. It provides a structure and criteria for content selection, but it is not a checklist or linear. • The curriculum must include all three NSE elements: content, engagement and position. • The NSE elements build cumulatively as students progress through the curriculum. • The focus is on human engagement with religion and non-religious worldviews, not studying them in isolation. • Statements can be broken down and units of work can focus on part of one (e.g. NSE d could be broken down to look at ontological questions about existence or origins, such as 'Is there a God?').	• Organised worldviews (e.g. religions) can be studied systematically to explore NSE elements. • Use case studies as microcosms to reflect broader worldview characteristics and NSE elements. • Include creative expressions, lived experiences, material religion and texts/teachings when deciding on material to select for use in the classroom. • Students should develop familiarity with multiple academic disciplines, but not all need equal emphasis. • Content should enable personal and critical engagement, with self-reflection as a key element.	• Rich enquiry questions help manage content overload, guide learning and shape appropriate methods and disciplines. • Enquiry questions should align with learning goals (e.g. preparing for visits, appreciation of diversity or developing nuanced understanding for GCSE). • Local context matters and can give a distinct identity to a curriculum – consider demographics, history, culture (e.g. religious diversity in London boroughs). • Compare local, national and global religious landscapes. Britain is atypical in its high proportion of non-religion. • Curriculum designers must be reflexive: question biases, diversify perspectives and include insider/outsider voices. Consider questions such as 'Are your sources diverse?', 'Are you including unfamiliar voices?'

Here are some advisory tips for devising your curriculum based on the toolkit:

Values and definitions
- Ensure your curriculum is aligned with your school or MAT's values and aims, e.g. religious ethos or curriculum philosophy.
- Give time to develop a shared understanding in your department of what is meant by key terms, e.g. religion, worldviews, disciplinary knowledge.
- Involve various parties in your discussions, e.g. SLT, governors, other departments.

Utilising the NSE
- Use the NSE as a starting point if building a curriculum from scratch or reviewing an existing one.
- Annotate it to highlight connections across statements, the way they can interlink and connect.
- Identify how local context can enrich engagement with the NSE.
- Use concentric circles or other tools to show how understanding, awareness and revisiting of concepts may occur over time.
- Recognise the gaps or areas covered in less detail, consider why this might be the case and what can be done to address this.

Develop structure and progression
- Break the content component of your overview into four or five key segments, to ensure clear progression and thematic consistency.
- Ensure that earlier learning prepares for later learning, and that later learning builds on earlier learning.
- Think about which segments suit different key stages and when best to introduce them.

Design questions that unlock learning
- Create or adapt enquiry questions appropriate for each age group.
- Ensure questions balance NSE strands (content, engagement, position) and identify which disciplinary method will be used to find out the answer.
- Use the mixing desk analogy to reflect on the balance of disciplines being used in your enquiry questions.

Draft your outline

- Draft a key stage outline or long-term plan populated with your exemplar questions and units, to ensure coherence across the years.
- Describe each unit's intent clearly – how it builds knowledge and develops understanding of religion and worldviews.
- Test how well you are exploring content, engagement and position by choosing a sample of enquiry questions from different phases and drafting units of work for them.
- Include a variety of case studies to reflect how worldviews operate in diverse, real-world contexts.

Developing enquiry questions

Enquiry questions are an excellent way of providing a clear focus for content, guiding choice of disciplines and personal reflections. These questions should grow in complexity as pupils progress through the curriculum.

A world religions approach may use enquiry questions to frame units of work, but the religion and worldviews approach looks to shift these questions to include a more evaluative element, recognising that different answers may be acceptable in different contexts.

The table summarises the differences:

Feature of enquiry question	World religions approach	Religion and worldviews approach
Question style	Communicates settled knowledge	Encourages interpretation and exploration of meaning
Context	Abstract and often context free	Context specific, e.g. particular people, time and place
Answer expectation	Implies one 'correct' or standard answer	Accepts multiple valid responses, reflecting diversity
Diversity	May acknowledge diversity but presents it as secondary	Diversity is central and expected in responses

Feature of enquiry question	World religions approach	Religion and worldviews approach
Evaluative element	Limited or absent	Built in – asks why different people respond differently
Purpose	Transmits information	Deepens understanding of how worldviews function and are lived

Based on the above, here are some examples of enquiry questions framed within a world religions approach, and how a religion and worldviews approach may frame these questions differently:

World religions approach	Religion and worldviews approach
What does Hinduism teach about life after death?	What differences does a belief in life after death make to the way Hindus live their lives?
Is there a God? What and why do people believe?	How do the Abrahamic religions understand God?
Are religions sources of peace or causes of conflict?	Why have Christians played a role in conflict and peace in the modern world?

Constructing a unit of work

The toolkit provides a sample process for constructing a unit of work. Here is an outline of the process with a focus on KS3:

Knowledge: What do pupils know and what do you want them to know?	Students will have explored the historical origins of different religious worldviews. They are going to explore how these beliefs shape identity and the lived reality of leading a religious life.
Use the NSE: Balance the three elements (content, engagement, position).	NSE e – values, commitments and morality NSE g – ways of knowing NSE k – personal worldviews: reflexivity

Topic: Identify an appropriate topic from the syllabus.	Ways in which worldviews may provide guidance on justice, value and goodness
Question: Create a question to frame the unit and the NSE focus.	Can different religious worldviews agree on what is good?
Disciplinary method: Choose the disciplinary tools to explore the question.	Discipline: Philosophy Method: Data from surveys and interviews; comparison of different ethical systems, e.g. Buddhist Eightfold Path and Christian agape
Personal knowledge: Decide on moments for developing and exploring personal knowledge.	Exploration of how different ideas of goodness mirror or differ from their own
Materials: Select sources, case studies and learning activities for the unit of work.	Case studies, e.g. responses to poverty, punishment or equality

The curriculum outline and case study below offer some examples of how the ideas discussed above can be followed. This curriculum is a model held up for illustration, not imitation. The questions asked in the case study would be useful for you to discuss with your team when reflecting on your own curriculum.

Case study of KS3 RE curriculum design
Charlotte Newman, Archway Learning Trust

How did your school context influence your curriculum design?

I am the trust lead for religious studies across eight secondary schools in a MAT spanning Nottingham and Derby. Although we are a Church of England trust, only three schools have a religious character. Since my appointment in September 2024, my main role has been driving 'curriculum convergence' – a shared curriculum and assessment framework across all schools to ensure equity, while allowing local adaptation. Our schools are diverse: some inner-city with mixed backgrounds, others predominantly white British, spread across four local authorities. While not bound to follow local agreed syllabuses, I believe aligning with statutory requirements is vital, so I serve on the working group reviewing the Nottingham City and Nottinghamshire syllabus. A key challenge has been creating a curriculum that reflects our wide-ranging demographics, beliefs and geography.

Another challenge is staffing: around 70 teachers deliver RE, but only 20 are specialists. Many teachers with other specialisms (TWOs) – from history, geography, social sciences, PE, English and art – teach RE, often without RE-specific CPD, as they prioritise training in their main subjects. I believe RE should be as ambitious as other humanities, so I've carefully designed our curriculum to support both specialists and non-specialists in delivering it effectively.

What was the vision for your curriculum?

Previously, the trust curriculum was designed for one religious school and rolled out across all, but this failed to meet the diverse needs of students and teachers. Many students disengaged, teachers lacked clarity on sequencing and units often didn't align with enquiry questions. The curriculum was also outdated, still rooted in a world religions paradigm, with poor resources and little explicit disciplinary knowledge, ignoring recent developments such as the religion and worldviews approach.

In response, I chose to start from scratch, involving teachers across all schools in the design so they understood and owned the curriculum, and could confidently articulate its intent to inspectors such as Ofsted and SIAMS. I introduced the team to a religion and worldviews approach, which became the foundation of our RE curriculum core principles.

Our vision is that RE begins with people, as Georgiou (2024) argues, moving from the particular to the general through lived religion case studies. Core substantive concepts run throughout to build schemas, made explicit and revisited regularly. All students, regardless of background, are entitled to the same core knowledge, captured in our 'need to know'. Theology, philosophy and social sciences are explicitly taught as disciplinary lenses, with students applying their methods to topics studied. Students also reflect on their own worldviews as they evolve and engage with rich texts, including original scholarly works like *Descartes' Meditations*. Finally, equitable and fair assessment ensures all students can succeed in RE.

What research has informed your curriculum design?

Many of our curriculum core principles are rooted in a religion and worldviews approach. Initially, I was sceptical, seeing it as an arbitrary rebrand, but reading the Commission on RE report (2018), Mark Chater's *Reforming RE* (2020) and the Ofsted *Research Review* (2021) showed me that RE must evolve to reflect today's religious and cultural landscape. For students to navigate life, they need to understand that everyone has a worldview – one that shifts as it is reshaped by study and experience.

Stephen Pett's *Developing a Religion and Worldviews Approach in Religious Education in England: A Handbook for Curriculum Writers* (2024) clarified how individuals interact with institutional worldviews in ways that may differ from orthodox teachings. This reinforced my commitment to ensuring students directly encounter diverse worldviews, avoiding misconceptions and presenting faiths in ways adherents would recognise. The multidisciplinary approach also enables students to interpret life through multiple perspectives using varied scholarly tools and methods.

Gillian Georgiou's *Teacher-led Framework* (2024) questions have been invaluable in reframing units, prompting us to reflect on disciplines, case studies and intended outcomes before writing or adapting schemes. I have also been influenced by Mary Myatt's call for curriculum to be 'collectively enough' (Myatt, 2018) and by Christine Counsell's emphasis on embedding the power of story throughout (Counsell, 2018).

What are the core concepts and 'golden threads' in your curriculum?

The substantive knowledge in our curriculum is organised according to the six core concepts below. They are repeatedly encountered as a part of a spiral curriculum and so these are the 'golden threads' that knit together the narrative throughout.

1. Continuity, change and diversity – recognising that religion/non-religion changes in response to new situations and challenges.

2. Meaning and purpose – recognising that worldviews/experiences produce a sense of identity and belonging.

3. Wisdom and guidance – beliefs and ideas are shaped by sacred texts and this impacts the lived reality of adherents.

4. Living well – beliefs and ideas shape the way in which people 'live well' and develop their morality.

5. Authority and power – how religious and non-religious communities interact with wider society and cultures.

6. Grand narratives – religious and non-religious worldviews provide accounts for how and why the world is the way it is.

In choosing our core concepts, I was guided by the SACRE framework in Stephen Pett's *Developing a Religion and Worldviews Approach in Religious Education in England: A Handbook for Curriculum Writers* (2024), which drew on the substantive knowledge section of the National Statement of Entitlement. I also took inspiration from Barbara Wintersgill's Big Ideas for Religious Education project (https://bigideasforre.org/), using both to shape concepts that align with what we want all students to know by the time they leave us.

What key knowledge and skills do you want students to retain by the end of each key stage?

Our end of key stage outcomes are shaped by the Nottingham City and Nottinghamshire local agreed syllabus and our core concepts.

By the end of key stage 3, students should be able to explain and analyse core religious and worldview beliefs and their impact on individuals and communities. They will engage with key sources of wisdom and authority through hermeneutics, learning how interpretation shapes belief. Students will also construct balanced arguments, explore moral frameworks from religious and non-religious traditions, and confidently apply the disciplinary tools of theology, philosophy and social sciences to understand belief, practice and lived experience.

Beyond GCSE requirements, by the end of key stage 4 we want students to reflect on others' worldviews, develop respect for difference and recognise how their own beliefs shape identity. Our aim is for students to be religiously literate, curious about traditions that have shaped the world, and able to evaluate and argue academically and empathetically. These skills are essential for fostering harmony in a multicultural, pluralist society.

Balancing breadth and depth is one of the biggest challenges in curriculum design, especially with only one hour a week at KS3. While some schools prioritise depth with one topic per term, we have opted for one per half term, to allow greater variety. We are clear that it is impossible to cover every tradition, so instead we build on what students have already learned at primary level, viewing the curriculum from early years to KS5 as a progression model leading to our end of key stage outcomes.

How do you find a balance between breadth and depth in your curriculum?

Some units focus on a single tradition for depth, such as 'Is it possible to follow Prophet Muhammad's teachings in 21st-century Britain?', 'Does Buddhist Dharma provide answers for why we suffer?' and 'What does it mean to be a Sikh in Britain today?' Here, carefully chosen knowledge enables students to revisit and answer the enquiry question. These foundations then support more thematic units, such as 'How do humans express their spirituality?', where students draw on multiple traditions through art, ritual and worship.

We ensure breadth by balancing disciplinary perspectives: philosophy units such as 'How do we know what is real?', theology units like 'How are the Abrahamic faiths connected through the prophets?' and social sciences units such as 'What is religion and is it dying?' Our enquiry questions are ambitious, introducing students to scholars and ideas often reserved for A-level or university, including Locke's room analogy, William James on religious experience, Linda Woodhead's 'values are the new religion', and feminist theology.

How do you sequence topics across the year(s)?

We begin KS3 with 'What is a worldview?', to give students a foundation they will return to throughout the course, recognising how worldviews shape perspectives. Alongside this, we explicitly teach the disciplines of theology, philosophy and social science as the 'lenses' they will apply. In Year 7, students study the Abrahamic prophets, different worldviews of Jesus, and the Prophet Muhammad, building solid knowledge of what connects these traditions. They then explore atheism, the 'nones' and finally how faith inspires action through figures such as Harriet Tubman, Dietrich Bonhoeffer and Esther.

In Year 8, we introduce Buddhism through the question 'Can it explain why we suffer?', linking back to Year 7 themes of faith in times of conflict. Students then explore 'Why is Christianity the way it is?' and 'What does it mean to be Sikh today?' through case studies of lived religion. Later units revisit all prior traditions in exploring 'How do humans express their spirituality?', before tackling philosophical questions on reality with Plato, Aristotle, Descartes, Locke and Turing. The year ends with 'How do Christians address modern challenges?', applying learning to issues such as poverty, sexism, racism, interfaith division and climate change.

In Year 9, with two hours a week, we address more complex questions before GCSE. Students examine 'Is religion dying?' through functionalism, cognitive science, census data and secularism, applying tools from earlier years. This leads into 'Does God exist?', covering philosophical arguments, Jewish theodicies and the impact of the Holocaust on faith. Finally, they study 'How do we know what is right and wrong?', applying religious and non-religious ethics to issues like genetic engineering, drawing on thinkers such as Hannah Arendt and Locke, and humanist perspectives on morality.

Across KS3, our core concepts act as golden threads, revisited to strengthen schemas. We sequence GCSE units in the same way – interleaving rather than teaching paper by paper – so that prior knowledge is continuously built upon.

How have you embedded or planned for disciplinary and/or personal knowledge in your curriculum?

As mentioned, each curriculum unit explicitly signals which discipline students will use to answer the enquiry question, primarily theology, philosophy and social sciences, though other disciplines such as psychology and history are occasionally incorporated to reflect the complexity of lived experience.

We teach these disciplines through a series of characters, inspired by Gillian Georgiou's work, which we adapted to reflect our context, age range and student diversity. Introduced in the Year 7 'Worldviews' unit, these characters reappear whenever their corresponding tools or methods are used. For example, Sunil the Social Scientist guides students through sociological studies, Philippa the Philosopher models Socratic questioning and Theo the Theologian leads hermeneutical analysis of texts using the LAaSMO model (Literary form, Author and Audience, Setting, Meaning, Our World Today). This approach helps students associate each discipline with a concrete method, gradually internalising what it means to 'be a theologian, philosopher or social scientist'.

Students are also encouraged to reflect on their own worldviews, considering factors such as religion or non-religion, era, culture, geography, personal experiences and family upbringing. These reflections are revisited across units when examining scholars' beliefs, enabling comparison with students' own perspectives. For instance, in 'How do we know what is real?', students complete an amended survey from the RE Today Studying Worldviews curriculum both at the start and end of the unit, to track shifts in belief. Similarly, the 'Who are the nones?' unit uses a snowflake diagram to help students visualise the extent to which they align with the perspectives studied.

How is diversity reflected in your curriculum?

As a diversity lead in my previous school, I am deeply committed to ensuring students see themselves reflected in the curriculum. This is particularly important in schools with students from a wide range of minority ethnic backgrounds and nationalities. We want the RE classroom to be an inclusive space where differences are respected and valued. To achieve this, we place lived religion case studies at the heart of our units, emphasising that students are engaging with real people's experiences, not just abstract ideas. For example, in the 'Why is Christianity the way it is?' unit, we study Reverend Naomi Mensah – a Black, British, liberal priest – who discusses questioning the Bible and applying it to modern issues, such as accepting LGBTQ+ couples in her church. Presenting this liberal perspective is vital in schools with a predominantly religious character, where students may be accustomed to fundamentalist interpretations, so they understand that religious belief is diverse.

In the 'How does Christianity address modern challenges?' unit, we explore liberation theology, feminist theology, Black theology, and Pope Francis I's approach to women priests and LGBTQ+ inclusion. In KS4 'Christianity beliefs', when examining the problem of evil and suffering, we include the story of Joni Eareckson, an evangelical paraplegic whose faith has strengthened through traumatic experiences. Philosophical explorations of God's existence include contributions from Islamic thinkers such as Al Ghazali and Ibn Rushd, as well as Jewish philosophers Moses Mendelssohn and Maimonides. Through these case studies and content choices, we aim to ensure students see themselves reflected in the curriculum, and avoid the misconception that Western thought and society have been shaped only by dead, white men.

How do you ensure your curriculum is implemented effectively?

As we are just a year into our curriculum journey, implementation is still in its early stages. However, trialling our first units has already provided valuable insights. A key lesson has been the importance of providing CPD directly linked to the content staff are delivering, to strengthen their subject knowledge. Many teachers, including specialists, have admitted that much of what we are developing is new to them. To support this, every lesson begins with a teacher information slide, outlining the 'need to knows' for the lesson, the disciplinary method being used, potential misconceptions, and signposting to additional resources such as YouTube videos, recommended books or podcasts. Lesson planning also includes subject-specific guidance in the PowerPoint 'Notes' section, covering discussion points, answers and examples that staff might use. This approach empowers teachers to deliver lessons confidently, and feedback has consistently highlighted its usefulness. In time, CPD sessions will build on this approach, and we plan to create short videos demonstrating how to teach each unit.

A particular challenge has been the number of TWOs teaching RE. These staff often have limited access to CPD, making it harder to communicate the vision of a religion and worldviews approach. Some have struggled to understand the use of disciplinary characters and the introduction of case studies. To address this, I created a guide for TWOs, detailing our curriculum aims and offering top tips on preparing to teach RE effectively.

As part of my role as trust lead, I regularly visit each school, often conducting learning walks with the head of department. These visits allow me to observe the curriculum in action and monitor how lessons are delivered. Planning intentions do not always match classroom realities, so ongoing monitoring is crucial to ensure the curriculum is implemented as intended.

How do you evaluate the success of your curriculum?

I have actively sought staff feedback throughout the curriculum's development. At the end of every lesson, staff can scan a QR code to provide specific feedback, highlighting what has worked well and suggesting any necessary adaptations. They can also upload resources showing how they have tailored lessons for their classes or schools, providing practical examples. Staff have commented on the increased engagement of students and the evident care taken in planning lessons to ensure accessibility and high quality. Student voice has also been gathered through surveys on the new units delivered so far. Feedback indicates that students enjoy the lessons and are learning about topics that interest them.

It is important to note that much of this work is still in the early stages. KS3 will be taught fully only from the next academic year, and in some schools, students have not yet fully embraced RE. However, given the positive feedback on the units delivered through a religion and worldviews approach, we are confident that students will begin to recognise its relevance. As lessons and resources continue to improve, staff become more confident and schemes of work become more engaging, we anticipate a positive impact on student attitudes and outcomes.

Assessment will be used to judge whether students have mastered the knowledge outlined in the curriculum. This will inform ongoing curriculum development, ensuring that any gaps in learning are addressed. We are also developing disciplinary assessments to evaluate students' application of specific tools and methods. For example, students may analyse an unseen set of data to test their skills as social scientists or interpret an unseen sacred text passage to test their skills as philosophers. This approach ensures that students are not only acquiring knowledge but also developing the practical skills associated with each discipline.

What changes have you made after reflecting on student outcomes and feedback?

I firmly believe that a curriculum is never truly finished; it should continually evolve and adapt as students engage with the knowledge and disciplines, and as new ideas and societal changes emerge. As a result, we are constantly refining our schemes based on feedback gathered through the QR codes mentioned earlier. Next academic year, we will teach 'What is a worldview?' for the third time. Changes have already been made between the first and second iterations of the unit, based on teachers' experiences and reflections on what worked well and what did not. Further adjustments will be made before the third iteration to ensure the scheme is the best possible version for our students.

Throughout this process, the curriculum's intent, design and implementation have been highly collaborative. All teachers across all schools have contributed to decision-making, which has been incredibly powerful. This collaborative approach ensures that we actively seek and act on feedback, giving everyone a sense of ownership over what we produce. While student outcomes will naturally inform future development, our curriculum intent and vision will always remain the primary driving force behind our work.

An overview of the Archway Learning Trust's key stage 3 RE curriculum is provided in the online resources that accompany this book. You can find these on the John Catt Extras page of the Hachette Learning website: www.hachettelearning.com/john-catt-archive/john-catt-extras

Case study of how to include diversity within the RE curriculum
Nikki McGee, Hethersett Academy, Inspiration Trust

For years I have had a timeline of key thinkers pinned to my classroom wall. One summer holiday I even spent a week balancing on a chair on top of a desk to get the timeline weaving around my classroom. That timeline was my first attempt at making philosophy feel real and relevant.

Then one day a sixth former asked me, with that bruising teenage tone, whether I only ever taught about dead white men. The comment stung, but it stuck. It forced me to look again at my curriculum and recognise how narrow the story I was telling really was.

Why does it matter?

In a diverse world we cannot hope to capture every child's exact belief system, but our curriculum should offer both window and mirror opportunities: chances for students to see themselves, and to see into the lives of others. A mirror might reflect a child's sex, race, faith, worldview or a place that feels familiar.

If our aim is to give students a nuanced understanding of religious and non-religious beliefs, then diversity is non-negotiable. Authenticity requires it. As I have shifted towards a religion and worldviews approach, I have used a wider range of case studies to achieve this.

I am fortunate to visit many classrooms. Defiance and disruption are rare, but I do sometimes see passivity or disengagement. Building a curriculum that students feel reflects them helps with that. This does not mean we only teach from their experience. Powerful knowledge asks us to go beyond, but touchstones that affirm students' identities can motivate and encourage.

It is not just about who we teach, but how. When I looked closely at my own resourcing, I realised Christianity was presented almost entirely through a white Church of England lens. Over time, I added case studies and images from other Christian traditions, and we are now applying the same approach to other faiths and worldviews.

Diversifying the curriculum can also add challenge. It allows us to revisit familiar stories through a fresh perspective. For example, Year 7s study Abraham and his family, and in Year 10 we return to the same story through a womanist lens.

What was my starting point?

For me, the first step was reading. I chose a unit and deliberately sought out diverse thinkers whose voices could enrich the teaching. That was more manageable than rewriting everything at once. For example, when teaching Abraham, I read Delores Williams' *Sisters in the Wilderness* (1993) and wove her insights into my lessons.

Reading is not enough. We need lived encounters. Trips are vital for students, but they are just as important for teachers. I sit on my local interfaith board and SACRE, attend open days and festivals, and have joined walking tours on Black History and Herstory. I keep everything I learn on my phone and return to it when planning.

I also talk to my students and families. The growing Islamic population in my own school community has been a gift here. Students help me with Arabic pronunciation and explain aspects of their faith. Parents send in books and resources. I run an interfaith group and a student advisory group, both of which help me shape an authentic curriculum. These relationships matter. They enrich what we teach and show students their voices count.

Examples of a more diverse and authentic curriculum

Year 7: What did the Ancient Greeks teach about wisdom, and are their ideas relevant today?
This began as a traditional philosophy unit on Socrates, Plato and Aristotle. In my first year, a girl asked if women could be philosophers, and another asked if any were alive today. Both questions echoed that sixth former's challenge and exposed the limits of what I was teaching.

Now we pair an Ancient thinker with a contemporary one. Socrates, who asked difficult questions and challenged authority, is studied alongside bell hooks, an American writer and activist who insisted on questioning systems of power and taught about education as a practice of freedom. She also enables us to introduce the concept of intellectual humility.

Plato's cave, with its shadows and illusions, is paired with Simon Critchley, a British philosopher who compares social media to the cave: a place where we see distorted reflections rather than reality.

Aristotle's ideas about persuasion are paired with Sunita Narain, an Indian environmentalist and campaigner. She uses Aristotle's ethos, pathos and logos in her fight for climate justice, showing students that these techniques are not just theory but living tools for change.

Year 8: Does the idea of God make sense?
This unit started with Aquinas and Paley, focusing on the Cosmological and Design arguments. Yet I knew from A-level teaching that Aquinas was influenced by Islamic and Jewish thinkers, and I wanted students to see this. It felt wrong to ignore contributions from Maimonides (a Jewish philosopher who argued for a rational understanding of God) and Ibn Rushd (Averroes, a Muslim philosopher who defended Aristotle's thought).

We now teach Aquinas in context. Students learn how Aristotelian ideas were preserved and developed in Islamic universities, and how Jewish and Islamic philosophy shaped Aquinas' work. This overlap means they revisit the Cosmological argument through multiple voices, strengthening understanding. It also links to what they know from history about the Crusades and the exchange of ideas.

By using Ibn Rushd in particular, we strengthen one of the wider narratives running through our curriculum: tracing the development of empiricism from Aristotle, through Aquinas, and later into the work of thinkers such as Bentham. This allows students to see empiricism not as a purely European tradition but as an idea that travelled, developed and was kept alive across cultures.

Year 9: Why are the Dharmic traditions so diverse?
This unit traces hinge moments in Dharmic traditions, moments that produced diversity. It also tackles debates around identity: should we even use the word 'Hinduism'? What about caste?

Students meet Sanjoy Chakravorty, who argues that the British colonial system made caste more rigid and fixed than it had been previously. They also encounter B. R. Ambedkar, the Dalit leader who rejected caste discrimination, criticised Hinduism and inspired the Dalit Buddhist movement.

To add authentic voices, we use media. A BBC video introduces Marichamy, a Dalit man who became a Brahmin priest through a state-sponsored programme. We also use interviews with Kaushal Panwar, a Dalit academic from Delhi University who researches caste and women's experiences. Her voice is powerful, especially when she speaks about her own struggles and achievements.

Year 10 (non-examined RE): Black and womanist theology
By Year 10 our students know the key biblical stories and how they shaped the Abrahamic faiths. Here we revisit those stories through Black and womanist theology.

We begin with the Civil Rights Movement, exploring Martin Luther King Jr and Malcolm X. Students see how Christian and Islamic worldviews shaped their approaches to justice.

Then we turn back to the Bible. We read the story of Hagar through Delores Williams, who sees her as a role model for survival and female empowerment. We look at the crucifixion of Jesus through James Cone, who compares it to the lynchings of Black men in the United States. We revisit Mary through Courtney Hall Lee, who presents her as a figure of strength and hope for women of colour.

This is some of the work of which I am proudest. Students see Hagar as a model of resistance, Jesus as connected to the suffering of the oppressed and Mary as an empowering figure for women today. These interpretations challenge, inspire and reframe stories the students thought they already knew.

Diversifying your curriculum means better RE

That sixth former's bruising question about 'dead white men' has stayed with me. It was uncomfortable, but it pushed me to see what my curriculum was missing.

Diversifying has not meant throwing everything out and starting again. Often it has meant weaving in new voices and perspectives to enrich what was already there. And it has added depth, not dilution.

Take empiricism. By bringing in Ibn Rushd, students see that the tradition of looking to evidence and experience did not simply leap from Aristotle to Aquinas to Bentham. It was preserved, debated and refined in Islamic universities before it reached Aquinas. This thread runs across cultures and centuries. It shows students that ideas travel, change and are shaped by many hands. That is powerful knowledge.

For teachers starting out, my advice is simple:

- Start small. Pick one unit and add a new voice.
- Read widely. A single book can reframe how you teach a whole story.
- Use the wider academic community – speak to your humanities and English colleagues, #TeamRE on social media and university departments.
- Connect with your community. Students, parents and local groups can offer authentic insight.
- Avoid tokenism. Choose thinkers who genuinely deepen understanding, not just to tick a box.

> Most importantly, keep asking yourself that sixth former's question. Who is missing? And what stories could help my students see both the mirrors and the windows in our subject?

Locally agreed syllabus

Looking at a locally agreed syllabus can also be incredibly beneficial to inform your curriculum design. Developed through SACREs, these are a collaboration between faith communities, teachers and local authorities. The following locally agreed syllabuses are just a few that have looked to implement some of the latest research on types of knowledge and aims of the subject:

- Coventry & Warwickshire Religion and Worldviews Agreed Syllabus for Religious Education 2024–2029: www.churchofengland.org/sites/default/files/2024-12/coventry-and-warwickshire-agreed-syllabus-2024-2029_0.pdf
- Plymouth Agreed Syllabus 2024–2029: www.churchofengland.org/sites/default/files/2024-12/plymouth-agreed-syllabus-2024-2029.pdf
- Norfolk Agreed Syllabus 2019: www.schools.norfolk.gov.uk/media/13960/download/pdf/norfolk-religious-education-agreed-syllabus-2019.pdf

CHAPTER 6
HOW CAN I EXPLAIN AND MODEL IN RE?

Explaining and modelling are vital elements in a teacher's repertoire of techniques. In the RE classroom, we want students to develop their knowledge of beliefs, practices and concepts, and to have the opportunity to apply their learning to a range of scenarios. RE is full of abstract concepts, such as monotheism, morality, justice and beauty. Therefore, we must think carefully about how we can make the abstract concrete to our students.

Explaining

Etymology and morphology

RE is full of complex and rich vocabulary that we want students to know, understand and be able to use independently in their work. For each lesson, we need to think carefully about what tier 3 vocabulary needs to be taught and understood. Teaching students the etymology of words can help with this.

Here are a few examples:

Root word	Meaning	Examples
Omni (Latin)	All	Omnipotent, omnipresent, omniscient
Mono (Greek)	One	Monotheism
Poly	Many	Polytheism, polygamy
Tri (Latin)	Three	Trinity, trimurti
Carne (Latin)	Meat/flesh	Reincarnation, incarnation

Similarly, you can support students with learning vocabulary by breaking words down:

Word	Different parts	Meaning	Overall meaning
Incarnation	In + carn	In + flesh	God taking human form
Atonement	At + one	At + one	Making amends for a wrong or injury
Transubstantiation	Trans + subs	To change + substance	In the Eucharist, the wine and bread become the body and blood of Jesus
Omnibenevolent	Omni + benevolent	All + loving	God is all loving
Reformation	Re + form	Again + make	Helping someone see what they've done wrong and trying to make them a better person

For words that have a memorable prefix, you can ask students for other words that have the same prefix. For instance, what other words do they know that begin with 'mono' or 'tri'? They may give examples such as monocle or tricycle.

Frayer model

This model helps students to consider a new piece of vocabulary by considering characteristics, examples and non-examples alongside its definition, as in the example shown in Figure 6.1. The use of non-examples also serves to address misconceptions.

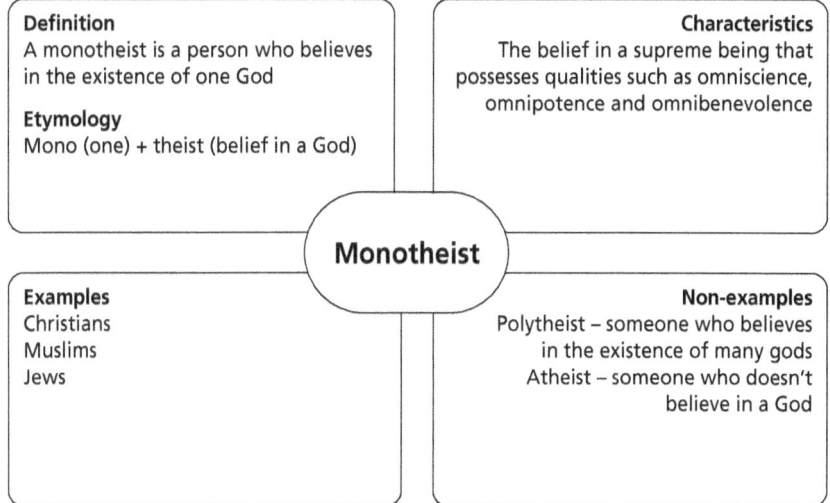

▲ Figure 6.1 Example of the Frayer model in use

Dual coding

As outlined in *Dual Coding with Teachers* (Caviglioli, 2019), Paivio's dual coding theory suggests that our brains process and represent verbal and non-verbal information in separate but related systems. As a result, we can give students information in two different ways: visually and verbally. This can create more retrieval cues for our students and, when designed well, can reduce cognitive load.

Dual coding can be beneficial when explaining an abstract concept such as salvation. Using a visualiser, I can present a step-by-step description of how I might use dual coding to explain salvation (see Figure 6.2):

1. Draw two platforms with a gap between them. Label one as 'God' and the other as 'humans'.
2. Label the gap between the two platforms as 'sin'. In addition, add that the gap is caused by the Fall, which led to a separation between humanity and God.
3. To connect the two platforms, draw the image of a cross. This is to represent the crucifixion of Jesus.
4. Use the four parts of the image to explain that sin causes a barrier between humans and God. God sent his son Jesus to atone for human sin and repair the relationship between humans and God.

SECONDARY RELIGIOUS EDUCATION IN ACTION

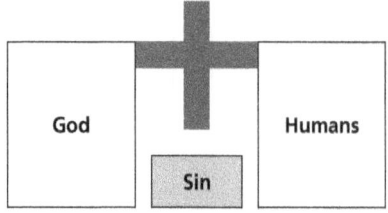

▲ Figure 6.2 How dual coding might be used to explain salvation

Dual coding can also work well when explaining what a concept isn't. When teaching the Trinity, I have used an image of the Shield of the Trinity (Figure 6.3) to support my explanation of the Trinity.

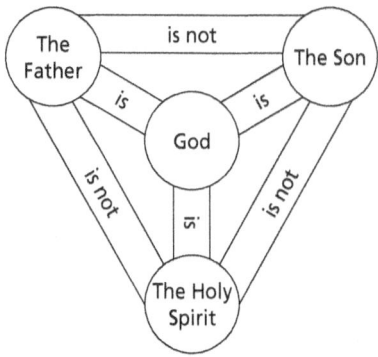

▲ Figure 6.3 An image like this may be used to support explanation

Building on this, I use diagrams to support my explanations of what the Trinity isn't. In Figure 6.4, each diagram contains a key misconception about the Trinity. As a class, we draw the diagrams and annotate what misconceptions are contained with them.

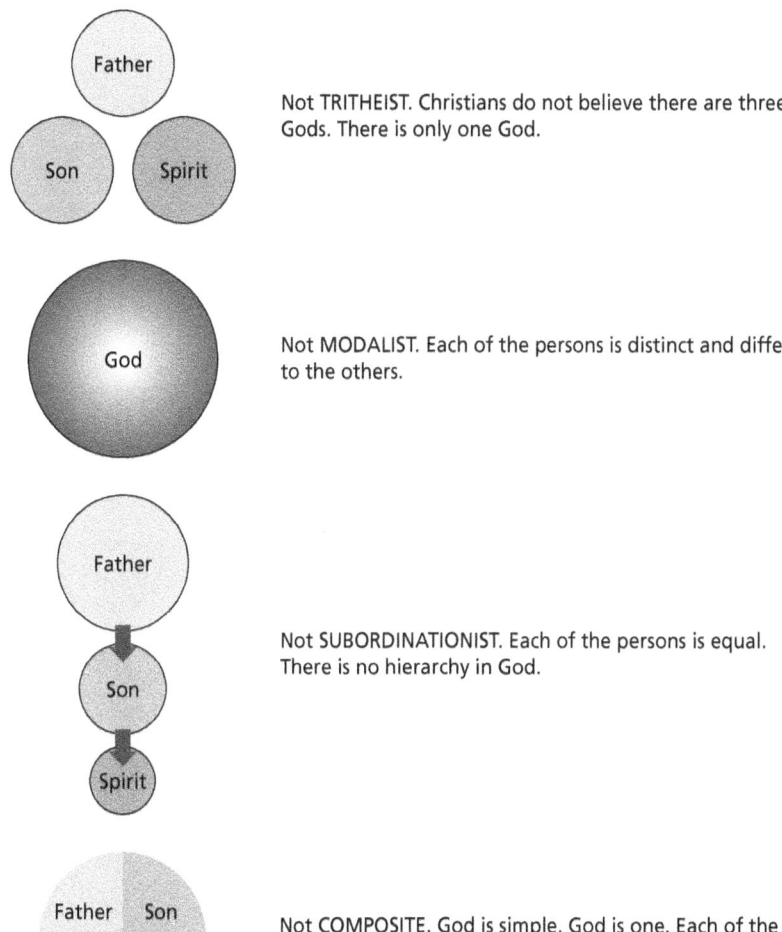

▲ Figure 6.4 Simple diagrams may also be used support explanation

Timelines

When teaching about the history of religions and beliefs, timelines can be a really effective way of explaining context and narrative. In the classroom, we can use timelines to illustrate the chronology, the significance of events and the relationship between them. By repeatedly referencing a timeline, students are able to have a visual reminder of how religions and beliefs have developed over time.

Figure 6.5 presents an example timeline. This one illustrates Siddhartha Gautama's path to enlightenment.

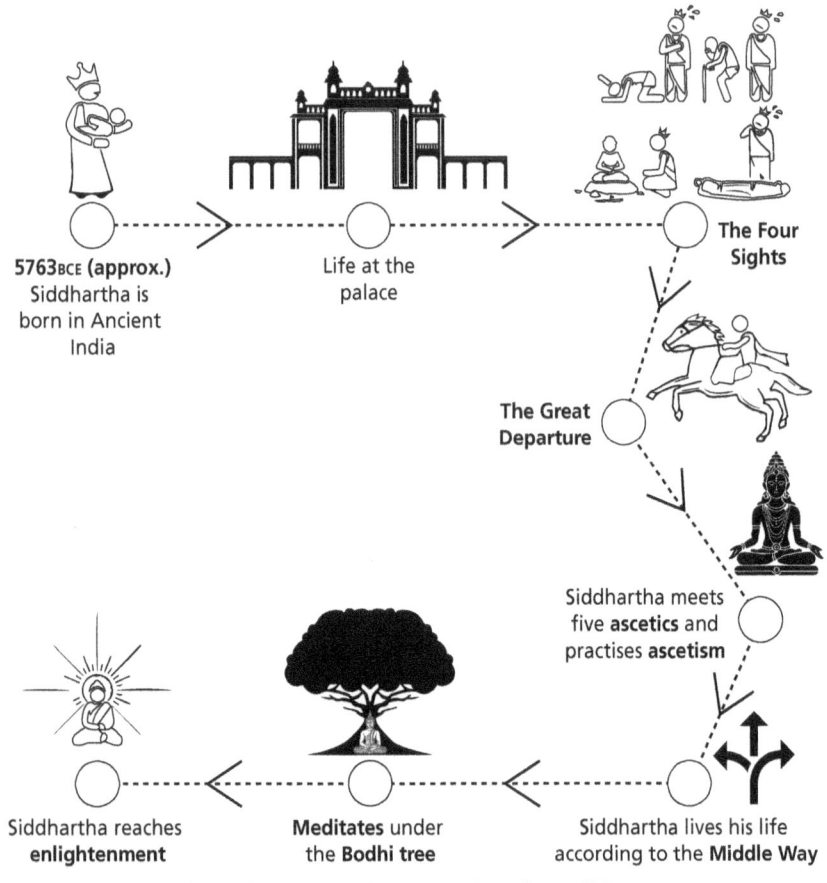

▲ Figure 6.5 Example timeline: Siddhartha Gautama's path to enlightenment

There are various ways in which you can use timelines in the classroom:

- **Pre-prepared timelines:** Provide students with a pre-prepared timeline to be used in a class activity. Websites such as TrueTube provide videos on the history of religions; these can be used alongside the timeline with students adding information to each key event to explain its significance.
- **Timeline quiz:** In a future lesson, ask students to recreate the timeline on a piece of scrap paper. They can look to include names of events, key

dates and the significance of each event. You could also test students' understanding of chronology by giving them the events of the timeline and asking them to arrange them in chronological order.

- **Influence of key events:** Get students to consider how each key event has influenced the beliefs or practices of the religion they are studying. For instance, how do the Four Sights influence what Buddhists believe about suffering?

Analogies

Analogies can serve as an explanation tool, as they involve comparing two ideas, one of which is already well understood. From Plato's analogy of the cave to the many analogies found within sacred texts, we can draw on analogies to make the complex more relatable to our students.

Here are some analogies it is helpful to use in the classroom:

Analogy	Application
The Church is like a body: Paul describes the Church as a body where each member is like a different part of the body with a unique role to play but all working together as one (1 Corinthians 12:12–27).	This analogy is useful for teaching about community, diversity, unity and the importance of each individual within the larger faith community.
The universe is like a watch: William Paley argues that the complexity and functionality of a watch implies it was made by a watchmaker. Just as a watch's design implies a watchmaker, the complexity, order and purpose of the natural world implies a designer – God.	This analogy is useful for teaching about the existence of God, natural theology, attributes of God and the theory of evolution.
Sin is like a stain: Just as a stain can mar the appearance of a piece of clothing, sin can mar the soul. But just as a stain can be removed with the right cleaner, so too can sin be cleansed by God's forgiveness.	This analogy helps to explain the concept of sin, repentance and forgiveness.

Analogy	Application
The Holy Spirit is like the wind: You can't see the wind, but you can see its effect, such as trees swaying or leaves rustling. Similarly, you can't see the Holy Spirit, but you can see the impact it has on people's lives.	This analogy helps to explain the invisible but powerful presence of the Holy Spirit in the lives of believers.
A McDonald's menu is like the diversity of religion: Across the world, there are some items that are found on every McDonald's menu. However, many menus will have items that cater to the culture or beliefs of the area.	This analogy helps to explain how religions can change and diversify as they spread across the world while still containing some essential features.

Similarly to dual coding, analogies can be helpful to give non-examples, address misconceptions and illustrate what something isn't. For example, the Trinity is often represented by the three forms of water: solid, liquid and gas. However, many Christians will argue that this is a poor analogy because it actually represents tritheism: the belief that the three persons of the Trinity are three distinct gods.

Compare, connect and categorise

It is essential for students to make links between key terms and see the relationships between them. This can be done in a variety of ways:

- **Venn diagram:** Ask students to complete a Venn diagram to show similarities and differences between two religions or within a religion. This could be based on a broad topic such as Christianity or Islam, or it could be on a specific topic such as beliefs on life after death.
- **Connecting concepts:** Give students a range of key words and concepts. Ask them to choose two that connect and explain the connection.
- **Grouping concepts:** Give students a selection of key words and ask them to create their own categories. In pairs or as a class, discuss the categories students have created and how they arrived at the links they have made.

Pictures and art

Pictures can help explain the lived reality of religion. They help engage learners, illustrate concepts and foster a deeper understanding of what is being taught. Pictures give students an insight into places, rituals and objects that they may never have encountered.

Here are some ways we can use pictures in the classroom:

- **Places of worship:** Students can see pictures of places of worship such as a synagogue, a langar or the Kab'ah. By seeing the features of a holy site, students are far better placed to understand an abstract concept. For instance, the mihrab in a mosque enables students to understand the direction of prayer for Muslims.
- **Religious rituals:** Students can see illustrations of people engaging in religious rituals such as prayer, baptism, communion or pilgrimage. For example, images of a baptism ceremony can help explain the process and its symbolic meaning.
- **Demonstrating cultural expressions:** Pictures can show how religious practices vary across different cultures, such as how weddings, funerals or festivals are celebrated in various religious traditions. For example, the use of images in Diwali celebrations in Hinduism can show how religious practices are intertwined with cultural identity.
- **Illustrating religious dress and symbols:** Pictures of religious dress such as a Sikh turban or a Muslim hijab allow for discussion of modesty, identity and the symbolic meaning behind clothing worn.
- **Showing diversity:** By using a range of pictures, we can highlight similarities and differences between key beliefs and teachings. For instance, students' understanding of pilgrimage is broadened by seeing a variety of places that a pilgrim may choose to visit.

If you are wanting to include artwork to support your explanations, the online Visual Commentary on Scripture is an excellent resource that provides more than 1000 artworks exploring concepts, stories and passages from the Bible. The artworks include commentaries from theologians, art historians and biblical scholars, which can help support your explanations in the classroom. Visit it here: https://thevcs.org/.

Modelling

Modelling is one of the most essential principles in effective teaching. As Rosenshine states in his article 'Principles of instruction' (2012), 'providing students with models and worked examples can help them learn to solve problems faster'. While it might sound simple and straightforward, the curse of the expert (teacher) is that we assume the novice (student) can do all the things that we take for granted. Modelled examples demonstrate to our students what success looks like in the RE classroom. This does not just pertain to written work, but also the skills and behaviours we wish to see from our students, such as asking good questions, humility, respect and intellectual curiosity.

There are a range of ways in which we can use modelling in the classroom and examples of excellence we want to model. Here are some examples:

'I do, we do, you do'

This is an approach to modelling that moves students from observing the teacher do something, to doing it together, to doing it independently. The technique has three steps and, in the RE classroom, I often find it is most effective with written work. The accompanying table outlines the process of 'I do, we do, you do' based on writing an answer to a GCSE-style question.

Step	Purpose	How does it work?	Why does it matter?
I do (teacher models)	Show exactly what success looks like.	Teacher demonstrates the skill, task or thinking process in full. This can be done on a visualiser, typed in a Word document or handwritten on the board. During this phase of modelling, explain the thinking and reasoning behind the decisions you have made, e.g. 'I have used the word Sawm here because ...'.	Removes ambiguity – students can see the process and product clearly before attempting it.

Step	Purpose	How does it work?	Why does it matter?
We do (guided practice)	Students try the task with teacher support.	Teacher and students complete an answer together for a similar style of question. Use questioning, cues and prompts to guide this step, e.g. 'What quote from the Qur'an would be most relevant here?'	Keeps cognitive load manageable as students are applying knowledge and skills with the teacher acting as the scaffold.
You do (independent practice)	Students take full ownership.	Students work individually to apply the skill without immediate help. As students work, the teacher circulates the class and provides live feedback where needed.	Students are practising skills independently using teacher model and guided practice examples to support.

After this process has taken place, you can select some examples from the class to share, and evaluate student responses in following the modelled examples. Use this time to explore what they've done well and any ways in which the work could be improved. If necessary, revert to doing more examples together to further build student confidence.

Pre-made and partial models

Models allow students to see what success looks like and to break down the specific elements that make a good piece of writing successful. Here are some tips to make this work effectively:

- Consider the best way to share the model, e.g. does everyone need a copy? Can everyone see it clearly if presented on the whiteboard? Would a visualiser be useful?
- Give students a variety of answers to a question to show that there is not one set answer.
- Focus on the features that make it a good answer. You can explain and get students to discuss the reasons why the exemplar is successful and how it could be even better still.

- Compare and contrast two exemplars, e.g. model answer A focuses on the question but model answer B has a better use of key terminology.
- From looking at a range of examples, discuss the specific features of excellence across all of them. These are the elements that students can look to include within their own work.
- Get students to carry out comparative judgement by giving them a range of examples and getting them to rank them with reference to a clear success criteria. Afterwards, discuss as a class their choices of ranking.
- After looking at a few full model answers, give students a partial model to complete. This could be the rest of a paragraph, the inclusion of a piece of scripture or a counterargument to what has already been provided.
- At the end of showing the pre-made and partial models, give students time to transfer ideas into their own work at the required standard using the success criteria previously established from looking at the models.
- For GCSE and A-level classes, exam boards will have a bank of model answers. These can be used to establish features of success.
- If you use online platforms such as Google Classroom, get students to write answers to exam questions as homework. In subsequent lessons, you can use answers as models. This saves you the time of writing model answers yourself!

Live modelling

Live modelling provides the means of showing your thinking to students. As the experts, we can demonstrate how to construct a piece of writing or complete a task. One of the key benefits of this is that it allows you to make your metacognitive process visible – sharing the self-questioning and decision-making that experts use. For example, 'What do I need to add into this paragraph?', 'Have I fully addressed the question?' By modelling both the task and the thinking behind it, we help students develop their own strategies for planning, monitoring and evaluating their work.

There are various ways you can live-model in the classroom:

- **Writing on the whiteboard:** The old-school and most traditional way allows you to write at the same speed as the students but does require good handwriting and provides only limited space.

- **Typing on a Word document or PowerPoint:** This is far easier for students to read, can be saved for future use and allows you to face students as you type.
- **Visualiser:** This feels like the best of both worlds. Your work is handwritten, so it's the same process that students go through, and you can observe students as you write. In addition, you can keep a copy of whatever work you produce, which can be used in future lessons.

Completing classwork in an exercise book with students

This technique encompasses a lot of aspects of modelling previously discussed. Give yourself a blank exercise book at the start of an academic year with a class and use a visualiser to model how all written work and activities are to be completed. This allows students to see exactly what is expected of them.

If you have used this approach throughout the academic year, the end product is what excellent classwork looks like in your subject. You have modelled your expectations for presentation and written work consistently. This also gives you a chance to review what written work has looked like across the academic year and any changes you wish to make moving forward.

Modelling language

Modelling encompasses how we want students to speak, as well as how we want them to write. Our subject is rich with academic language and the aim is for our students to use this language confidently in the classroom. As teachers, we may receive answers from students that are partially correct but do not offer the richest response.

Here's an example:

Teacher: Why is the Qur'an important to Muslims?

Ryan: The Qur'an is their holy book.

The student's answer is correct but we want an answer that provides more academic language. If I accept Ryan's answer and just move on, I am not modelling the expectation of what I want in verbal responses from students.

We can do this in three ways:

1 **Ask why:** The most powerful question to pose to a student, and it encourages them to give a richer answer.

2. **Ask for something specific:** If you know what was missing from Ryan's response, ask a specific question that can prompt him to respond better, such as 'How is the word revelation relevant to the importance of the Qur'an?'

3. **Bounce the question to another student:** Acknowledge Ryan's answer and then pose the question again to another student, asking them if they can add more to what has been given. Once you have received a better response, return to Ryan and ask him to repeat the better response.

There may be times when a student gives a fully correct answer but it omits key vocabulary.

Here's an example:

Teacher: What is a similarity between Judaism and Islam?

Remi: They are religions that both believe in one God.

In this example, we might return to the student and ask:

Teacher: What is the key term for believing in one God?

If they answer correctly, we can then ask the student to repeat the answer with the key word included:

Remi: They are both monotheistic religions.

CHAPTER 7
WHAT DOES QUESTIONING LOOK LIKE IN RE?

In Plato's *Apology*, Socrates is quoted as saying 'The unexamined life is not worth living.' This helps to illustrate how the very nature of our subject is founded on questioning. The same questions the Ancient Greeks were considering, such as 'What is goodness?', 'What is justice?' and 'What is real?', are the very same questions we are introducing to our students in the classroom. Questioning helps to explore complex concepts, challenge assumptions and stimulate critical thinking.

In this chapter we will look at the role of questioning in the RE classroom.

Checking for understanding

Rosenshine states that 'checking for student understanding at each point can help students learn the material with fewer errors' (2012). Using questioning to check for understanding allows us to see what students do know, and enables us to identify misconceptions and decide the next steps of the lesson.

You can use questioning to check for understanding in a range of ways, as described next.

Cold calling

This technique involves the teacher selecting students to answer questions without them volunteering first. Instead of asking a question and waiting for hands to go up, the teacher strategically names a pupil to respond.

This technique is beneficial as it ensures all students are thinking. If you allow 'hands up' or calling out, you only get responses from a few. At its best, it can be an inclusive questioning technique that gets the whole class involved and gives the teacher a far better insight into the understanding of the class.

Given our subject involves dealing with sensitive and controversial issues, the use of cold calling needs to be carefully considered and appropriate. Here are some tips that may help.

1. **Explain the rationale for using cold calling:** Explaining to pupils when and why you will be using this technique can help create trust and engagement with your class. Consider introducing it like this: 'In our RE lessons, I won't always ask you to put your hands up. Instead, I want *everyone* to think deeply about the questions I ask, and then I'll choose someone to share their answer. That's because your ideas matter, and we can learn a lot from hearing different views – even if the answer isn't perfect. If I call your name, it's because I'm genuinely interested in what you think. And if I don't call you this time, I will soon.' In RE, where discussion of beliefs, values and ethical dilemmas is central, cold calling helps make space for a range of voices and ensures everyone stays engaged. To make the technique effective:

2. **Consider when best to use it:** The often personal nature of RE can make cold calling more challenging because it often asks students to engage with sensitive topics – such as religion, morality, identity and belief – that may feel deeply personal, emotionally charged or culturally significant. In this context, students may be reluctant to share their thoughts publicly. In light of these challenges, RE teachers must think carefully about when to use cold calling. This can involve small tweaks such as:

   - using cold calling for conceptual or factual questions
   - allowing students to 'pass' or contribute later if they need
   - prefacing questions with supportive language, such as 'There's no one right answer here, I'd love to hear what you think …'.

3. **Ask the question before saying the name:** This small change can transform questioning as it keeps everyone thinking. If pupils hear the name before the question, only the named pupil has to engage. But if the question comes first, all pupils have to be prepared to respond:

Less effective	More effective
Teacher: Aaliyah, what is the concept of the sanctity of life?	Teacher: What is the concept of the sanctity of life, Aaliyah?
Only Aaliyah has to think.	*The whole class has to think before you name the respondent.*

4. **Give adequate wait time before taking the answer:** This tweak helps to ensure that all pupils have time to think and prepare a response, which improves the quality of their answers. Many questions we ask in RE are complex and require interpretation or empathy.

By pausing, we give pupils the time they need to process the question and formulate a thoughtful response:

Less effective	More effective
Teacher: What might a Buddhist say about the nature of suffering, Yusuf? *Yusuf is expected to answer immediately, but this answer is likely to be of limited depth.*	Teacher: What might a Buddhist say about the nature of suffering? … [pause] … Yusuf? *The pause allows pupils to mentally prepare, and increases the chance of a thoughtful, reflective response.*

Think pair share

Paired discussion allows all students to rehearse and share ideas as part of responsive teaching. It encourages all of them to process complex ideas, articulate their thoughts and engage with different viewpoints.

For this to work effectively, preface the task with how you want it to be done. Here's an example:

Think:

Teacher: *In silence,* you have *30 seconds to note down* some points for the following question: 'How might karma influence a person's actions?'

At this stage, the teacher can observe the class from the front to ensure all pupils are writing.

Pair:

Teacher: You've now got *30 seconds to discuss* with your partner, how might karma influence a person's actions?

You may also wish to specify in advance which student is going to talk first, e.g. the person closest to the door or the person whose name is first in the alphabet.

At this stage, the teacher can circulate around the class as pairs share ideas, listening out for particularly interesting points, examples or misconceptions.

Share:

Teacher: Sarah, what were you and Abeba discussing?

This use of cold calling allows the teacher to choose which pair to select. Based on the quality of Sarah's answer, the teacher can decide the next steps – probe further, address a misconception or move on to another pair.

Probing questions

RE teachers can use probing questions to develop pupil understanding and thought processes. Probing questions push students to think more deeply, clarify their ideas and extend their reasoning.

Here are some examples:

Category	Purpose	Examples
Clarification	To clarify meaning or unpack vague terms	• Can you say more about that? • What do you mean by 'sacred'? • Could you give an example from a religious tradition?
Justification	To prompt reasoning or evidence	• What evidence from scripture supports this view? • Why do you think that teaching is important to Sikhism? • Why might a Muslim go on Hajj?
Challenge	To consider other views or question assumptions	• Is that always true or just in this case? • What might someone from another religion say? • Does that belief still apply today?
Elaboration	To encourage students to expand their thinking	• Can you tell me more about that? • What other teachings link to that idea? • Can you provide another example?
Comparison	To make connections across beliefs and traditions	• How is that similar to karma in Hinduism? • Do other religious traditions share a similar idea? • Are there non-religious parallels to that view?

Category	Purpose	Examples
Consequences	To explore implications and possibilities	• What are the consequences of believing in an afterlife? • How might this belief affect the way people live their lives? • How do evil and suffering challenge those who believe in God?
Personal reflection	To develop personal knowledge of the pupil	• How would you feel in this situation? • Has this changed your view of the issue? • What further questions do you have?

Say it again better

This questioning technique serves to develop the quality of verbal responses we receive from students. Sometimes, pupils may offer an answer that is half-formed. By encouraging high-quality responses when short responses are given, we maintain high expectations of pupils and can gain a better sense of their understanding.

When a pupil has given a half-formed answer, acknowledge and if possible praise their first response. Next, use questioning to invite them to consider how their response could be improved, as illustrated in the following examples.

Example 1:

Kesia: Muslims believe God is kind and helps people.

Teacher: Yes, that's a good start. Can you improve this answer by using more precise religious language?

Kesia: Muslims believe Allah is beneficent and merciful, always guiding and helping His followers.

Example 2:

Alex: Hindus believe you come back after you die.

Teacher: You're on the right track. Can you say it again using the terms Hindus would use?

Alex: Hindus believe in reincarnation, where the soul is reborn in a new body based on karma from past lives.

Using questioning when a pupil says 'I don't know'

We have all experienced the situation where we pose a question to a pupil and receive this response. There are a number of reasons why this might be the case, such as lack of understanding or lack of motivation. To keep our classroom culture strong, we need to ensure that this pupil eventually provides the answer.

We can do this in a range of ways:

No opting out

If the pupil is unsure, we can encourage them to give it a go, remind them of something related to the question, or give them extra thinking time and say you will return to them. For example:

Teacher: What is a fundamentalist Christian ... Jon?

Jon: I don't know.

Teacher: Think back to last lesson when we talked about how different Christians may interpret the Bible. I'll come back to you in a minute. I want you to have a go because I know you can do it. While Jon is thinking, what is a liberalist Christian ... Lucy?

Lucy: A liberalist Christian is a believer who views the Bible as the authors' interpretation of God.

Teacher: Yes, that's correct, Lucy. Well done. Jon ... I'm coming back to you now.

A strategy like this communicates to Jon that you value his learning and want to check his understanding in all circumstances.

Make the question less high stakes

Our subject is full of highly complex, controversial and contested material. Sometimes a pupil may reply with 'I don't know' because the question feels high stakes and/or is about subject matter that may have a multitude of interpretations. By revising the question to make it lower stakes, we can remove some of the pressure and also show that there are many ways in which some questions may be answered.

Here are some examples:

Initial high stakes question	Revised lower stakes question
Why do we dream?	Why do you think we dream?
How does a belief in reincarnation influence Buddhists today?	How might a belief in reincarnation influence Buddhists today?
What is the best way we can improve this paragraph?	In what ways can we improve this paragraph?

As shown in one of the examples above, one of the most powerful ways we can make the question less high stakes is by adding the word 'might'. This can help remove the fear of getting the answer wrong, which often can cause the initial response of 'I don't know.'

Tell me something you do know

In some cases, probing questions related to the topic might be helpful to tease out what foundational knowledge the pupil has. These probing questions can help chunk the initial question down and eventually lead to the answer we are looking for.

Here's an example:

Teacher: Why is the Qur'an important to Muslims ... Maisie?

Maisie: I don't know.

Teacher: Tell me something about the question which you do know about this topic which might be helpful.

Maisie. The Qur'an is the Muslim holy book.

Teacher: Good. Who was the book revealed to?

Maisie: Prophet Muhammad.

This approach can help build pupil confidence as they are showing correct understanding of ideas related to the topic. At this point, you may wish to call on another pupil to give a partial answer before returning to the original pupil.

Diamond 9 activities

This activity is a great way to promote discussion and critical thinking, and provide pupils with a space to evaluate different opinions or perspectives. It involves ranking nine items (e.g. concepts, statements, beliefs) into a diamond-shaped grid based on how much pupils agree or disagree with each item in response to a given question or prompt. The one they most agree with goes at the top, the one they agree with least goes at the bottom and all the other items are placed in the boxes in the middle.

Figure 7.1 shows an example of a diamond 9 activity. This one is on animal rights.

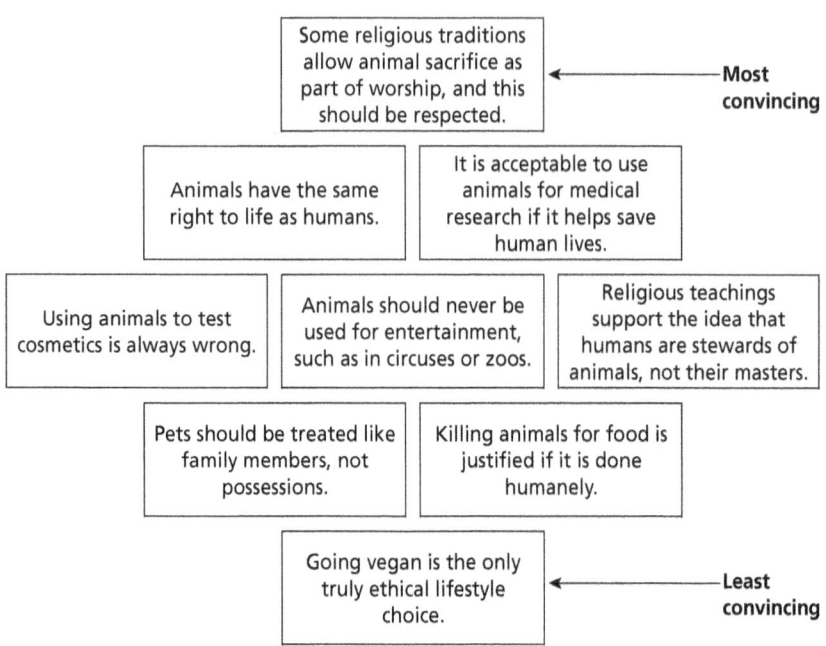

▲ Figure 7.1 Example of a diamond 9 activity

After pupils have had some time to rank the statements, some helpful follow-up questions as part of whole-class discussion could be:

- Which argument did you most agree with and why?
- Which argument did you most disagree with and why?
- Which argument was hardest to place?
- How might we challenge this argument?
- What examples could be given to support this view?
- Are there any extra arguments to consider?

Metacognitive questions

Metacognitive, or process, questions are often defined as questions on 'thinking about thinking' – getting pupils to plan, monitor and evaluate their own learning. The Education Endowment Foundation (EEF) guidance report on metacognition (2018) recommends that teachers ask metacognitive questions because these help students become more independent and reflective.

There are various ways this can be done in the RE classroom:

1. **Diamond 9 activities:** After pupils have completed a diamond 9 activity, get them to explain their reasoning:
   - 'That's interesting, Simon – why did you think that was the most important reason?'
   - 'How did you decide which arguments were stronger?'
   - 'Jakub, can you explain why you thought this was a weak argument?'

2. **Interpretation of texts:** If a lesson has been spent exploring interpretations of a religious text or parable, ask pupils to explain their idea:
   - 'Nice idea, Louise. What made you think of that?'
   - 'Lovely point, Bilal. Where did that idea come from?'
   - 'How did your own worldview affect the way you interpreted this, Andy?'

3. **Personal reflection:** As a tool for further developing personal knowledge, metacognitive questions can be especially fruitful:
   - 'How did comparing religious views shape your own view on forgiveness?'
   - 'After learning more about the Sikh view of the afterlife, has your perspective changed?'
   - 'What similarities are there between your view on this issue and the views of religious believers?'

4. **Modelling:** When writing a live-modelled answer or sharing exemplar work, metacognitive questions can be really helpful to explain thought processes:
   - 'Why did I choose to start my sentence like this?'

- 'What's a better word or phrase I could use here?'
- 'Is there another way we could explain this extract?'

You can find more on modelling and metacognition in chapter 6.

How best to do class discussion

Class discussion is at the very heart of a great RE classroom. It is a rich way of checking for understanding, and provides pupils with the opportunity to form their own arguments and hear different points of view.

Here are some ways to best utilise questioning as part of classroom discussion for the benefit of all students:

- **Decide on the purpose:** Before the lesson, decide on the function of the class discussion. Is it to deepen understanding of a specific concept? Get student opinions on a moral issue? Discuss the relevance of a Biblical passage in the modern world?
- **Pose big questions:** The joy of the RE classroom is that every lesson involves consideration of big questions. The best class discussions are framed around thought-provoking questions that invite interpretation, different opinions and perspectives, e.g. 'What does it mean to live a good life?'
- **Use structured discussion protocols:** Use think pair share to help create an inclusive classroom. This technique ensures that everyone can think and verbalise their ideas, and that everyone's voice matters, from the confident pupils to the shy ones.
- **Cold calling and hands up:** A healthy mix of both creates a good flow to a class discussion. Cold calling keeps students focused and encourages participation, while hands up is good for gaining alternative viewpoints and creating spontaneity.

Asking questions framed around ways of knowing

In the RE classroom, we may want to ask questions that are framed around 'ways of knowing'. The types of question we ask may depend upon the disciplinary focus of the topic, but each discipline provides a different type of question we can pose in the classroom.

Here are some examples based on a range of religious beliefs and practices:

Belief or practice	Theological question	Philosophical question	Social science question
Original sin	How is original sin understood in Christian theology?	Does original sin undermine the concept of free will and moral responsibility?	How has the belief in original sin influenced social norms and morality?
Mitzvot	Why are the Mitzvot considered a central way of expressing devotion to God?	Should moral laws evolve, or are eternal commandments more trustworthy?	How do observant Jews navigate the Mitzvot in modern, secular societies?
Zakah	What is the theological significance of Zakah in purifying the soul?	Can obligatory moral acts lead to social justice?	How does the practice of Zakah influence Muslim communities?
Meditation	How does meditation facilitate the Buddhist path to enlightenment?	Can meditation provide a valuable insight into the nature of reality?	What are the social and psychological benefits of meditation?
Seva	Why is Seva considered a spiritual duty in Sikhism?	Is an act ever truly selfless?	How does Seva shape Sikh engagement in charitable and community life?

Each of these questions is ripe for discussion and a range of perspectives can be considered. As the teacher, you are in the best position to decide which questions to ask at what time in your classroom.

Creating a strong questioning culture in the RE classroom

Many of the strategies referenced in this chapter work best when there is a strong questioning culture in the classroom.

Here are a few ways we can foster this in the RE classroom:

Model intellectual curiosity

As teachers, we should often ask our own questions aloud, to model that we are still learning and questioning things ourselves – for example, 'I often wonder why this belief is so important ...'. On a similar note, it can be really powerful to model intellectual uncertainty – for instance, 'I'm not sure where this practice originated, but I'm going to find out for next lesson.'

Modelling to our pupils in this way shows that questioning is hard for all and learning is an ongoing process throughout life.

Getting students to ask questions

Young people are naturally inquisitive and we want to encourage intellectual curiosity as much as possible in our classroom. To do this, we want to give students opportunities to ask questions. These questions might be to clarify their own thinking, check their own understanding or just intellectual inquiry. We can really help to promote love for our subject by answering pupil questions, so look to give some space for this in your lessons.

Here are some ways we can do this:

- **Ask the author:** If pupils have read a piece of scholarship, get them to formulate questions they would like to ask the author if they had the opportunity.
- **Social science data analysis:** If pupils have analysed social science data in response to survey questions, get them to write follow-up questions they would pose in a hypothetical future survey.
- **At the end of a lesson:** As an exit ticket, you could get pupils to write one question they have based on the day's learning. These questions can be collated by the teacher. Some questions might be ones the teacher needs to explain in the next lesson; some might be worthy of class discussion and some might reveal misconceptions that need to be addressed.
- **Explore what makes a good question:** You may wish to ask pupils how to analyse and construct good questions. To do this, introduce them to four types of question, with a non-RE example of what each looks like:
    1. Textual questions – ones that are easy to find the answer to. The answer can easily be found in a source, e.g. book. Example: 'What are the names of the Harry Potter books?'
    2. Intellectual questions – ones that require deep thinking, reasoning and interpretation. They may require an expert to be asked about the matter. Example: 'What makes the Harry Potter books so successful?'

3   Closed questions – ones that typically have a specific or factual answer, often 'yes or no'. Example: 'Is Harry Potter a wizard?'
4   Open questions – ones that have multiple possible answers that invite explanation, opinion or interpretation. Example: 'How does friendship shape the story of Harry Potter?'

Place these four styles of question in a quadrant, like that shown in Figure 7.2, and give pupils a big list of questions. They are to place each question in the appropriate section of the question quadrant, e.g. A closed textual question.

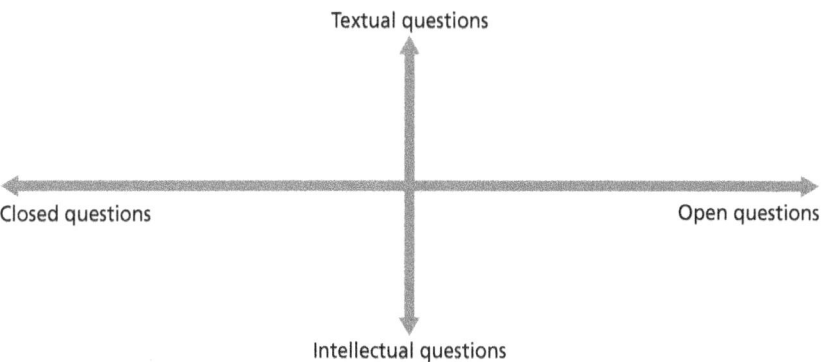

▲ Figure 7.2 A question quadrant

You can get students to create criteria for what open intellectual questions have in common. Their criteria may include the following:

- Does the question challenge us?
- Is the question about something that really matters?
- Does the question contain a big concept?
- Is the question contestable?
- Will the question engage people?

Reward and celebrate good questions

Our students will often ask great questions in lessons, so make sure you praise thoughtful and challenging questions. This can help create a strong questioning culture where pupils posing questions is encouraged. You may look to give awards or merit points for excellent questions. You could create a 'question wall' or a 'wonder board' where pupils post questions related to their learning.

CHAPTER 8
WHAT DOES WRITING LOOK LIKE IN RE?

How to teach students to write is a challenge which all subjects face and RE is no different. Alongside time teaching new content, we need to give students the time to write about the knowledge they encounter in our lessons.

In their book, *The Writing Revolution* (2017), Hochman and Wexler offer various reasons why it is important to explicitly teach writing:

- Writing is both the process of learning and the product.
- Writing involves retrieval and elaboration of knowledge.
- It gives students time to think and develop their ideas.
- The content of the curriculum drives the rigour of the writing.
- Teaching writing is difficult.

They offer a range of strategies on how to explicitly teach writing in a way that serves to develop students' ability to write sentences, paragraphs and extended pieces of writing in all subjects. Below you will find some ways in which these strategies can be adapted to an RE context.

Writing sentences

One of the key takeaways from the book is the importance of sentences as the foundation for excellent writing. We want our students to write knowledge-rich essays, but we must recognise the amount of scaffolding needed for this. By starting with the sentence, we lay the foundation for students to demonstrate their knowledge.

Because, but, so

With this strategy, you give students a sentence stem (beginning of a sentence) that remains the same and ask them to turn it into three complex sentences. When introducing this task, it is important to make sure students understand the meaning of each conjunction:

- The conjunction *because* explains why something is true.
- The conjunction *but* indicates a change of direction.
- The conjunction *so* tells us what happens as a result of something else.

This task requires students to think deeply about the knowledge they have been looking at and consider how their knowledge is applicable to the sentence stems they are given. Rather than giving students an open-ended question to answer, the use of *because, but, so* offers the teacher a more precise measure of checking student understanding. There is no one way in which these sentences can be completed. The quality of written responses will indicate the quality of understanding.

Example 1

Within an RE classroom, this strategy can be used in a range of ways. Within a key stage 3 topic exploring the history of Islam, students may explore the religious, political and military influence of Muhammad. To check student understanding, pose the question, 'Why is Muhammad best understood as a prophet?' After checking student understanding of each conjunction, ask them to complete following sentence stems, which are rooted in knowledge explored in the lesson:

- Muhammad is best understood as a prophet because … after the Night of Power, he began preaching his message in Mecca.
- Muhammad is best understood as a prophet but … the leaders of the Meccan tribes did not like his monotheistic message.
- Muhammad is best understood as a prophet so … Muslims show respect to Muhammad by saying 'peace be upon him' after his name.

The *because* sentence tests students' ability to explain why Muhammad is a prophet. The *but* sentence tests their ability to give a counterargument or point of opposition to Muhammad being seen as a prophet. The *so* sentence tests students' ability to give a way in which Muhammad's prophethood is significant or how it influences the lives of Muslims. The completed parts of each sentence after the ellipsis are just an example of how students may complete these sentences, but a range of answers is possible.

Example 2

This sentence-level strategy can also serve to develop students' ability to write within a discipline. For example, theological writing may involve explaining the origin of a belief or concept, elaboration on how a text may be interpreted, or exploring the significance of a particular idea.

For example, a KS4 lesson may explore key teachings of Genesis and how different Christians may interpret these. Afterwards, you could provide students with the following sentence stems to complete.

- Literalist Christians believe God created the world in six days because ... 'all scripture is God breathed'. This means that every word in the Bible comes from God.
- Literalist Christians believe that God created the world in six days but ... non-literalist Christians believe that each day represents millions of years.
- Literalist Christians believe that God created the world in six days so ... they are provided with further evidence of God's omnipotence.

Example 3

Finally, the strategy can work nicely when students have looked at key quotes from scholars. In this example, students may have been taught about critiques of religion and we can test the depth of their understanding by seeing if they can explain the quote, give a counterargument and provide implications of the perspective:

- Richard Dawkins claims 'Faith is the great cop out, the great excuse to evade the need to think and evaluate evidence' because ... he believes that questions about reality can be explained with scientific evidence.
- Richard Dawkins claims 'Faith is the great cop out, the great excuse to evade the need to think and evaluate evidence' but ... theists might argue that arguments for God's existence make faith reasonable.
- Richard Dawkins claims 'Faith is the great cop out, the great excuse to evade the need to think and evaluate evidence' so ... people should feel free to challenge and criticise religious beliefs.

Using subordinating conjunctions

Subordinating conjunctions are conjunctions that introduce an adverb clause and signal the relationship between the class and main idea, e.g. although, while, if. The use of subordinating conjunctions promotes the use of complex sentences, boosts vocabulary development and encourages close reading/references to a key text. In addition, it serves to check student comprehension. Students become better able to understand complex texts and their oral language becomes more sophisticated.

Many of these conjunctions are very useful in composing argumentation and essay writing:

Subordinating conjunctions		
After	If	Though
Although	In order that	Unless
As	Now that	Until
Because	Once	When
Before	Since	Whenever
Even if	So that	Where
Even though	Than	Wherever
How	That	While

Within an RE classroom, there are a range of ways in which we can get students using subordinating conjunctions in their writing. In the following example, students may have been exploring the life of Siddhartha Guatama and we can check their understanding by getting them to complete the sentences.

Example

- Although the Buddha's teachings are important … he never claimed to be a God.
- After Siddhartha spent six years practising asceticism … he realised that spending his life denying his body what it needed was as bad as being surrounded by luxury.

In the first sentence, the conjunction *although* is testing students' ability to provide a counterargument. In the second sentence, the conjunction *after* is testing students' understanding of the chronology of events in the life of the Siddhartha.

To make this writing activity more challenging, you can provide students with just a subordinating conjunction with a key term and ask them to write a complex sentence.

Here are some examples based on a topic focused on the philosophy of religion:

- As Plato …
- Since Descartes …
- Although William Paley …

Writing a paragraph

When getting students to write an excellent paragraph, there are various steps involved.

1. Identify your topic or question

It is important to decide exactly what question you want students to answer. Consider the length, wording and complexity of the question.

2. Annotate the question

Let's imagine students are planning an answer to the question 'What are the key teachings of the Genesis story and how do Christians interpret it?' As a class, we need to make some annotations to address key elements of the question and identify prerequisite knowledge. For instance:

- What is the Genesis story?
- What are the key teachings of the Genesis story?
- What is meant by the word 'interpret'?
- What are the different Christian interpretations?

The class annotations may look something like those shown in Figure 8.1.

The first book in the Bible, it literally means 'origin'.

What are the key teachings of the Genesis story and how do Christians interpret it?

- God created out of nothing (ex nihilo).
- God pre-existed the world – he is transcendent (outside time and space).
- God was the sole creator, it was a deliberate planned creation. It is ordered and not chaotic.
- All parts of the Trinity were involved in creation (therefore God's triune nature pre-existed it too).
- All that He created was good (perfect).
- Humans are made 'imago dei', in the image of God, reflecting his qualities.
- Humans are created last as they are the most important and have dominion (control) over all living things.

How something is understood or explained.

Literalist view – Bible is the direct word of God, therefore what is written is *literally* true.

Non-literal view – scripture is the *writers' interpretation* of the word of God.

▲ Figure 8.1 Annotating a question

3. Create a single paragraph outline

The Writing Revolution advocates for a single paragraph outline (SPO) as a means of getting students to plan and eventually write their paragraph. This consists of three parts:

1. Topic sentence – a sentence that introduces the theme of the paragraph.
2. Supporting details – evidence that supports the theme of the paragraph.
3. Closing sentence – a sentence that links back to the theme of the paragraph.

You may wish to provide a physical copy of the SPO that looks like this:

Topic sentence	
Supporting details	
Closing sentence	

1. Topic sentence

The first step is to write the topic sentence for the paragraph. The key ingredients are for it to reference the question clearly and introduce the topic of the paragraph. After some brief 'think pair share', we may arrive at 'Literalist Christians interpret the Genesis story to be literally true and historical fact.'

If students struggle with this task you could write a topic sentence yourself and explain why it is good, or alternatively, provide two or three examples and ask them to explain which one is best.

2. Supporting details

Next, students need to provide supporting evidence for their paragraph. The term 'evidence' can be somewhat vague, so I usually provide prompt questions to guide their thinking and help them to elicit relevant knowledge:

- What is the origin of this literalist Christian belief?
- According to literalist Christians, who authored Genesis, and why is that important?
- What are the implications for saying Genesis is not authoritative?

With reference to their prompt questions and classwork, students complete the supporting details section of their SPO.

3. Closing sentence

The closing sentence serves to remind the reader of the topic sentence, but it should not repeat it word for word. To create an effective closing sentence, I often stress for students to use a subordinating conjunction such as *since, therefore* or *as a result*.

A completed SPO may look something like this:

Topic sentence	Literalist Christians interpret the Genesis story to be literally true and historical fact.
Supporting details	'All scripture is God breathed' – this means that every word in the Bible comes from God.
	If Genesis is merely symbolic, then what's to stop the rest of the Bible being symbolic too? If this is the case then the Bible doesn't have any authority.
	The Bible is a trustworthy and authoritative source for Christians – why should we interpret what is written in it differently?
	If the Bible says God created the sun on the fourth day, then he created it on the fourth day.
	The Genesis story illustrates God's omnipotence as the universe was created 'ex-nihilo' (from nothing).
Closing sentence	Since literalist Christians believe the words of the Bible come from God, the Genesis story could be interpreted as literally true.

For a subsequent paragraph, students can follow the exact same process and complete a SPO for a different interpretation of the Genesis story. If students are looking to include evidence about the non-literalist interpretation, I may provide the following prompt questions:

- Why do some Christians reject the Genesis story as literally true?
- If not literally true, how do some Christians interpret the Genesis story?
- If Genesis lacks authenticity, what meaning does it provide for Christians?

With their answers to the prompt questions and class notes, students' SPOs may look something like this:

Topic sentence	Non-literalist Christians interpret the Genesis story to be a myth that offers spiritual truths.
Supporting details	Genesis is quite poetic in nature, with repeated passages throughout, e.g. 'and he [God] saw it was good'.
	Each day of creation represents millions of years.
	The Genesis creation story misses out so much, e.g. there is no mention of dinosaurs, which is strange as dinosaurs existed before humans.
	The Genesis story does not say specifically how God created the world – perhaps the Big Bang could explain this?
Closing sentence	As the Genesis story omits key details, non-literalist Christians interpret it as a myth offering spiritual truths.

Write the paragraph using their SPO

Once the SPO is complete, students are now in a position to write their paragraph. Depending on your students you could do this in various ways:

- Students have their SPO in front of them and write the paragraph in the lesson.
- Students put their SPO away and write the paragraph without looking.
- Students can review their SPO for homework and write the paragraph at the start of the next lesson.

Whenever they complete the paragraph, students can then revisit their SPO to check that they have included all their relevant evidence and effective topic/closing sentence.

Writing an essay

The process for writing an essay or extended piece of writing can follow a very similar pattern to that for writing a single paragraph.

1. Unpack the question

When preparing for extended writing, the first thing I would do with students is briefly explain the success criteria. In KS3, I might give students an essay question such as 'Explain key Muslim beliefs about Muhammad and Allah.' For a question like this, success criteria might include:

- Explain key events in the life of Muhammad.
- Explain Muslim characteristics of God.
- Reference Muslim teaching, e.g. the Qur'an.
- Use key terminology accurately and consistently.

Afterwards, as a class, we would look to unpack the three key terms in the question and how they are relevant:

- What is a Muslim?
- What do Muslims believe about Muhammad?
- What do Muslims believe about Allah?

Using my visualiser, we would annotate key parts of the question together and make some brief notes of some key beliefs. Through direct questioning, this allows me to check student understanding and provides the class with an initial insight into ideas they could explain in their essay.

2. Show a model paragraph

The next step is to show students a model paragraph. There is little point in getting students to write if they do not know what is expected of them or how the writing should be structured.

The model paragraph can be pre-written or you may choose to write it live with the class. Regardless of which approach you choose, include success criteria for what you want to see in the paragraph, as it is essential to break down what makes the writing successful. Using my visualiser, we highlight as a class the role that each sentence or phrase of a sentence serves. I explain to the students why I have included certain pieces of evidence and key terminology, and how every element of the paragraph contributes to the topic sentence and answering the question.

3. Plan the next paragraph in a SPO

Now, students can look to plan the next paragraph for the essay using a SPO. We start by working together to craft a topic sentence that is focused on the question. I encourage students to refer to their annotated question plan to help them in identifying a new belief to write about.

After giving students some time to craft their topic sentence, they are now at the stage of looking for evidence and supporting details for it. Students can use their class notes and/or textbooks to find relevant evidence for this. In addition, I share a list of key terminology with students. This vocabulary will have been pre-taught and should act as a trigger for them. Some may not be relevant for the paragraph they are planning, but some of it will. Students are to add all the supporting details to their SPO in bullet points.

4. Write the paragraph

After the planning stage, I give students 5–10 minutes of silent writing time to translate their SPO into a written paragraph. To help them link their evidence, and to encourage fluidity in their writing, I might share on the board a bank of phrases that can be used to illustrate ideas and emphasise points. For example:

Words used to illustrate ideas	Words used to emphasise points
For example	Especially
For instance	In particular
Specifically	Obviously
Particularly	Above all
As an illustration	Most important
Namely	Primarily
Such as	Certainly
Expressly	Particularly
Like	Moreover
Including	Notably
In particular	Keep in mind

As they write, I will circulate the room and check in with students who may need extra support or encouragement to start the writing.

Once the silent writing time is finished, I will share a couple of examples of student writing under the visualiser. As a class, we will discuss how well the paragraph has met the success criteria.

5. Complete a multi-paragraph outline (MPO)

At this point, students are ready to complete a MPO. This follows the exact same structure as the SPO but allows students to plan multiple paragraphs. I usually give students the rest of the lesson to complete their MPO. Once the MPO is complete, I set a homework task where students are to read/review their MPO in preparation for writing the essay next week without notes.

Here is a template you could use for a MPO (the blank spaces shown here are just an indicator – they should be much bigger in the actual MPO, to allow students sufficient room to make notes):

Paragraph 1		
Topic sentence	Supporting details	Closing sentence
Paragraph 2		
Topic sentence	Supporting details	Closing sentence
Paragraph 3		
Topic sentence	Supporting details	Closing sentence
Paragraph 4		
Topic sentence	Supporting details	Closing sentence

How can we develop evaluative writing?

Especially at key stage 5, there is an expectation that students can evaluate knowledge and concepts they encounter within lessons. Many RE teachers will find that their students are naturally good at evaluating verbally but sometimes struggle when putting this into writing.

The following strategies are designed to support them with this.

Evaluating criticisms

At A-level, students are required to know the strengths and weaknesses of various philosophical arguments. However, evaluation requires them to comment on how effective these points are. In the example shown here, students read a criticism of teleological arguments given by David Hume. Afterwards, they give the criticism a mark out of 10 for how strong it is, then they justify their choice with a clear reason.

> In his dialogues, Hume made several criticisms of the idea that design in the world gives strong evidence for the existence of God:
>
> 1 Hume believed that teleological arguments that relied on using analogies were weak. Hume says we can conclude that a house has a builder and architect. However, we cannot deduce a builder or architect of the universe in the same way, as there is no similarity between the two.
>
> **If we apply this, then, to Paley:** Characteristics of purpose and design might be obvious in a house, but they are not nearly so obvious in the world.
>
> **Note:** This critique does not apply to Aquinas' argument, as this focuses on things following natural laws.
>
> **Mark out of 10:**
> _____
>
> Reason:
> _____
> _____

Snowflake evaluations

This strategy provides students with a visual representation (like that in Figure 8.2) of what arguments are more successful than others. Students read each argument and place an X along the line to illustrate how successful they think it is. The nearer the centre, the less successful; the nearer the outside, the more successful. Students join up the Xs to make their unique snowflake shape. In the space underneath, they justify their choices for how successful they think each response is.

SECONDARY RELIGIOUS EDUCATION IN ACTION

Can God be defended in the face of evil?

1. Put an X on each of the lines connecting the responses to the central question, to illustrate how successful you think each response is. The nearer the centre, the less you agree. The nearer the response, the more you agree.
2. Join up the Xs to make your unique snowflake shape. In the spaces within your snowflake, justify your decision for how successful you think the response is.

Augustine's theodicy defends God by claiming evil is a privation. God cannot create a lack of something and so cannot have created evil. Augustine transfers the blame of both moral and natural evil to the free will of humans and angels.

The logical problem of evil highlights the logical inconsistencies in believing in the omni-God despite the existence of evil and suffering. If, as Augustine claims, God created the world perfectly, how could it go wrong?

The evidential problem of evil points out the overwhelming amount of pain, suffering and evil evident in the world. Even if some suffering is needed to warn us of the dangers, or to make natural laws predictable, is there too much?

Swinburne argues that God should not be held responsible for evil because free will is essential to being human.

Can God be defended in the face of evil?

McCabe supports Augustine's claim that evil is a privation and that God could not have created it. Evil and suffering arise because things do not live up to expectations.

Dostoevsky asks how dysteleological suffering, particularly of innocent children, could serve any purpose. What kind of God would allow innocent suffering and not intervene? If God is not responsible for evil, he is not worthy of worship.

Hick's theodicy suggests that while God allows evil and suffering for a purpose, God is not wholly to blame. Free will is so valuable that humans must be able to make choices, both good and bad.

Hume asks, could the world be a little more hospitable and still teach us or enable us to learn? Could God have created a world with less evil? Or is it equally possible to learn from goodness?

What is the most successful response? Why?
What is the least successful response? Why?
What questions do these responses raise?
Are there any other responses that might be more successful?

▲ **Figure 8.2 A snowflake evaluation**

Evaluative sentences – JQR

The JQR method, suggested by Arabella Saunders, enables students to write more evaluative sentences at the start of their paragraphs.

This technique gets students to consider three things when writing an opening sentence:

1 **Judgement** – How successful is the argument?
2 *Question* – Where is my link to the question?
3 Reason – What is the reason for my judgement?

For example, the essay question 'To what extent does Plato's allegory of the cave have convincing ideas?' might include opening sentences such as 'Plato believed in the importance of having a critical and philosophical attitude to knowledge.' This sentence is far too descriptive and has no clear link to the question.

After applying the JQR method, the revised sentence could read:

> Plato **successfully** argues for the importance of having a critical and philosophical attitude to knowledge. *This is one of the most convincing ideas in the allegory of the cave because* knowledge is essential in the quest for truth and meaning in life.

With just a few more words, the sentence becomes more evaluative and tied to the question.

After trialling this with one opening sentence, you can have students practise this skill further by giving them a bank of descriptive opening sentences and getting them to use the JQR method to make them more evaluative.

To further support the students, you may wish to provide them with a bank of evaluative language, like this:

Adjectives to describe strong arguments	Adjectives to describe weak arguments
Sound	Limited
Persuasive	Poor
Convincing	Unconvincing
Reasonable	Flawed
Significant	Inadequate

CHAPTER 9
WHAT DOES ASSESSMENT LOOK LIKE IN RE?

Assessment is essential for teachers to find out whether students have learned the things we want them to learn. The purpose of assessment in teaching is to support and measure student learning effectively. *Formative assessment* is used throughout the learning process to monitor progress, provide feedback and guide teacher instruction. It helps teachers identify areas where students may need additional support, and allows learners to reflect on and improve their performance. In contrast, *summative assessment* occurs at the end of a learning period and is designed to evaluate what students have learned by a given point, e.g. end of unit, term or key stage. While formative assessment is diagnostic and developmental in nature, summative assessment is evaluative, providing a summary of learning outcomes. Together, both types of assessment serve to enhance teaching effectiveness and ensure that learning goals are being met.

The following table summarises some of the differences between formative and summative assessments.

Formative assessment	Summative assessment
To improve learning and inform future teaching	To evaluate learning by a given point
Ongoing, during the learning process	At the end of a unit, term or key stage
Immediate, easy to administer and assess	Takes time and can detract from teaching new content in curriculum time
Provides quick, specific feedback for teacher and student	Provides feedback on a wider domain of knowledge
Low stakes, usually not graded	High stakes, often contributes to a final grade
Diagnostic – allows teacher to make in-lesson decisions and decide next steps to further support student progress	Holistic – allows teacher to make judgements about student attainment and progress made towards curriculum end goals
Allows for short-term actions by teacher and student in lesson	Allows for macro evaluation of curriculum and pedagogical approach

Formative assessment in lessons

There are a variety of ways in which we can assess within a lesson to check student understanding. These diagnostic tools are really helpful to determine students' security with the ideas they are encountering in a lesson.

Here are some of the methods we can use to formatively assess in the RE classroom:

Key word quizzes

Quizzing students on key words is an excellent way to help them retrieve knowledge regularly. At the start of a lesson, you may have a recap activity with key words that you want students to write definitions for. These words might relate to previous lessons or the lesson about to take place. For example, a key word quiz at the beginning of a lesson on Hajj may consist of:

- Prophet
- Mecca
- Kab'ah
- Allah.

To save time on marking, you could put the correct definitions on the board and have students peer mark.

As an alternative way of quizzing key terminology, you may wish to provide definitions and ask students to note down the relevant key word. For example:

- What is the term for the Jewish place of worship?
- Which Jewish festival celebrates the Exodus from Egypt?
- What is the name for the day of rest in Judaism?
- Which prophet founded Judaism by making a covenant with God?

You may wish to prepare students for key word quizzes by getting them to self-quiz using a knowledge organiser and creating flashcards. The Leitner system is a really effective way of self-quizzing in preparation for a key word quiz. There is a video explaining how it works here: www.youtube.com/watch?v=C20EvKtdJwQ.

Quote quizzes

As students will look at sources of authority across the key stages, quizzing on quotes is essential. Here are some ways you can test their understanding of quotes:

Activity	How?	Example
Fill the gap	Give students a quotation with key words missing, and ask them to fill in the gaps.	'For ___ so loved the _____, he gave his only ___' (John 3:16) '_____ is _____ with God' (Luke 1:37)
Topic application	Provide students with a topic and a religion. They have to provide a quotation that could be used in relation to that topic.	Abortion – Christianity Creation – Islam
Match explanation to the quote	Give students an explanation of a quote and ask them to identify the quote being explained.	This quotation teaches Christians to worship only one God and not commit idolatry. Answer: 'You shall have no other gods before me' (Exodus 20:3)
Source check	Provide students with a question about a quote and ask them to recall the source or reference.	• In which book of the Bible is the creation story found? • Who said 'Love thy neighbour as thyself'? • In which book of the Bible are the Ten Commandments found?
Topic links	Provide students with a quote and ask them to identify topics within the unit that this quote would link to.	'Whatever you did for the least of these brothers and sisters of mine you did for me' (Matthew 25:31, The Parable of the Sheep and the Goats) Topic links: • Life after death • Judgement • Heaven and hell • Salvation through good works

Multiple-choice questions

These are excellent diagnostic tools for checking understanding, misconceptions and interpretations. When written well, they can be really effective in illustrating how well knowledge has been understood.

Here are some tips for making the most of multiple-choice questions in your classroom:

- Ensure your question is designed to test student knowledge related to what you want them to have learned, and not irrelevant material.
- Include answers that you know will reveal common misconceptions.
- Ensure possible answers are of similar length.
- Three or four possible answers is considered to be optimal.
- Include questions with a variety of challenge.
- Ensure all possible answers are plausible, e.g. Which prophet was tested by God to sacrifice his son? (a) Moses (b) Abraham (c) Adam
- Use a range of formats to pose the multiple-choice question, e.g. Which of the following gives the best explanation of the Big Bang theory? Which of the following statements are reasons for why Zakah is important?

If you want to push student thinking with multiple-choice questions, you can design follow-up tasks based on the incorrect answers. Here is a key stage 5 example:

Why did Thomas Aquinas conclude that there was a designer God?
(a) When we look at the natural world, we see clear evidence of complex design that cannot have come about by chance.
(b) The universe is structured in such a way for life to develop.
(c) Everything in nature that is moving but that has no intelligence must be directed to its telos by God.
(d) The human ability to detect and appreciate beauty must be something that is given to us by God.
Incorrect answer ___ Why might someone incorrectly choose this answer?
Incorrect answer ___ Rewrite the question to make this the answer.
Incorrect answer ___ Which scholars are associated with this conclusion?

Mini whiteboards

These are an excellent way of checking whole-class understanding and can be combined with probing questions. The idea is that pupils write on boards in response to a set question or series of questions, and then, simultaneously, show the teacher their responses. This provides the teacher with lots of instantaneous feedback.

Here is an example of a mini whiteboards activity that could be used as a do-now task to check depth of understanding and prior knowledge, and to look for misconceptions. For context, this would be for a Year 10 lesson on Islam, which began with a review of learning on Prophethood.

1 Islam is a monotheistic religion. True or false?
2 What is a prophet?
3 What is the term for a message sent from God to humans?
4 Who was the archangel who delivered the revelations to Prophet Muhammad?
5 What is the name of the night when the Qur'an was first revealed to the Prophet Muhammad?

After scanning boards for responses, the teacher can engage with a sample of answers to discuss, probe or correct.

Karen Steele (2023) has written an excellent blog about the use of mini whiteboards in the RE classroom. Find her blog by entering 'Miss Eva RE Teacher' in a search engine, or use this link: https://missevareteacher.wordpress.com/blog/.

Connecting concepts

This is a really sophisticated way of allowing students to investigate links between key concepts explored within a sequence of learning by encouraging them to identify the relationships between ideas.

There are two ways this could be done:

Example 1

Provide students with a bank of concepts that have been studied. Get them to identify two concepts that connect and explain why.

The example in Figure 9.1 is taken from key stage 4, where students will have studied Christian beliefs and practices.

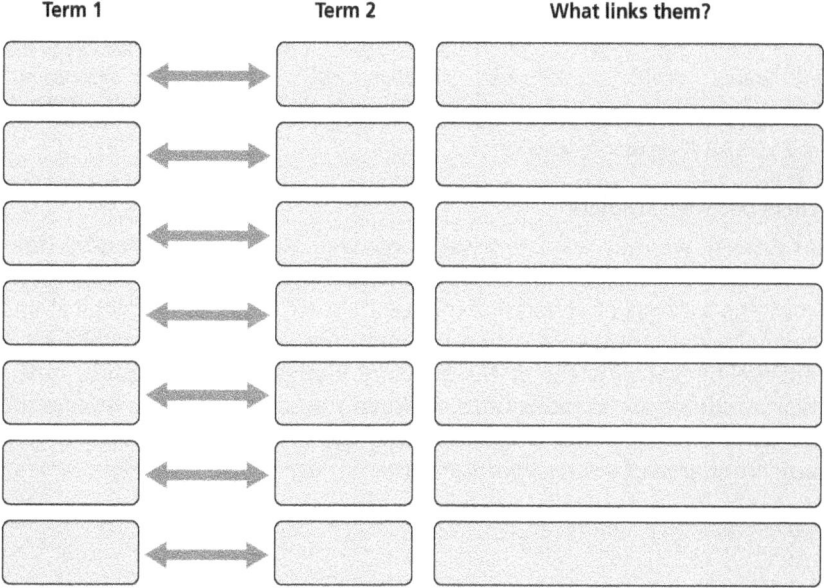

Worship	Holy Communion	Believers' baptism	God	Sacrament	Day of Judgement
Sin	Christmas	Pilgrimage	Resurrection	Atonement	Omnipotent
Prayer	Baptism	Forgiveness	Incarnation	Easter	Salvation
Crucifixion	Liturgical worship	Jesus	Heaven	Infant baptism	Original sin

Challenge:
Don't repeat your explanation for what links the two different terms.
Don't choose a term more than once.
See if you can use quotes or examples, where appropriate, to develop your explanation.

Term 1   Term 2   What links them?

▲ Figure 9.1 Connecting concepts activity

Example 2

Give students a chain of concepts, key words or scholars, with some blank spaces. Students have to identify a concept that connects to the previous and subsequent one. They then have to explain the connection between the ideas.

The example in Figure 9.2 is taken from an A-level topic where students study the theology of Augustine.

SECONDARY RELIGIOUS EDUCATION IN ACTION

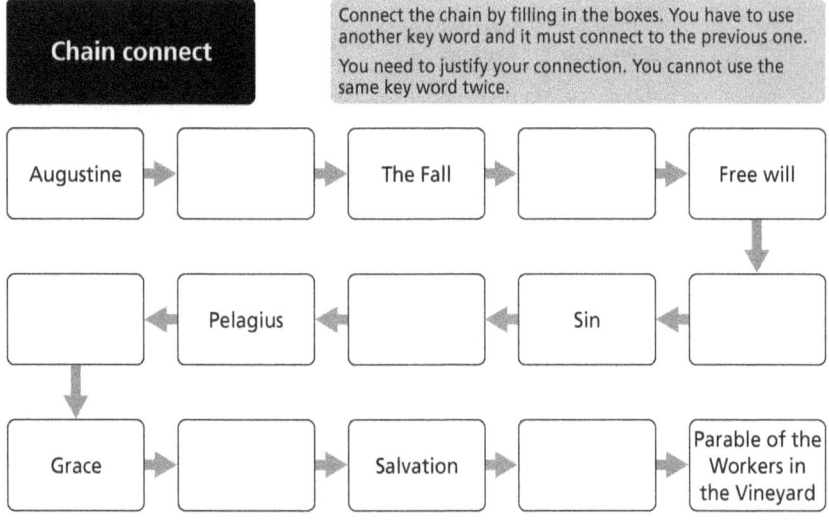

▲ Figure 9.2 Chain connect activity

Links between scholars

At A-level, we may want to assess how well students can identify links between philosophers they have studied. The example in Figure 9.3 contains a range of scholars explored in their study of teleological and cosmological arguments (when running this activity, you might like to include relevant images of the scholars alongside their names). In the task, students are to make links between the scholars. These links could be based on a view they share, how they have responded to each other or any other area of similarity/difference.

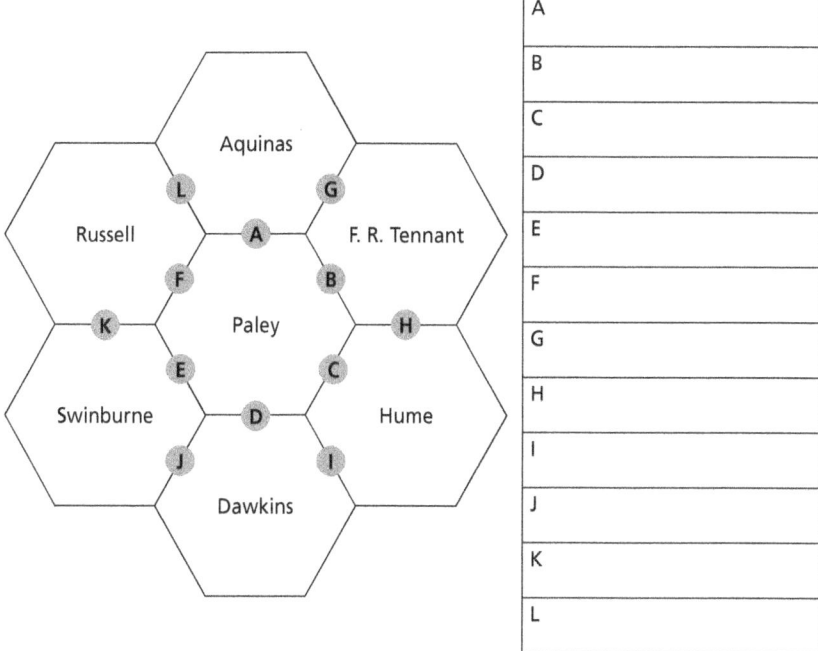

▲ Figure 9.3 Linking scholars activity

Summative assessment

The purpose of summative assessment in RE is to evaluate students' understanding and application of both substantive and disciplinary knowledge at the end of a unit or course. It takes place at the end of a piece of learning or final assessment of learning. This may include end of unit/year tests, or GCSE or A-level examinations. Summative assessment measures how well students can recall and explain key religious content (substantive knowledge), and how effectively they can use methods of enquiry and argument (disciplinary knowledge) to engage with religious and ethical issues. This assessment helps teachers determine if students have met the curriculum aims of the unit of work.

Tips for designing summative assessments

When designing a summative assessment for a unit of work, keep in mind the following:

- **Alignment with learning outcomes:** Focus on the objectives of the unit of work and ensure that the assessment gives you the opportunity to directly measure what students were expected to learn.
- **Make expectations and instructions clear:** Use precise wording in your instructions for the assessment and the tasks set within, so that students understand what is expected of them. If the assessment includes a piece of extended writing, ensure that students are clear on the success criteria to produce the best work possible.
- **Ensure accessibility:** Include a mix of tasks with different degrees of challenge so that students can demonstrate some success while still differentiating levels of understanding among the class.
- **Use a variety of question types:** In key stage 3, there is a lot of freedom for the format of an assessment. You could include types of questions such as multiple choice, short answer questions, extended writing or text analysis, to name but a few. At key stages 4 and 5, the format of an assessment should draw upon the exam-style questions that are set by the exam board you follow.
- **Review and pilot:** Review the assessment with the department for clarity and alignment. A worthwhile CPD opportunity would be to complete the assessment yourself or as a department. This can help you identify flaws but also allows you to see what excellence could look like for the assessment.
- **Consider the feedback:** In advance of marking the assessments, you may want to consider how you will be giving feedback to students on the assessment. Guidance on how best to give feedback can be found in chapter 10.
- **Workload:** RE teachers often have a lot of key stage 3 classes. It is important to find a style of assessment that provides a healthy challenge for students while not being incredibly onerous for teachers to mark.

Examples of summative assessments

Here you can see an example of a Year 9 assessment on the history and beliefs of Buddhism. The assessment consists of four parts:

1. Multiple-choice questions
2. Key word definitions
3. Short answer questions
4. Extended writing questions.

Buddhism (history and belief): assessment

Name:

Answer all the questions. You have 30 minutes to complete this assessment.

Part 1: Multiple choice: Circle the correct answer.

Question	Answer options			✓/✗
1. How many followers does Buddhism have around the world?	a) 500 million	b) 6 million	c) 1.3 billion	
2. On what continent do the majority of Buddhists live today?	a) Europe	b) Asia	c) Africa	
3. The teachings and sayings of the Buddha are contained in which book?	a) Parinirvana	b) Sanskrit	c) Dhammapada	
4. The idea that our actions affect our future is called:	a) Karma	b) Samsara	c) Anatta	
5. The Buddha's teachings are called:	a) Anicca	b) Dharma	c) Anatta	
6. Which term describes the suffering and dissatisfaction of all living beings?	a) Impermanence	b) Anicca	c) Dukkha	
Total: /6				

Part 2: Key words: Define the following:

Key word	Definition
Ascetic	
Enlightenment	
The Middle Way	
Samsara	
Total: /8	

Part 3: Knowledge: Answer all the questions.

Question	Answer
1. What did Siddhartha achieve under the Bodhi tree?	
2. What is the name of the four teachings of Siddhartha that form the basis of Buddhism?	
3. Name one relative of Siddhartha other than his mother.	
4. What four sights did Siddhartha see after leaving the palace?	
5. Siddhartha gave eight instructions for people to follow in order to achieve enlightenment. What are they known as?	
6. What is meditation?	
Total: /6	

Part 4: Extended answers: Answer these questions in as much detail as possible.

1. Explain each of the Four Noble Truths in your own words. [8]

_____

_____...

2. Explain how following the Eightfold Path is different to following a set of rules in another religion you know about. [4]

_____

_____...

3. 'Buddhism is more of a philosophy than a religion.' Discuss. [8]

_____

_____...

Total: /20

Part	1	2	3	4	Total	Percentage
Mark	/6	/8	/6	/20	/40	

[The answer spaces provided for Part 4 are for illustrative purposes only. In an actual assessment, they would be much larger, depending on the level of detail required.]

For more guidance on how to teach writing in RE, read chapter 8.

Assessing at key stages 4 and 5

As mentioned previously, summative assessments at key stages 4 and 5 often take the form of a set of exam questions or an essay. However, these forms of assessment do not always sample the full domain of knowledge within a unit of work. Therefore, you may wish to consider a form of summative assessment that allows you to assess a wider domain of knowledge.

The additional benefits of doing this are:

- It's quick to mark.
- When giving feedback, you can show a model set of answers on the visualiser and talk through the successful answers.
- It provides students with confidence in the knowledge they have looked at within a unit. This can help build confidence prior to answering a set of exam questions or an essay, which can seem daunting.
- Students can use it to self-quiz as they go, throughout the course.

SECONDARY RELIGIOUS EDUCATION IN ACTION

Here is a key stage 4 example based on their study of Christianity beliefs:

▼ **Christianity beliefs and teachings: knowledge recall**

Question	Answer	✓/✗
1. What term describes God as 'all-powerful'? [1]		
2. What term describes God's nature as fair and tells us he will treat us fairly at judgement? [1]		
3. What does omniscient mean? [1]		
4. 'God so loved the world that he gave his one and only son, that whoever believes in him shall not perish but have eternal life.' – John 3:16. What quality of God does this passage best show? [1]		
5. Define Trinity. [2]		
6. Which person of the Trinity is often regarded as the creator? [1]		
7. The first book of the Bible contains the creation account. What is this book called? [1]		
8. What is the difference between a literal and non-literal (liberal) interpretation of the Bible? [2]		
9. According to a literalist Christian, how many days did it take God to create the world? [1]		
10. Many Christians believe that humans were the most important part of God's creation. Identify two reasons why someone might argue this. [2]		

Question	Answer	✓/✗
11. The term 'The Word' is used to refer to God the Son in which gospel? [1]	a) Matthew's gospel b) Mark's gospel c) Luke's gospel d) John's gospel	
12. Which of the following does not describe The Word's role in creation? [1]	a) was there in the beginning b) was with God c) was God d) some things were made without him	
13. Define incarnation. [1]		
14. Identify **two** features from the nativity story that highlight Jesus' birth was special and unique. [2]		
	Total marks /18	

Here is a key stage 5 example based on their study of Ancient philosophical influences:

▼ Ancient philosophical influences: knowledge recall

Question	Answer	✓/✗
1. What does it mean to call Plato a rationalist? [1]		
2. In which book does Plato's analogy of the cave appear? [1]	a) Meno b) Timaeus c) Republic	
3. Which term is the Greek word meaning end or purpose? [1]		
4. Which of these is *not* a characteristic of Aristotle's Prime Mover? [1]	a) Eternal b) More knowledge of it can be gained after death c) Perfect	
5. What is motus? [1]		

Question	Answer	✓/x
6. Which term best describes Aristotle's understanding of reality? [1]	a) Rationality b) Empiricist	
7. In Plato's analogy, what does the Sun represent? [1]		
8. Identify and explain each of Aristotle's four causes. [8]		
9. Give **two** ideas that Plato is illustrating in his analogy of the cave. [2]		
10. Identify **three** strengths of Aristotle's understanding of reality. [3]		
11. Identify **three** weaknesses of Aristotle's understanding of reality. [3]		
12. Why does Plato think we can gain certain knowledge of the Forms but cannot gain certain knowledge of the physical world? [1]		
13. Explain **one** difference between the Form of the Good and the Prime Mover. [2]		
14. Give **two** characteristics of Aristotle's Prime Mover. [2]		
15. What does Aristotle mean by the formal cause of something? [1]	a) It explains what something is made from b) It explains the purpose of something c) It explains what shape and identifying features something has	
16. What does Aristotle mean when he says that the Prime Mover must have necessary existence? [1]		

Question	Answer	✓/X
17. In Plato's analogy, what is represented by the prisoner arriving in the daylight of the outside world? [1]		
18. Why did Aristotle think that the Prime Mover must be perfectly good? [1]		
19. Identify **three** strengths of Plato's theory of forms. [3]		
20. Identify **three** weaknesses of Plato's theory of forms. [3]		
21. 'I see no reason whatsoever to suppose that the total has any cause whatsoever … what I'm saying is that the concept of cause is not applicable to the total. … I should say the universe is just there, and that's all.' – Bertrand Russell Explain Bertrand Russell's criticism of Aristotle. [2]		
	Total marks	**/40**

Case study on assessing disciplinary knowledge and skills
Alice Thomas, Blue Coat School

Assessment methodology

The Curriculum and Assessment Review (DfE, 2025a) asks us to consider 'how the assessment system can best capture the strengths of every child and young person ... with the right balance of assessment methods ...'. We are, as a result, asked to recognise whether all pupils may be assessed in the same way and, as leaders and teachers of RE, we may assess our pupils through a wide range of methodologies, including formative and summative. This will therefore give our pupils opportunities to secure mastery of disciplinary knowledge and skills in RE, which are vital for raising standards and enabling future expertise.

When creating an assessment, we want to capture the strengths of each pupil, but moreover, we also want to capture the breadth of the curriculum that pupils have studied. When we assess our pupils, we want to strike the right balance of assessment. This includes considering the use of oracy as a method in which we could capture pupils' substantive and disciplinary knowledge. This ensures that pupils have every opportunity to fully master the fundamental knowledge and disciplinary skills the locally agreed syllabus demands.

The process of assessment

One of the key principles to assessment being successful throughout the pupil's learning journey and across our curriculum phases is the centrality of assessment to planning. Ultimately, as teachers, our planning should provide opportunities for both learner and teacher to obtain and use information about progress towards their learning goal. As a result, when planning, we should include strategies to ensure that learners understand the goals they are pursuing and the criteria that will be applied in assessing their work: 'planning becomes about more than the accumulation of knowledge, but about progress in knowledge, skills, attitudes and concepts' (Holt, 2022). Therefore, when considering how we assess our pupils, the underlying principles should underpin the planning, teaching and learning that takes place within RE. We identified that for assessment to be effective our approach needs to be 'a learning journey ... as such the teacher should be able to articulate how each element of the curriculum builds on/is built upon other aspects of the content being taught' (Holt, 2022). As a result, we recognise our assessment methodology is to highlight the progress pupils have made within each key stage in the way of disciplinary knowledge and skills. We therefore want to create a model of assessment that will stand independently but also help lay the foundations for progress at key stages 4 and 5.

Proposed models of assessment
- The use of assessment is to help build students' understanding within day-to-day lessons.
- The use of assessment is to provide information on students' achievements to those on the outside of the student–teacher relationship: to parents, further education institutions and employers.
- The use of assessment data to hold individuals and institutions to account, including through the publication of results that encourage outsiders to make a judgement on the quality of those being held to account.

The Ofsted *Research Review* (2021) draws upon three different types of knowledge that are found in the curriculum:

1 **Substantive knowledge:** Knowledge about various religious and non-religious traditions.

2 **Ways of knowing:** Pupils learn 'how to know' about religion and non-religion.

3 **Personal knowledge:** Pupils build an awareness of their own presuppositions and values about the religious and non-religious traditions they study, but this is not assessed formally.

The Coventry and Warwickshire Locally Agreed Syllabus outlines the journey of disciplinary knowledge and skills in which pupils will be assessed throughout their religion and worldviews journey by the end of key stage 3. You can view this on pages 53 and 54 of the full document, which is available for download on the Church of England website: www.churchofengland.org/sites/default/files/2024-12/coventry-and-warwickshire-agreed-syllabus-2024-2029_0.pdf.

Example of assessment practice from the Coventry and Warwickshire Religion and Worldviews Locally Agreed Syllabus

As part of my research for the Stage 2 Culham St Gabriel's Leadership Scholarship programme, I have had the opportunity to gather evidence of assessment practice from both the primary and secondary phases this academic year to identify how RE practitioners are assessing disciplinary knowledge and skills as a result of the successful implementation of the Religion and Worldviews Locally Agreed Syllabus.

SECONDARY RELIGIOUS EDUCATION IN ACTION

Here is an example of part of a pupil's response to K3.5, with a focus on assessing the disciplinary knowledge and skills covered within the teaching of this unit. Pupils were given an opportunity to be able to demonstrate knowledge and skills using a variety of methodologies, including both formative and summative methods of how philosophies may be used through the theological lens:

How might philosophies drawn from sacred texts impact on the way people choose to live today?

Philosophies from sacred text end of unit exam

Section 5 – 'Sacred texts provide a good guide to morality today.' Analyse and evaluate this statement. [12 marks]

I think theists would agree with this because their sacred texts show them what they should and shouldn't do and they believe in what their God teaches them. Most Christians, for example, would believe in this because they have the seven commandments from God that are supposed to instruct them about what is right and wrong.

I think atheists would disagree with the statement. Because they don't believe in a God none of the instructions or guidelines in sacred texts about how to live will matter to them. For example, theists are taught to believe that everything said by their God is morally right, but atheists don't have any God for them to listen to.

Sacred texts offer a good guide to morality today. Because I am a Christian myself, I believe everything that God teaches is morally right and I use what he says to guide me in how I should live my everyday life.

Religious teaching teaches theists how their God wishes them to live their lives. Most holy books have instructions about what their God wants them to do and so theists use this to guide them and they believe that, because this is what their God wants them to do, it is morally right.

You can view the assessment guidance on page 53 of the full document, which is available for download on the Church of England website: www.churchofengland.org/sites/default/files/2024-12/coventry-and-warwickshire-agreed-syllabus-2024-2029_0.pdf.

Conclusion

Considering how we assess pupils from within a religion and worldviews approach instigates complex thinking and empowers pupils to engage in conversations that are informed, because of the implemented curriculum. As a result, pupils experience the breadth of knowledge, understanding and balance of the disciplinary knowledge and skills that have been assessed as they make their journey through the key stages, becoming religion and worldviews explorers and experts.

Case study on assessing student progress when teaching personal knowledge
Arabella Saunders, Derby High School

In the past, GCSE RE exam criteria have included the requirement of learners to present their own opinion on an issue and give reasons for their opinion. Explicit teaching of personal knowledge offers much more rigour. It requires the pupil to unpack why it is that they have come to that opinion. Explaining a perspective is a preliminary task, and unpacking the reasons for the occupation of that particular worldview requires deeper reflexivity.

When assessing pupil progress in personal knowledge education we want to see the development of a deepening 'awareness of their own presuppositions and values' and evidence of a 'critical positionality' (Pett, 2024). That is, we want students to be more reflective about their own position by developing their ability to explain why they hold the views that they do. In addition, when engaging with the personal worldviews of others, we want students to show an increasingly nuanced understanding of the diversity within and between religious and non-religious beliefs. In short, students should be able to articulate why a Muslim may or may not wear hijab, why a Roman Catholic may or may not be supportive of homosexual marriage, and everything in between.

One teaching tool that might offer up a way to demonstrate the development of personal knowledge is a bookend task. This would see students set the same questions at the start and end of a unit of study, so the teacher is able to assess their progress. This task would need the prerequisite knowledge of the factors that influence a worldview:

- Topic question

- What are my ideas about this question?

- What factors have influenced my ideas?
- How did I come to have those factors?

This example shows how engaging with the topic has enabled the student to explain their position with greater clarity and insight:

Y7 Spring Term	Response at the start of the unit	Response at the end of the unit
Topic question	Are Jesus' teachings about love relevant today?	Are Jesus' teachings about love relevant today?
What are my ideas about this question?	Jesus' teachings are not that relevant today. Although I agree that caring for others is important, Jesus' teachings are in the Bible, which is an old document containing stories that I do not believe are true.	I don't believe in life after death or that being kind helps you get to heaven, but I can see that being kind leads to a peaceful society. So, I do not agree with all of Jesus' teachings, but I think agape love is still important in the modern world. For example, the values of love and kindness link to current laws such as the 2010 Equality Act.
What factors have influenced my ideas?	I am an atheist, so I do not believe in God or the Bible. I think that Jesus might have existed, but his message is not that important to me. I think we should be kind to others, but we don't need Jesus to teach us that – it is common sense.	Jesus was highlighting the importance of looking after other people in his time and culture. I do not believe in Jesus, but Linda Woodhead explains how Jesus' values have been 'unbundled' over time so they can still be a bit relevant, even to non-Christians like me.

Y7 Spring Term	Response at the start of the unit	Response at the end of the unit
How did I come to have those factors?	My family are atheists and we do not follow a religious tradition. I have learned about Jesus' message of care at school and I know that England has a Christian heritage, but I cannot see how reading parables from 2000 years ago in a distant country can possibly relate to modern life in the UK.	I am not Christian, but I see that respect for others might be relevant. For example, in the Parable of the Good Samaritan Jesus shows the lawyer how unkindly he has been treating others just because of their cultural differences. This parable teaches the importance of equality and respect, which are relevant values today.

Case study on creating trust-wide assessments
Nikki McGee, Hethersett Academy, Inspiration Trust

The importance of centralised trust-wide assessments

At Inspiration Trust, every KS3 student sits the same end-of-year assessment. Designing a test for thousands of students across several schools is a serious responsibility. It takes time, mental energy and a lot of consultation. I present our assessments to our heads of department months before they will be used, and they go through multiple rounds of quality assurance, both within and outside of the trust. Ideally assessments should be the product of professional subject-specific conversations.

Why did we rethink our assessments?

I inherited rigorous assessments, but my perspective as both a trust lead and a classroom teacher influenced how I saw them. I remembered marking hundreds of essays at the most exhausting point in the year. I felt resentful, and I doubted the accuracy of my marking.

I wanted assessments that told us something useful about how effective we were in teaching our curriculum, without overwhelming teachers. Our students and parents also want to know how well students are doing in comparison to their peers. A project from Culham St Gabriel's and Ormiston Academies Trust helped shape my thinking. It encouraged me to design assessments that made students think hard, without demanding too much writing.

I was also aware that we had a growing number of teachers delivering RE who spent most of their time teaching another subject. When you rely on teachers with other specialisms to deliver your curriculum you are relying on hard-won goodwill, and so I wanted assessments that they could mark with a feeling of confidence.

At the same time, our curriculum was shifting. We wanted students not just to learn about theology, philosophy or history, but to actually use the tools of these disciplines. This meant our assessments had to be explicitly disciplinary.

What do we test?

Our starting point is a 'scheme of knowledge' – an idea I took from Dawn Cox. We do not have centralised schemes of work, but we do set out the knowledge and skills students are expected to have at the end of each unit. All assessment questions are drawn from this. Schools in our trust have different amounts of curriculum time, so being clear about what can be tested is essential. The purpose of assessment is not to catch students out; it is to check whether the curriculum is working. I want every child to open their assessment and feel like they have been prepared.

How did we reduce teacher workload?

One major change was to remove essays from centralised assessments. This was controversial, particularly in departments that had invested in teaching essay writing. However, essays can still be set at other points in the year. I think it is unreasonable to expect one teacher to mark hundreds of essays at once, especially at the end of a term or academic year, when they are at their most tired.

Our RE assessments are now 30 minutes long. Students peer mark about half the paper in the lesson, while teachers spot check. Instead of essays, students write one or two paragraphs. For example, a previous essay asked students to compare Martin Luther and Guru Nanak. Now they explain two ways their reforms were similar. I provide an example paragraph, usually giving the most obvious point, which means students have to think harder for themselves.

Multiple-choice questions remain, although I reduced the number from 10 per test to 5. Creating good multiple-choice questions is time-consuming and challenging, and I often found myself scraping the barrel for the last few, sometimes having the opposite of a plausible distractor or testing something niche rather than something that was essential for our students to understand. My starting point when crafting multi-choice questions is to think about the words or ideas that students have to know in order to access our curriculum – both the units they have just studied and those that will follow. For example, our Abrahamic faiths units require an understanding of monotheism and our philosophy units require an understanding of the term empiricism.

I also wanted students to generate more of their own answers. Following the Ormiston approach, we now include descriptions of thinkers or ideas that students must identify. These are quick to mark and suitable for peer marking. Here are two examples:

1 This Hindu word can be translated as 'duty' or 'right way of living'.
2 This leader from the Dharmic traditions spent three days under a river before reappearing and saying, 'There is neither Hindu nor Muslim, so whose path shall I follow?'

These can take a while to craft because you want a question that has only one correct answer and assesses the key knowledge of your curriculum. This is not about creating niche questions that catch students out.

There are no GCSE-style questions in our assessments because they are not testing a GCSE curriculum. We choose question types that suit the material at hand. The students receive a percentage and an average for the class and year group. There are no flight paths or projected grades. However, the students' scores have proven to be quite a reliable indicator of GCSE success. This is because, in my opinion, any broad, balanced and challenging RE is good preparation for GCSE; there is no need for GCSE-style questions.

How do we assess disciplinary knowledge?

All of our trust-wide assessments now have a disciplinary section, broken down into philosophy, theology and social sciences. Each section includes a mix of knowledge and skills. It is important that these are not new skills or knowledge. Students should have practised the disciplinary skills in lessons and met the required knowledge. It is worth repeating that our assessments are not about catching students out but checking that they have the knowledge and skills that we have taught them.

Here are some examples:

- Philosophy: In Year 7, students practise Socratic questioning by writing a question that exposes a flaw or assumption in a scripted dialogue. In Year 8, they read dialogues and have to identify specific arguments for the existence of God and explain criticisms of them. In Year 9, they apply different moral theories to ethical dilemmas.

- Theology: In Year 7, students study extracts from the Abrahamic faiths and explain what these reveal about God. In Year 8, they use the Nicene Creed to explain beliefs about the Trinity and identify disagreements the Council resolved. In Year 9, they turn to the Dharmic traditions and explore how figures such as the Buddha or Guru Nanak changed beliefs within their communities.

- Social sciences: This is the area we are still developing. Writing questions showed us that we had been teaching about the social sciences but not teaching students to use their methods. At present we ask students to connect theories with religious beliefs, stories or practices.

Example disciplinary questions
Philosophy:

- Read the dialogue between Lily and Ben. Suggest a Socratic question that would make them think more deeply.

- Below is the Design argument as a syllogism. Complete the conclusion.

Theology:

- Give two examples of what this story reveals about God.

- The Nicene Council was called to settle arguments within the Church. Give one example of a disagreement Christians were having in the fourth century CE.

- Identify one way a Dharmic figure (for example, the Buddha or Guru Nanak) changed beliefs within their community.

Social sciences:

- Give an example of a religious story that is easy to remember because it uses familiar ideas but also challenges our understanding of the world.

- Below is a diagram of the varna system. State two ways in which the varna system can prevent society from changing.

Why do our assessments draw across the curriculum?

The purpose of our curriculum is to build a narrative about the complexity of belief, not to collect isolated facts. Our assessments therefore end with questions that ask students to make links across units. These questions were previously essays, but for workload reasons the students now answer in one or two paragraphs. To get into the top marking band, they have to draw from across our curriculum. From Year 8 this means drawing from a topic from a different year. We want to check that our students are building a body of knowledge.

For example, once students learn that Peter Berger argued religion helps people feel safe in an uncertain world, they can revisit stories from previous units through this lens. In Year 8, our students ask whether religion acts as a conservative force in society, using Marx and Durkheim. They can revisit stories from Year 7, asking if these stories encourage revolution or obedience. This means that in the final section of the assessment, students have an opportunity to reinterpret for themselves, to create knowledge that is new to them.

Our students tell us that these 'cross-curricular' questions are challenging, but they also help students think more deeply.

Example questions
- Choose one figure from the Abrahamic faiths (Abraham, Moses, Jesus, Paul or Muhammad). Explain how their story might help believers feel safe in an uncertain world.
- Explain one similarity between Guru Nanak and Martin Luther.
- Choose one figure from the Abrahamic faiths and explain how they tried to change society.

What are our next steps?

After further consultation with teachers and students, we have agreed three priorities for the future:

1. Adding history: Assessments will now include a history section, so that all four of our disciplines are represented.
2. Increasing challenge: Mark schemes will reward more complex and developed answers, encouraging students to stretch themselves.
3. Strengthening social sciences: Our long-term goal is to look again at how we teach and assess the social sciences, moving from teaching about them to teaching students how to use their methods.

CHAPTER 10
WHAT DOES FEEDBACK LOOK LIKE IN RE?

Feedback happens all the time in the classroom – it is a reciprocal and responsive process. Throughout our lessons, we find out things that students do not know and then do something to address this. This feedback could be written or verbal. The most effective feedback is that which tells a student what to improve and how to improve it.

What are the principles of effective feedback?

Some principles of effective feedback, proposed by Dylan Wiliam (2011), include:

- Feedback is only useful if it leads to action. The most important thing is what students do with the feedback, not what the teacher writes or says. If the feedback doesn't cause a change in the student's thinking or performance, it's a waste of effort.
- Feedback must be more work for the student than the teacher. Students need to actively engage by revising, reflecting or applying suggestions given, rather than receiving corrections.
- Feedback should come before or without a grade, so that students have a reason to do it. Giving grades alongside comments can often lead to student disengagement, as they focus on the grade, not the feedback.
- Feedback must cause thinking and prompt students to figure out how to improve.
- The quality of the feedback matters more than the quantity. A small, focused piece of actionable feedback is often best.

For the RE teacher, providing meaningful and effective feedback can be difficult alongside the sheer number of classes we teach. Here are some strategies that you can use in the classroom to enable you to provide meaningful feedback alongside a manageable workload:

Exam assessment criteria

In GCSE and A-level classes, it is wise to use the assessment criteria provided by the exam boards to inform the way you provide feedback for students. These can offer clear guidance about what is expected to be included within certain styles of answer.

If using these with students, we have to be aware that the language used by exam boards is often ambiguous and not student-friendly. To deal with this issue, you can either explain what the assessment terminology means or translate it into student-friendly language.

Assessment descriptor	Simplified descriptor
Evaluate	Judge how good or bad something is and explain why
Coherent	Clear
Influence	How something affects what someone does, believes or feels
Explain	Provide a clear point with reason to support
Reference to sources of wisdom and authority	Quotation from a holy text
Justified conclusion	Conclusion summarises the argument with reasons
Thesis	Main argument being presented in a piece of writing
Compare	Say how things are similar
Contrast	Say how things are different

Tick sheets

Tick sheets are a really effective feedback tool for reducing workload and providing students with clear feedback on how to improve their work. When marking a piece of work, complete the tick sheet appropriately. This can then be given to students with clear guidance on what they need to improve.

Here is an example from a GCSE 6-mark question:

Criteria	Done
Gave two simple explanations of Hindu beliefs about reincarnation	✓
Gave two detailed explanations of Hindu beliefs about reincarnation	✓
Gave an accurate reference to a Hindu sacred text	✓
Applied reference to a Hindu sacred text to question	
Gave an accurate reference to a Hindu sacred text to support explanation of one belief	✓

Live feedback

Live feedback provides students with immediate feedback in the classroom. As you walk around the classroom looking at student work, you might identify some misconceptions. For example, some students may have written that 'A belief in the Trinity means that Christians worship three gods', or that 'All Christians reject the theory of evolution.' Instead of waiting until the end of the lesson, you can intervene immediately to address the misconceptions that have been made.

Live feedback may also involve celebrating the things that students are doing well. When circulating the room as students carry out an extended piece of writing, you may see that a student has effectively used references to a source of authority in their first paragraph. In this scenario, you could point this out to them individually to celebrate their success, or you could pause the class while you put the paragraph under the visualiser and ask them to identify the excellence within it. This can give the whole class specific feedback on what they need to include within their writing.

Selective marking

This technique allows students to absorb precise feedback and helps to reduce teacher workload – a big issue for RE teachers at key stage 3. This form of feedback involves you being clear to students that they will receive feedback on only a selected aspect of their writing, e.g. their use of examples to support their explanations, evaluation of arguments or accurate references to scholarly views. However, don't tell the students what you will be selecting to mark, as this will ensure they apply themselves fully to all aspects of the work they are producing.

When you are marking the piece of work, identify misconceptions or areas for improvement in it. You want to provide students with feedback that is specific, actionable and will enable them to improve. For example, their evaluation of arguments may be better if they considered a counterargument from a humanist perspective. The benefit of this feedback technique is that it allows the teacher to give very specific feedback on a selected section of work without overwhelming the student.

When you return the work, provide the students with some time in lesson to look at their marked work and act upon the feedback. The goal of this feedback time is for students to improve the piece of work. After some lesson time, you may wish to show examples of improved work under the visualiser and discuss how the improvements were made.

Spot your mistakes

This feedback technique encourages students to generate their own feedback by spotting areas of misconception in order to discover areas for improvement in their work.

This feedback process begins with the teacher reading student work and identifying areas for improvement. You should look to identify a maximum of three or four key areas for improvement and highlight them on the student work. When giving back work to students, you may wish to provide some prompts as to the type of error they are looking for, such as incorrect use of key vocabulary, confusion of appropriate scholars or insufficient development of a point.

At this point, give students some time to find and correct the errors in their work. As they engage with this task, you may need to provide scaffolds to support the process. These could include key word lists, success criteria or showing exemplar work. This will enable students to evaluate their work more quickly and effectively, and understand it.

Whole-class feedback

This technique is an excellent way to give students prompt, detailed feedback while minimising teacher workload. It replaces writing individual comments on student work with feedback given to the class as a whole, based on trends noted by the teacher.

After deciding on the piece of work you wish to give whole-class feedback on, here is a simple process from taking in student work to the feedback lesson itself:

1 Take in student work and make notes on the following:
   a) Common areas of strength (and why)
   b) Student examples of excellent work to use as models in feedback lesson
   c) Common misconceptions
   d) Common knowledge errors
   e) Common spelling errors
   f) Key areas for improvement and next steps

A template for making notes for whole-class feedback might look something like this:

Class:	
Date:	
Areas of strength	**Student examples of excellent work**
Common misconceptions	**Common knowledge errors**
Common spelling errors	**Key areas for improvement and next steps**

2. You can now plan a feedback lesson that allows students to address these issues. Here are some ideas of things you may wish to do for the feedback lesson:

- Use a PowerPoint or visualiser to run through your feedback notes.
- Copy the feedback sheet to give to students as a record.
- Break down examples of excellent work via a visualiser, a photo of the work or a typed version.
- Provide students with time to act on feedback and make improvements.
- Have one-to-one conversations with students about their work if they have specific issues.

Alongside this general process for whole-class feedback, here are some additional tips and tricks to ensure it is as effective as possible:

- Have a blank copy of the assessment or test next you that you can annotate. As you are marking, if you notice that a lot of misconceptions are being made on question 4, you can write your observations in the answer space indicating where students have gone wrong or any features of excellence in answer to that question. These annotations can form the basis and focus of the whole-class feedback you provide on particular questions.

- In *Tips for Teachers*, Craig Barton (2023) gives the strategy of 'Reteach' and 'Retrieve' to really focus whole-class feedback. This involves the teacher reviewing student work alongside a piece of paper with two columns, one labelled 'Reteach' and the other labelled 'Retrieve'. In the 'Reteach' column, note down any topics that students have really struggled with and where class time is necessary to address these through teacher explanation or examples. You can consider where in the next lesson or future lessons this will be addressed. In the 'Retrieve' column, note down topics that were troublesome but some understanding was evident. These topics can be translated into a few retrieval practice questions at the beginning of a lesson to help students further progress.

- Take pictures or scan student work to really enrich the whole-class feedback lesson. You can give a copy of the work to each student so that they can annotate it themselves based on what they think is good about the answer, or you can show the answer on the board. By explicitly showing students what excellence looks like, such as use of scripture or detailed evaluation, they can see more clearly the standard of work they should be striving for. These examples of student work can also be used in future years to show subsequent students what excellence looks like.

- To ensure that students focus on the feedback and how to improve, don't give the work back straight away. By giving the work back at the start of the lesson, many students will only want to know their grade or how their mates have done, or to question something in your marking. Moreover, the incentive to listen is lost if students think feedback doesn't apply to them. For example, Jem will be unlikely to listen to the feedback on question 2 if they know they scored full marks. We want to ensure that all students are focused on the next steps to improve, and handing back their work after the feedback has been given enables this.

Examiner's reports

This technique involves the teacher writing their observations from marking student answers to each question on a set assessment. All points of excellence are noted down, e.g. good use of key vocabulary, accurate use of scripture. Any misconceptions or errors are noted down too, e.g. incorrect use of structure, inconsistent use of capital letters. These comments are typed and given back to students at the start of a feedback lesson, along with their work.

Students are tasked with reading their work and highlighting the comments on the examiner's report that apply to them. Students then use the highlighted feedback to improve their answers to the set questions.

Assessment reflections

This form of feedback works especially well for high stakes assessments such as mock exams in key stage 4 or 5.

Reflection sheets are completed in class by the students when their assessments have been returned. This gives them an opportunity to review their performance by considering the following:

- how they prepared for an exam, e.g. what revision techniques did they follow
- a breakdown of marks for each section
- analysis of their performance, e.g. which types of questions or topics they lost marks on
- targets for moving forward based on their performance
- anything specific they need help with that the teacher may not have addressed with the whole class or individually with them.

When we use reflection sheets in my department, we collect them at the end of the lesson and they form the basis of our discussion at parents' evening. This is really beneficial for the teacher, as it gives them a simple resource that reminds them of the performance of the student. For the student, it offers them a detailed piece of feedback on their mock exam. This assessment audit is returned to the student and can be revisited later in the academic year when another assessment has taken place, to see if the targets have been met or progress has been made.

Here is an example of an assessment reflection based on a Year 11 mock exam:

Class teacher:

Name:

YEAR 11 RELIGIOUS STUDIES – STUDENT REFLECTION

Prior to Mock:

On a scale of 1–10 (10 being well prepared), how prepared were you for this exam? In other words, how much effort did you put into preparing for the RS exam? *Why?*

_____

_____

What did your revision look like?

_____

_____

Tick all that apply:

- I gave myself plenty of time to prepare for this exam
- I had a revision plan, e.g. revision timetable, knew what to revise and which revision activities to do for X and Y, etc.
- I utilised my time effectively in preparation for the exam
- I looked after myself in the lead-up to this exam (food, water, sleep, exercise)
- I was able to revise in a quiet space and was not distracted, e.g. by family, friends or mobile
- I read carefully the AQA specification for each topic, so I was aware of what content could come up in the exam
- I revised thoroughly topics or specific content within a topic that I found especially difficult or I was not confident in
- I revised past exam mark schemes
- I practised answering exam questions

- I asked my teacher to look over my answers/plans or asked for further support with content I found difficult
- I made a point to learn the definitions of key vocabulary
- I made a point to learn some religious teachings off by heart

Mock:

Topic	MCQ [1]	Give [2]	Explain [4]	Explain with scripture [5]	Evaluate [12]	Total /24
Christianity beliefs						
Christianity practices						
Islam beliefs						
Islam practices						
Total	/4	/8	/16	/20	/48	

Comment on what you notice from the grid, e.g. which types of questions did you tend to lose marks on/do well? 4 markers/5 markers, etc. What topics highlighted knowledge or lacked knowledge?

Strengths:

_____

_____

Weaknesses:

_____

_____

Post-Mock:

What grade did you achieve in the re-Mocks?

Were you happy with the grade you achieved in the Mocks? *Why?*

_____

_____

The overall grade I am aiming to achieve in the real GCSE in RS is:

Targets for the future

Now set yourself three targets to improve your performance in your Year 11 exam and to achieve your goal, e.g.

- Learn the key terms accurately
- Learn Biblical or Qur'anic passages to include in the 5-mark and 12-mark questions ('In the Qur'an it says …')
- Make sure I include both sides of the argument in the 12-marker and reach a clear conclusion
- Make sure I include religious views in the 12-marker and be explicit in this reference ('In the Bible it says …')
- Learn a specific topic in more detail (state topic)
- Extend my 4-marker answers to include detailed, rather than a 'couple of words'-style, explanations
- Extend my 5-marker answers to include detailed, rather than simple, explanations, and make sure I include reference to scripture
- Read the questions more carefully in the exam
- Work on my time management
- Focus on the spelling of key terms
- Spend more time on my revision
- Revise specific religious concepts on the specification that I have found difficult to answer a question on, e.g. stewardship, dominion, sanctity of life, revelation

	Target
1	
2	
3	

Use this space to indicate if there is anything you feel you need specific help with in terms of the RS exams:

_____

_____

Model answers

As discussed in chapter 6, model answers are very effective as part of a rich diet of feedback. Instead of providing vague feedback, such as 'explain the quote clearly', a model answer shows what this looks like in practice. It gives students the chance to compare their own work to the model and spot specific differences. This puts the onus back onto the learner and makes the feedback actionable, as the student can imitate the excellence within the model answer. As mentioned earlier when we explored whole-class feedback, a model answer can give whole-class feedback by addressing common issues, saving teacher time and making feedback more concise. In essence, it shows students what excellence in our subject looks like.

Here is an example of three model answers to a GCSE exam question. I designed each model answer to include specific features of excellence and specific misconceptions I noticed from student answers.

Explain two ways in which a belief in God the creator influences Christians today. [4]

First way:	
• simple explanation of a relevant and accurate influence	1 mark
• detailed explanation of a relevant and accurate influence	2 mark
Second way:	
• simple explanation of a relevant and accurate influence	1 mark
• detailed explanation of a relevant and accurate influence	2 mark

Answer 1

One way belief in God influences Christians today is through prayer. Christians believe that God is always present and listens to their prayers, which encourages them to communicate with Him regularly through church services, or seek guidance during difficult times.

Another way a belief in God influences Christians is through moral decision-making. Believing in an all-knowing and just God can lead Christians to follow His teachings and commandments more closely because they believe God sees their actions and will judge them accordingly.

What went well	Even better if	Mark /4

Answer 2

One way a belief in God the creator influences Christians is that they may try to care for the environment.

Another way is that they might feel a sense of purpose because they believe God created them.

What went well	Even better if	Mark /4

Answer 3

One way a belief in God the creator influences Christians is that they try to care for the environment. They believe God gave them the role of stewards in Genesis, so they protect the planet through actions like recycling and reducing waste.

Another way is that they may feel a sense of purpose in life. Christians believe they are made in the image of God, so they may believe that all human life has value.

What went well	Even better if	Mark /4

As a class, we would do the following:

- remind ourselves of the success criteria for this question
- read each answer, identifying examples of excellence and areas to improve
- give the answer a mark.

Each model answer is designed to include specific features of excellence and misconceptions noticed from marking work.

Here is another example model answers activity, this one based on an A-level essay:

How convincing is the ontological argument for the existence of God? [40]

	Assessment Objectives	
AO1	Demonstrate knowledge and understanding of religion and belief, including: • Religious, philosophical and/or ethical thought and teaching • Approaches to the study of religion and belief	40%
AO2	Analyse and evaluate aspects of, and approaches to, religion and belief, including their significance, influence and study.	60%

The existence of God is a topic philosophers have grappled with for centuries. The ontological argument, originally formulated by Anselm, and later developed by Descartes, centres around the nature of God. The argument claims that existence is a predicate and a fundamental attribution of God, so he must therefore exist. The argument relies on a priori reasoning which means it draws conclusions based on reason. This essay will argue that the success of the ontological argument is restricted as it comprises numerous logical fallacies that have been highlighted by scholars such as Kant and Russell. Pure a priori logic carries little persuasion. Evidence from observation is required to convince us of the existence of God.

Read through the introduction and highlight the following:

☐ General statement – introduces the topic of the essay and gives context.

☐ Specific statement – addresses the question directly, uses key terms and scholars.

☐ Thesis statement – makes clear the line of argument.

The ontological argument is a fundamentally flawed argument because it is absurd to say that any object in its superlative form must exist. Anselm, writing in his book *Proslogion*, uses the ontological argument to try to prove God's existence. He states that we can all define God as 'that than which nothing greater can be conceived'. A real existent being would be greater than any imaginary, illusory being. Therefore, the concept of God is surpassed by an actual, existent God. It seems logical to say that yes, an existing God is greater than one who doesn't exist because we can accept that things in reality are better. For example, thinking about your favourite chocolate bar is far inferior to actually eating that chocolate bar and getting the taste of it. In turn, a priori arguments can be appealing and persuasive; if their premises are true and the reasoning is sound, then they lead to a certain truth.

Read though the opening sentence of each paragraph and highlight the following:

☐ Judgement – is it a convincing argument?

☐ Question – link to the question?

☐ Reason – reason for judgement?

What is good about this paragraph?

However, the ontological argument offers little to convince us that we can move from conception to reality. Although we can think of any object as 'the greatest' in our mind, it doesn't make it any more real. As much as we define something (including God) as the greatest, it can't possibly prove existence. Gaunilo (a contemporary monk of Anselm) successfully pointed out the logical problems with Anselm's argument. He imagined the 'most excellent island' and fully understood this definition. By using Anselm's logic then you would have to say that if the island imagined is truly the most excellent, it cannot have inferiority that comes from it being a concept only and thus, it must exist in reality. But of course, there is no such island in reality.

What counterarguments are offered in this paragraph?

Anselm offered a response of limited appeal by appealing to the unique essence of God's existence. Anselm's definition of God as 'the greatest being' entails that God has 'necessary existence' (not relying on anything else for existence) as a necessary being is superior to contingent beings (relying on other things for existence, such as humans relying on parents to be born). With God having necessary existence he can very easily exist but the island cannot. The island (or anything else in the world) is dependent on other factors to exist. The island depends on sand, water, vegetation etc. so it is possible for it not to exist, unlike God.

How does this paragraph present an opposing view?

Note down three excellent features of this paragraph:

Ultimately, Anselm's argument is still greatly unconvincing for proving the existence of God because the additional predicate of 'God has necessary existence' does little to further justify his conclusion. What if, similar to Gaunilo's island, I imagined one that was so great it relied on nothing but itself to come about. It would be absurd to say that that has made my island real. Moreover, for Anselm's argument to work, we have to accept that God is defined as the greatest possible being and possesses necessary existence. As Aquinas said 'perhaps not everyone who hears the name "God" understands it to signify something than which nothing greater can be thought'. This further highlights the failures of the ontological argument.

This model answer is a section of an essay. The aim of the model answer was to develop student understanding of how to explain ideas fully and to consistently use evaluative language in their writing.

CHAPTER 11
HOW CAN I USE TEXTS AND SCHOLARSHIP IN RE?

As the Ofsted *Research Review* (2021) states, academic scholarship is central to high quality RE. The RE curriculum should be firmly grounded in what is known about religion and non-religion from academic study, helping to guard against misconceptions and oversimplifications. RE must be academically rigorous. Therefore, curriculum design and teaching should rely on scholarship and academic texts to secure accurate, in-depth learning.

The use of text and scholarship allows us to reflect on the resources we provide students in our classroom. Mary Myatt (2023) argues that the resources we use in the classroom should look to stretch our students. We want to use resources that make pupils think deeply about their learning. Myatt recognises that high-quality texts and visuals spark intellectual curiosity. Our students deserve the very best and the resources we use should have value in the sense of making them think. This highlights the importance of beauty: a curriculum rich in complex, beautiful ideas should be mirrored in the resources we provide and the work students create.

What is scholarship?

Scholarship refers to the use of academic study, research and expert perspectives to explore religion and worldviews in a deep, rigorous and informed way. It goes beyond just learning facts about beliefs or practices – it involves engaging with the thinking, debates, methods and evidence used by scholars in disciplines like:

- theology – studying beliefs within a faith tradition
- philosophy – analysing the coherence and chains of reasoning
- social sciences – exploring religion as a social and cultural phenomenon.

In practical terms, this involves:

- using academic texts and extracts from scholars
- engaging with sacred texts, such as the Bible and the Qur'an, to explore how they inform belief and practice
- engaging with big questions relating to religion through a variety of academic lenses, e.g. theological, philosophical, sociological
- understanding methods scholars use to study religion, such as textual analysis, ethnography and philosophical reasoning
- avoiding simplifications or stereotypes by representing religion with depth, nuance and academic rigour.

When used effectively in the classroom, scholarship helps to:

- **Unpack concepts and ideas with further details:** Using extracts from scholars, such as Karen Armstrong, allows students to explore the theological and historical implications of the ideas being studied.
- **Develop literacy:** Academic texts encourage students to grapple with complex language, helping them to learn, decode and discuss challenging texts.
- **Provide diverse interpretations of concepts:** Looking at various interpretations of concepts, such as karma, shows students that religious concepts are understood differently across and within traditions
- **Allow for consideration of wider arguments:** By looking at contrasting arguments, students develop their understanding of competing perspectives and the reasoning behind them.
- **Raise the level of challenge, to encourage academic rigour:** Reading simplified texts from academics pushes students to engage with abstract and intellectually challenging material.
- **Lower the level of threat:** Providing guided reading questions, prompts and other scaffolds alongside the text allows students to explore the big questions that texts grapple with in a supportive way.

Below you will find some examples of how we can do this in the RE classroom.

Story, source, scholarship

This model was first used in history classrooms by history teacher Dan Warner Meanwell, and some RE teachers have adapted it to fit the demands of our subject. The model is framed around an enquiry question and enables students to engage with a clear overview of a concept or question, a relevant source and the views of scholars who have contributed to the question. It is a really powerful activity for showing students how the concepts studied sit as part of a wider academic conversation.

As illustrated by the example in Figure 11.1, the model is broken down into three sections:

1. **Story** – an overview of the key question you are studying. This is a narrative account that gives students a clear foundational reference point for engaging with the source and scholarship later. Students complete a guided reading of a text by creating a title and bullet-point summary for each paragraph. (We include only a sample of the narrative account here, to give you an idea of how the model works; in reality, the section would be around three times longer.)

2. **Source** – this provides contextual knowledge from the 'story'. There are a wide range of things you could draw upon to decide your source. For instance, it could be an extract from a source of authority, a piece of artwork or social science data. Students answer the set questions based on the source given.

3. **Scholarship** – students engage with arguments made by academics who have contributed to the big question, highlighting the most important phrase or sentence in each.

Can the need to create a 'vale of soul-making' justify the existence or the extent of evil?

Story

Create a title for each paragraph.	Read through each paragraph and highlight the key points.	Summarise each paragraph in one or two bullet points.
	One argument against an Irenaean view is that some people suffer a lot more than others; does this mean that God wants some people to grow to spiritual maturity, but does not care whether those who lead peaceful and contented lives learn very much? Some people are unable to benefit from suffering, but they still experience it. For example, someone with severe learning difficulties might be hurt in a fire, or a tiny premature baby might have a painful infection, and they may not be capable of gaining new insights from their experiences. ... John Hick's view of salvation for all has perhaps been the most controversial aspect of his theodicy. Although there are many who welcomed this inclusive approach and who see it as a way forward for religious acceptance and diversity, there are others who would argue that it undermines the whole value of Christianity. Why would Christ have died on the cross to save humanity from sin, if there were also lots of other ways to reach God, and if everyone gets to God in the end anyway? The same outcome of salvation for all would have happened without the sacrifice of Jesus, which makes the whole gospel story appear pointless. ... [The ellipses (...) used here indicate that a full text of several paragraphs would normally be included in the 'Story' section; the shorter sample included here is just for illustrative purposes.]	

Source

Why is Christ submerged in darkness?		How might the viewer feel when looking at this artwork?
Why are no people present in this artwork?		How might this artwork support Hick's soul-making theodicy?
Why has de Zurbarán focused on the image of Christ on the cross?	**Francisco de Zurbarán,** *Christ on the Cross,* **1627**	How might this artwork reject Hick's soul-making theodicy?

Scholarship

Richard Swinburne, *Is there a God?* (1996)
The central core of any theodicy must, I believe, be the 'free-will defence', which deals – to start with – with moral evil, but can be extended to deal with much natural evil as well. The free-will defence claims that it is a great good that humans have a certain sort of free will which I shall call free and responsible choice, but that, if they do, then necessarily there will be the natural possibility of moral evil. ... A God who gives humans such free will necessarily bring about the possibility, and puts outside his own control whether or not that evil occurs. It is not logically possible ... that God could give us such free will and yet ensure that we always use it in the right way.

Fyodor Dostoevsky, *The Brothers Karamazov* (1880)
In this famous scene from Chapter 35, Ivan Karamazov visits his younger brother and challenges his faith by giving him examples of innocent suffering:
Imagine that you are creating a fabric of human destiny with the object of making men happy in the end, giving them peace and rest at last, but that it was essential and inevitable to torture to death only one tiny creature – that baby beating its breast with its fist, for instance – and to found that edifice on its unavenged tears, would you consent to be the architect on those conditions? Tell me, and tell the truth.

D. Z. Phillips, *The Problem of Evil & the Problem of God* (2005)
What I am going to argue is that even if we grant that things are as theodicies and defences depict them, even if the ultimate good did necessitate all the evil in the world, and even if the ultimate good somehow redeems all evil, it would still be impossible to attribute perfect goodness to God.

Task 1	Task 2	Task 3
Read through the **Story** critiquing Hick's soul-making theodicy. For each paragraph, you need to create a 'title' on one side and a short summary (two bullet points maximum) on the other.	Look at the **Source**, Francisco de Zurbarán's *Christ on the Cross*. Answer the questions around the artwork.	Read through the **Scholarship** of Swinburne, Dostoevsky and Phillips. Highlight what you think are the three most important sentences. In your book, write a short paragraph justifying your choices of the most important sentences.

▲ Figure 11.1 Story, source, scholarship model, used at key stage 5

Tips to make the most of story, source, scholarship:

- Carefully consider the big question the model is looking to answer, as each part helps students to answer the question.
- Model each stage of the process clearly and discuss key ideas as you go.
- Use challenging material as part of the 'story' component.
- When choosing your source, consider what can provide students with new insights to the big question.
- When choosing your scholars, aim to include a wide range of interpretations to illustrate diversity of views.

Guided reading

First shared by history teacher Simon Beale, this is an approach to reading that scaffolds pupils' thinking in how they analyse a body of text. Research (Chang and Ku, 2015) shows that note-taking from reading improves student learning. Note-taking requires effort and encoding, which stores the information more firmly in long-term memory.

Prior to the lesson, select a body of text appropriate for students to read. In the lesson, students are to do the following for each paragraph:

- Highlight the key information, with a focus on being very selective.
- In the right margin, summarise the paragraph's contents in two to three bullet points.
- In the left margin, give the paragraph a title that best summarises its overall message.

This process is to be repeated for each paragraph in turn, as shown here:

What do Muslims believe about Jesus?

Read through this article exploring what Muslims believe about Jesus. After reading each paragraph, you are to do the following:

- Highlight the key information.
- Summarise the paragraph in 2–3 bullet points.
- Give the paragraph a title that best summarises it.

What title would you give this paragraph?	What is the key information in this paragraph? Be brief – do not highlight everything!	How would you summarise this paragraph in 2-3 bullet points?
	Muslims honour Jesus Christ as a great **prophet**. They believe that God has always sent prophets to humankind, from Adam onwards. Muslims believe in the same prophets as Jews and Christians, and the names of Noah, Abraham, Moses and others can be found in the **Qur'an**. **Muhammad** is seen as the Last Prophet, or 'the Seal of the Prophets', whose message has been faithfully preserved in the text of the Qur'an. He closes the line of profits, as a wax seal used to seal and close a letter.	
	In Arabic, in the Qur'an Jesus is called Isa ibn Mariam Al Masih – 'Jesus, son of Mary, the **Messiah**'. Jesus was the prophet before Muhammad, and a special reverence is given to him. Muslims believe that he was a perfect human being who was born from a virgin. Allah performed a miracle in Mary's womb as a sign that this boy was to be a special prophet. The Qur'an teaches that Jesus worked miracles, healing people. He is also called 'Messiah', 'God's special chosen and anointed'.	
	In the Qur'an, Jesus says, 'I am the servant of Allah. He has given me the gospel and ordained me as a prophet. His blessing is upon me wherever I go, and He has commanded me to be steadfast in prayer and to give almonds to the poor as long as I shall live.' (19:29)	
	Muslims do not believe that Jesus was **divine** – Christians say that he was God living in a man (this belief is known as the '**incarnation**'). Muhammad once said, 'Do not **extol** me as the Christians have extolled the son of Mary. I am only God's servant. Refer to me as the servant and messenger of God.'	
	Most Muslims believe that Jesus was too holy to die on the cross: they believe another died in his place, or a trick was played upon the crowd, and he was taken up to heaven to be with God. Muslims expect Jesus to return before the final judgement. Muhammad once said, 'I swear by Him who holds my life between His hands, the son of Mary will come back down among you very soon as a just judge.'	

What title would you give this paragraph?	What is the key information in this paragraph? Be brief – do not highlight everything!	How would you summarise this paragraph in 2-3 bullet points?
	Whatever exactly happened to Jesus, all Muslims believe that he was taken to be with God and will one day return. Christians called Jesus 'the Son of God'. Muslims disagree, for the Qur'an teaches that Allah has no son. The Qur'an does say that Jesus was specially blessed by Allah, born of a virgin, a worker of miracles, and he is even described as a 'word sent from Allah'.	
	The Christian term 'Son of God' is often misunderstood – it is not meant in a physical sense. It is more poetic, meaning that Jesus was the most holy person who ever lived, filled with God. There are still major disagreements between Muslims and Christians about Jesus, but many try to respect each other's beliefs as they share and talk together.	

In one paragraph, summarise what Muslims believe about Jesus:

_____

_____

Key vocabulary:

Prophet	A messenger of God
Qur'an	The holy book of Islam, which Muslims believe contains the word of God; it literally means recitation
Muhammad	The final prophet, who received God's full revelation; he lived from 570–632CE
Messiah	Anointed one
Divine	Relating to, coming from, or like gods
Incarnation	God coming to earth as a human
Extol	To praise enthusiastically

Tips to make the most of guided reading
Carefully model how you want the note-taking to be done, using the first paragraph as a whole-class model:

- Go through the activity a paragraph at a time.
- Provide further scaffolds where needed to support all learners, e.g. key word vocabulary box.

Using shorter extracts of scholarship
You can use prompt questions to draw students' attention to ideas contained within a shorter piece of scholarship. Instead of just giving them a section of scholarship and asking them to explain it with no guidance, provide the following scaffolds:

- Give context for the scholarship, e.g. when it was written, the author.
- Highlight sections of the text and ask questions based on what is highlighted.
- Provide a key vocabulary box.
- Use a follow-up writing task to check understanding.

The context for the example shown in Figure 11.2 is a unit on the philosophy of religion. Students had been exploring arguments for and against the existence of God. I wanted a piece of scholarship that would revisit knowledge from the previous lesson, give students the opportunity to think about how religious beliefs they have encountered in their KS3 curriculum would support Freud's hypothesis and provide a stimulus for evaluation of Freud's thought.

Why was Freud critical of religion?

Sigmund Freud was the founder of **psychoanalysis**. In his book, *Civilization and Its Discontents* (1930), Freud explores the clash between the desire for individuality and the expectations of society. Freud argues that the friction stems from the individual's quest for freedom and civilisation's contrary demand for conformity and repression of our instincts. In this extract, Freud outlines his critique of religion:

Why does Freud describe religious beliefs as infantile?

What examples could be given to support Freud's view that religious belief is 'foreign to reality'?

'The whole thing is so **patently infantile**, so foreign to reality, that to anyone with a friendly attitude to humanity, it is painful to think that the majority of mortals will never be able to rise above this view of life'

What aspects of religion might be appealing to the majority of people?

Why might it be impossible for people to escape religious belief?

For Freud, why is religion not good for humanity?

Freud was critical of religion because _____

Freud was critical of religion but _____

Freud was critical of religion so _____

Key words	
Psychoanalysis	The primary assumption of psychoanalysis is the belief that all people possess unconscious thoughts, feelings, desires and memories. The aim of psychoanalysis is to make the unconscious conscious.
Civilisation	Human civilisation, with its well-developed social organisations, or the culture and way of life of a society at a period in time.
Patently	Clearly, without doubt
Infantile	Childish

▲ Figure 11.2 Using prompt questions with shorter extracts of scholarship in key stage 3

With this quote from Freud, several phrases or ideas are pre-highlighted for focused thinking and questioning. With each phrase, we looked to establish two things:

1. What is Freud saying here?
2. What examples are there to support this?

The first question allows students to use knowledge from previous lessons. The second allows them to use knowledge from across their KS3 study – for example, from our RE lessons in key stage 3, what beliefs might Freud say are foreign to reality?

After completing work on the quote itself, students complete a 'because, but, so' writing activity. This sentence-level task allows me to check for student understanding of Freud's ideas, counterarguments and the implications of his ideas.

This works well across all key stages. The example in Figure 11.3 is taken from key stage 5, where students grapple with primary texts written by scholars such as Aquinas, Augustine and Kant.

SECONDARY RELIGIOUS EDUCATION IN ACTION

Is Aquinas right to argue that God caused the universe?

Way 1 – Motion
The existence of movement, growth and change

St Thomas Aquinas (1225–1274) was a major influence on religious philosophy and theology. He attempted to combine the ideas of Aristotle with the teachings of Christianity. In *Summa Theologica*, he wrote Five Ways of arguing for the existence of God.

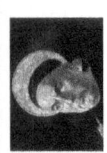

1. What does Aquinas observe about things in the world?

2. How must motion occur?

3. How does Aquinas define motion?

4. What is the difference between actuality and potentiality?

The first and more manifest way is the argument from motion. "It is certain, and evident to our senses, that in the world some things are in motion. "Now whatever is in motion is put in motion by another; for nothing can be in motion except it is in potentiality to that towards which it is in motion; whereas a thing moves inasmuch as it is in act. For "motion is nothing else than the reduction of something from potentiality to actuality. But "nothing can be reduced from potentiality to actuality, except by something in a state of actuality.

Thus "that which is actually hot, as fire, makes wood, which is potentially hot, to be actually hot, and thereby moves and changes it. Now it is not possible that the same thing should be at once in actuality and potentiality in the same respect, but only in different respects. For what is actually hot cannot simultaneously be potentially hot; but it is simultaneously potentially cold. "It is therefore impossible that in the same respect and in the same way a thing should be both mover and moved, i.e. that it should move itself. Therefore whatever is in motion must be put in motion by another. If that by which it is put in motion be itself put in motion, then this also must needs be put in motion by another, and that by another again. "But this cannot go on to infinity, because then there would be no first mover, and, consequently, no other mover; seeing that subsequent movers move only inasmuch as they are put in motion by the first mover; as the staff moves only because it is put in motion by the hand. "Therefore it is necessary to arrive at first mover, put in motion by no other; and this everyone understands to be God.

Thomas Aquinas, *Summa Theologica*

5. How does Aquinas use the example of wood and fire to illustrate his argument?

6. Why does Aquinas argue that something cannot change itself? Use the example of wood.

7. Why can they not be an infinite chain of movers?

8. What is Aquinas' conclusion?

▲ **Figure 11.3** Using prompt questions with primary texts in key stage 5

Here, I have taken Aquinas' 1st Way as written in his *Summa Theologica*. As students read the text, I have highlighted certain phrases to identify the premises in his argument. As a class, we read the extract and answer the questions as we go.

Using texts in the classroom

Hermeneutics is the study of interpretation; it is used across many fields, including religion. In RE, it involves interpreting sacred texts like the Bible by examining language, context, audience and meaning. This form of scholarship helps students understand how texts have been interpreted over time and how they can engage with them thoughtfully. The goal is to help students become responsible interpreters of religion by using careful, informed approaches to understanding religious texts and ideas.

In some cases, students' exposure to sacred texts can be limited to learning specific quotations to support moral or ethical issues. For example, the commandment 'Thou shalt not kill' is often used as scriptural reference for a Christian view against abortion, euthanasia or the death penalty. However, this is sometimes taught without any reference to the context in which it was written. Without this contextual knowledge, students can be prone to misuse a quote or to try to apply it without any understanding of its meaning. All RE teachers will have come across the student who uses 'Love thy neighbour' as a quote to try to justify anything and everything.

The use of hermeneutics allows students to unpick and analyse a text to explore its layers of meaning. This can be done with short quotes or longer pieces of text. Hermeneutics encourages students to ask questions of a text, to discuss its meanings, and to consider how meaning can change with time, place and the person engaging with the text.

Texts and Teachers: The Practice Guide (Bowie et al, 2020) offers an excellent insight into how to use hermeneutical tools to help students interpret sacred texts more deeply and contextually. You can download this via the searchable Research page of the Canterbury Christ Church University (CCCU) website: https://repository.canterbury.ac.uk/item/8vzy1.

There are a range of ways we can use hermeneutics in the classroom.

Example 1

In this example, we provide students with a longer piece of text. We read the text collectively and complete the tasks shown in Figure 11.4.

How can we link this text to wider knowledge?	How might this text influence the lives of Christians today?
How might some Christians interpret this text?	How might non-Christians interpret this text?
What is the context?	What are the key points being made?

Genesis 1:26

'And God said, let us make man in our image, after our likeness: and let them have dominion over the fish of the sea, and over the fowl of the air, and over the cattle, and over all the earth, and over every creeping thing that creepeth upon the earth.'

Who is the audience?	What key terms are used?
Is this teaching for everyone and for all the time?	Does it reflect the overall message of the Bible?
Do these ideas make sense?	What questions do you have about the text?

▲ **Figure 11.4** Analysing a text by exploring layers of meaning

With this activity, there are three layers of questions to explore. The inner layer focuses on key ideas within the text; the middle layer focuses on interpretations; and the outer layer focuses on the coherence and influence of the text.

The questions are all designed to get students to think about the text in a variety of ways. As students develop their skills in this area, they may come up with their own questions to ask about the text.

Example 2

In the style of activity shown in the Cain and Abel example in Figure 11.5, we start with a Biblical extract that we read collectively. Afterwards, students complete the comprehension questions to ensure they have an understanding of key events in the story.

Chapter 11 How can I use texts and scholarship in RE?

Cain and Abel

Understanding		Interpretation
		How might these people read the text differently?
Why did people in the Old Testament make offerings to God?	After some time, Cain brought some of his harvest and gave it as an offering to the Lord. Then Abel brought the first lamb born to one of his sheep, killed it, and gave the best part of it as an offering. The Lord was pleased with Abel and his offering, but he rejected Cain and his offering. Cain became furious, and he scowled in anger. Then the Lord said to Cain, 'Why are you angry? Why that scowl on your face? If you had done the right thing, you would be smiling; but because you have done evil, sin is crouching at your door. It wants to rule you, but you must overcome it.'	A literalist Christian
What did Abel sacrifice to God?		A non-literalist Christian
What happened after Cain's sacrifice was rejected?	Then Cain said to his brother, 'Let's go out in the fields.' When they were out in the fields, Cain turned on his brother and killed him. The Lord asked Cain, 'Where is your brother Abel?'	An agnostic
	He answered, 'I don't know. Am I supposed to take care of my brother?' Then the Lord said, 'Why have you done this terrible thing? Your brother's blood is crying out to me from the ground, like a voice calling for revenge. You are placed under a curse and can no longer farm the soil. It has soaked up your brother's blood as if it had opened its mouth to receive it when you killed him. If you try to grow crops, the soil will not produce anything; you will be a homeless wanderer on the earth.'	An atheist
Meaning		
What does this story teach us about human nature?	And Cain said to the Lord, 'This punishment is too hard for me to bear. You are driving me off the land and away from your presence. I will be a homeless wanderer on the earth, and anyone who finds me will kill me.'	An English literature teacher
What does this story teach us about the nature of God?	But the Lord answered, 'No. If anyone kills you, seven lives will be taken in revenge.' So the Lord put a mark on Cain to warn anyone who met him not to kill him. And Cain went away from the Lord's presence and lived in a land called 'Wandering', which is east of Eden.	A pastor/vicar
What are the similarities between this story and the story of the Fall?	**Genesis 4:3–16**	

▲ **Figure 11.5** Biblical extract interpretation task

The meaning questions in this example are designed to get students to think about the key philosophical and theological questions posed by the Cain and Abel story, to make them think deeply and make links with their study of the Fall in the previous lesson.

The interpretation task is prefaced with the teacher explanation that sacred texts can be read in many different ways, depending on the reader. We can challenge the assumption that only religious people would read sacred texts and that multiple meanings can be drawn from the same text.

Students are provided with different interpretive lenses and asked to think about how each lens may view the text differently. As a class, we discuss how each might respond to the text. As teachers, we can also emphasise that, even with one group, interpretations can vary and shift. This activity works well in helping students see that sacred texts are rich, complex sources that offer multiple layers of meaning.

Example 3

This playful approach works well for looking at different interpretations of parables.

In the example shown here, students will have spent some time looking at the Parable of the Prodigal Son. The task is designed to get them thinking about how the meaning of the parable may shift if we change its name.

Similarly, the meaning of the parable may change depending on who is reading the text. As a class, or in small groups, students discuss how the meaning shifts depending on the parable's name or audience. A blank space is left at the bottom of each column for students to choose an additional name and audience for the parable and then decide on what the potential meaning could be.

What's in a name?	Who's reading and why?
What would be the most important meaning if the parable were called:	*How might these people read the text differently?*
The Prodigal Son?	A Christian?
The Lost Son?	A 'sinner'?
The Forgiving Father?	An English teacher?

What's in a name?	Who's reading and why?
The Foolish Father?	An atheist?
The Loyal Son?	A pastor/vicar?

Example 4

This activity works well at GCSE as it encourages students to make links between pieces of scripture. Over the course of a unit, they will have encountered various pieces of scripture to support their understanding of different beliefs and practices. In this activity, they revisit these, explain them and identify what topics within the unit they link to.

We refer to these as 'Magic Teachings', to remind students that they do not need to know a different quote to support every single point on a GCSE specification (see Figure 11.6). The same quote can be used to illustrate different beliefs and practices, and this task gets them thinking about what connections can be made.

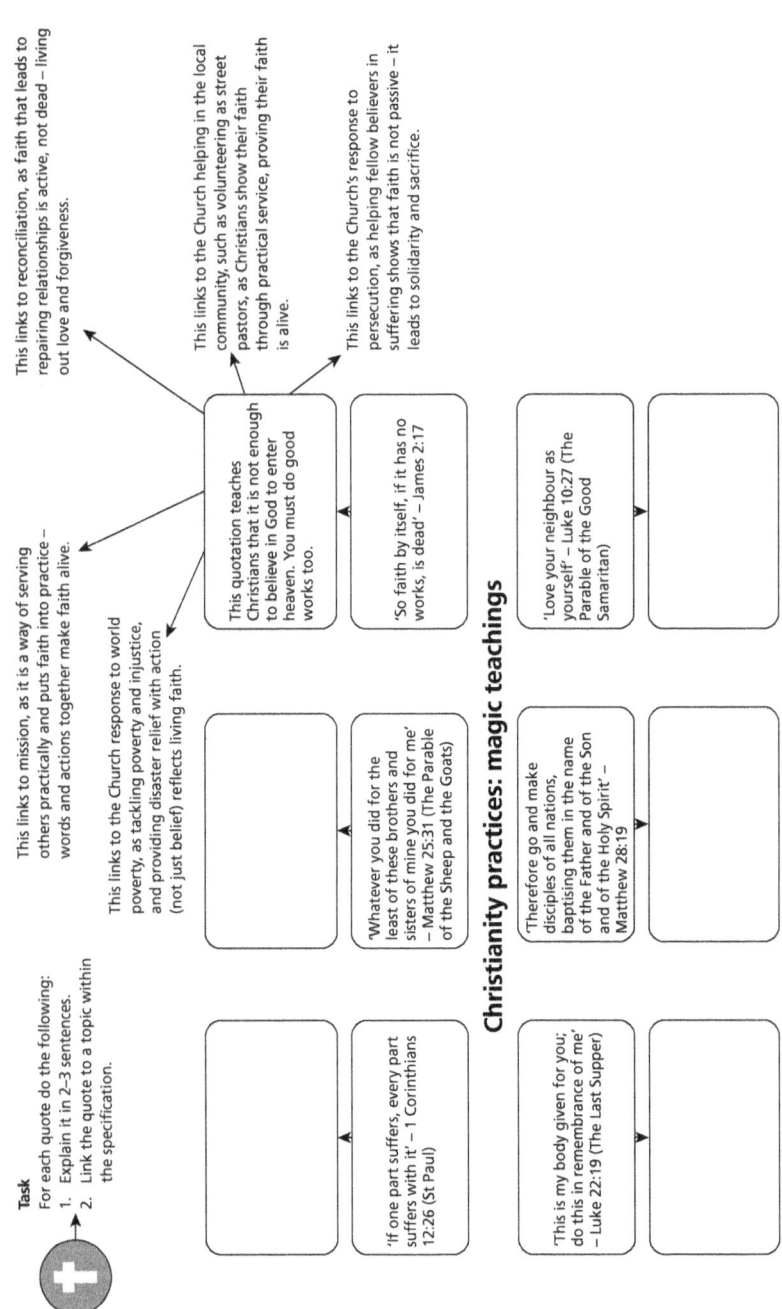

▲ Figure 11.6 'Magic teachings' encourage students to make links between pieces of scripture

Example 5

Similar to Example 4, this task gets students making connections between quotes. For instance, in the space shown in Figure 11.7, we explain each quote in two or three sentences. Afterwards, students look to draw lines of connection between the quotes. You can give students the following question prompts to help guide their thinking in finding connections:

- Are these quotes expressing similar beliefs?
- What actions do these quotes encourage?
- Do these quotes link to any pillars of faith?
- What actions or attitudes do these quotes encourage?
- How might these quotes influence how a Muslim lives their daily life?
- Are there similar meanings in these quotes?
- How do these quotes link to broader themes in the Qur'an or Hadith?
- Do these quotes raise similar questions about the nature of God?

SECONDARY RELIGIOUS EDUCATION IN ACTION

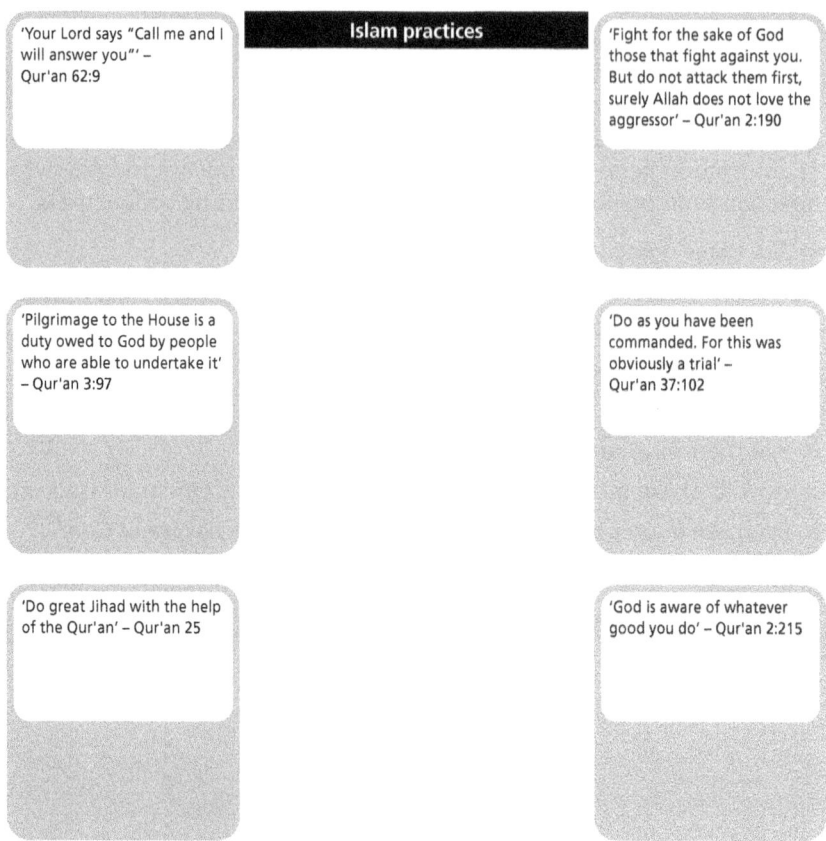

▲ Figure 11.7 Making connections between quotes

Other forms of scholarship

Outside of the traditional form of academic texts or scripture, we can also introduce students to scholarship through resources such as podcasts. Especially at key stage 5, podcasts such as *The Panpsycast Philosophy Podcast* and *In Our Time* provide students with the opportunity to hear theologians, philosophers and other experts engage in conversation about a range of big questions that we explore in the classroom.

The same principles of scaffolding need to apply when getting students to listen to podcasts. Many podcasts are lengthy, rich with detail and speakers can talk quite quickly. Therefore we need to provide students with a clear task or instruction for what to do when listening to a podcast.

The example in Figure 11.8 refers to the first part of an episode of *Panpsycast*. Although only part of the worksheet is shown here, referring to the first 20 minutes or so of the podcast, I provide students with questions about the whole episode and they need to listen carefully for the answers. As an additional scaffold, I provide a time stamp for when the answer is given. At the end, I give students the task of writing a summary paragraph of the key ideas from the episode.

Dualism and materialism

This episode explores Plato and Aristotle's beliefs about the soul, plus an overview of dualism and materialism.

- What did Plato believe about the soul? (1:56)
- Why does Plato believe the soul existed? (2:50)
- What does it mean to say the soul is intelligible? (3:30)
- For Plato, why is the soul immortal? (5:05)
- What is Plato's tripartite soul? (7:00)
- What is the appetite part of the soul? (7:15)
- What is the spirit part of the soul? (9:15)
- What is the reason part of the soul? (10:30)
- According to Aristotle, what are the different types of soul? (14:10)
- Who was Descartes? (18:40)
- What was Descartes' fascination with existence? (19:00)

…

Write a short paragraph summarising the key ideas from the podcast.

▲ Figure 11.8 Scaffolding can be used to support students as they listen to a podcast

Source: *The Panpsycast Philosophy Podcast*, www.thepanpsycast.com/panpsycast

CHAPTER 12
HOW CAN I TEACH CONTROVERSIAL TOPICS AND SENSITIVE TOPICS IN RE?

What do we mean by a 'controversial topic'?

There are many different topics within the RE classroom that generate controversy. Kerr and Huddleston (2015) and Claire and Holden (2007) define controversial topics as issues that provide strong, conflicting views, and that are often connected to moral, social, political or culturally sensitive subjects. These topics typically do not have straightforward or universally agreed upon answers, and may challenge students' values, beliefs or identities.

The latest research tells us that controversial issues are:

- **Open to dispute and debate:** They lack consensus in society.
- **Connected to values and beliefs:** Often involving a moral, ethical or ideological dimension.
- **Emotionally charged:** People care deeply about these issues, which can lead to intense discussions.
- **Real-world and relevant:** Tied to current events and societal debates.
- **Politically or socially divisive:** People take different sides based on political views, religious background or personal experience.

Examples of controversial topics might include abortion, euthanasia, human rights or religious expression.

Why teach controversial topics?

All RE teachers will encounter the aforementioned topics and many more which will evoke strong, definite and controversial opinions from our students. The RE classroom has a unique and important role in teaching controversial topics. It is important that RE teachers are prepared to take on these topics, presenting evidence and challenging stereotypes. The RE classroom connects students with real-world issues such as extremism, abortion and gender roles. By teaching controversial topics authentically, we empower our students to have a better understanding of themselves, the world around them and their relationship to it. We can help to challenge prejudice and encourage respectful intellectual discussion, even when opinions differ.

By tackling controversial issues, students learn how to participate in democratic debate and consider multiple viewpoints without hostility. Ultimately, we want our students to be informed, global citizens, and so helping them to understand multiple perspectives so that they can participate in a pluralistic society is essential.

What common approaches can teachers use in the RE classroom?

Controversial topics should never be taught for the purpose of engagement or relevance.

The fundamental principle underpinning the approach to teaching controversial topics should be one of learning. We want students to engage with controversial topics as theologians, philosophers or social scientists. They should be directed to think intellectually about these issues, and provided with the environment to maturely engage with complex subject matter. Wherever these debates go, it should remain firmly in the realm of learning.

Naturally, many RE teachers may feel uncomfortable teaching controversial topics. Here are some tips to support you:

Before the lesson

Plan in advance

Before the lesson, spend some time predicting what controversial opinions or questions students might come up with, and practise your responses. You might wish to make a few brief notes for specific explanations or plan your responses to questions that may arise. Being able to anticipate sensitive areas will allow you to maintain a calm, respectful learning environment.

Know your subject

Controversial issues are surrounded by misinformation, bias and emotion. By having a strong grasp of the topic, you can provide accurate information that distinguishes between fact and opinion. There are times when students may intentionally ask tough questions. If you understand the subject well, you can ensure that your responses are thoughtful and well informed. This helps to build your intellectual credibility and trust with students.

Ensure all voices are heard

As with teaching a lesson on any topic, certain voices can dominate class discussion. Plan to make space for all voices and opinions to be heard during the lesson. This could be done by using sticky notes, 'think pair share' or talking tokens, where a student receives a limited number of tokens they can 'spend' to speak.

Speak to the pastoral team

If teaching a topic such as life after death or euthanasia, it might be helpful to know in advance about any students who have suffered a bereavement. You can ask your pastoral team, such as head of year, for any information they may have. With this knowledge, you will be better placed to know the needs of your students. Prior to teaching the lesson on this emotive topic, you could speak to the student privately to inform them of the upcoming lesson and provide alternative arrangements if they do not feel comfortable sitting in the lesson.

Phone parents

Phoning parents in advance before teaching a controversial topic helps build trust and avoids potential misunderstandings. It shows professionalism, respects any sensitive personal or cultural contexts, and reassures parents that the lesson is being handled thoughtfully and appropriately. This communication can also encourage support and discussion at home.

Consider your own positionality/worldview

Just like the students, we may have strong opinions on certain topics that we teach. As teachers, we need to acknowledge this and be conscious of how we present these topics. Being aware of this helps you avoid unintentionally presenting a one-sided view or steering the conversation in a particular direction.

During the lesson

Promote open-mindedness

When introducing a lesson on a controversial topic, you might wish to make some initial comments about the importance of being open-minded.

Some opening remarks like this might be helpful:

> 'Today, we're going to explore a topic that people often feel very strongly about. In RE, we don't avoid difficult questions – we explore them so we can understand different beliefs, values and perspectives. My goal isn't to tell you what to think, but to help you think more deeply, respectfully and with greater understanding. Being open-minded doesn't mean you have to change your views – it means being willing to listen, reflect and consider other perspectives fairly.'

Find out what they already think

At the start of the lesson, you might want to get some initial insights into what students already think about aspects of a controversial topic.

Activities such as the one shown here allow students to offer their initial responses to a range of statements pertaining to an issue.

Animals: What do you think?

Read the following statements and circle the number that most closely represents your viewpoint.

1 = Strongly disagree; 2 = Disagree; 3 = No opinion either way; 4 = Agree; 5 = Strongly agree

1. Animals should have equal rights to humans.	1	2	3	4	5
2. Horseracing is a morally acceptable form of entertainment.	1	2	3	4	5
3. Religious people are more likely to protect animal rights than non-religious people.	1	2	3	4	5
4. Animals can make moral decisions.	1	2	3	4	5

5. It is hypocritical to be angry at someone for eating dog if you eat beef burgers, pork chops, chicken, etc.	1	2	3	4	5
6. Animals have purely instrumental value.	1	2	3	4	5
7. Zoos should be abolished.	1	2	3	4	5
8. Everyone should strive to be vegan.	1	2	3	4	5
9. It is unacceptable in today's society to make, sell and buy leather.	1	2	3	4	5
10. It is okay to use animals for testing medicine.	1	2	3	4	5
11. To be a good person is to look after all animals.	1	2	3	4	5
12. Animals and humans have more similarities than differences.	1	2	3	4	5
13. Humans are more important than animals.	1	2	3	4	5
14. Society would change for the better if nobody ate animals.	1	2	3	4	5

After the lesson, they could revisit their initial responses and reflect upon how their view may have become more informed or changed as a result of the learning in the lesson.

Provide time out

There might be times when a student feel overly emotive or uncomfortable during a lesson on a controversial topic. If you notice this, give the student a brief time out to allow them to regulate their emotions before returning to the classroom.

Challenge vague views

While everyone is entitled to an opinion, students must have informed opinions. If a student offers a vague view with little reasoning, challenge it and ask them to substantiate it. Based on the response you get from the student, you can use further questioning to probe the view further.

Frame the lesson

For some controversial topics, getting students to think about how the topic should be interpreted can be really helpful.

For instance, if teaching about the relationship between science and religion, you could start by giving them various words synonymous with a debate, asking them to define each and then discussing the similarities between them:

- dialogue
- conversation
- argument
- debate.

Following this task, you could ask the students to discuss how the relationship between science and religion should be understood.

This task can work well with a range of controversial topics, such as life after death, personhood or religious freedom.

Explicitly teach discussion skills

Class discussion will occur naturally with many topics we teach, and we want to manage this as best as possible. A good discussion is one that adds to, builds on or challenges (ABC) previously heard ideas. Look to teach this to your students by modelling discussion skills. One way in which this can be done is with 'sentence starters', which pupils use before providing their contribution.

ABC can be a useful discussion tool for this because it promotes active listening, encourages respectful dialogue and helps students think more deeply. It supports balanced participation, making it easier for all students, including quieter ones, to join in. It also models how to disagree thoughtfully, which is especially important in RE when exploring diverse and sometimes sensitive worldviews.

Discussion skill	Purpose	Sentence starters
Add	Suggest further examples or reasons	• I agree with … because … • The point by … reminds me of … • Another example of that is …
Build	Provide explanatory reasons or points of view	• Building on what … said … • The point by … can be further supported by … • This links to the concept of …

Discussion skill	Purpose	Sentence starters
Challenge	Offer contrasting or directly opposing points of view	• I see it differently to … because … • I want to question the idea by … because … • A different interpretation could be …

Provide counterpoints

As a teacher, providing counterpoints to controversial student opinions is important to encourage critical thinking while maintaining respect. You can do this in various ways:

Provide a counterpoint by …	You can say …
Staying neutral and respectful: Acknowledge the student's opinion without judgement, then gently introduce alternative viewpoints.	That's an interesting perspective. Another way to look at it is …
Asking open-ended questions: Encourage students to think more deeply about the view they have given.	What might someone who disagrees say?
Showing benefits: Make it clear that different opinions help us understand the topic more fully, rather than trying to prove someone wrong.	Let's explore another perspective to broaden our understanding.

Provide information they wouldn't know

As the subject expert, we should feel empowered to give students information that they wouldn't know, and taking a multidisciplinary approach can be particularly helpful for this.

For instance, when teaching abortion, you may wish to look at the data on the number of abortions per year in the UK and UK abortion law, to introduce the topic. This will provide students with some of the realities and statistics regarding abortion.

Dawn Cox has compiled an extensive list of social science data sources. You can access these via her 'Social science data sources 2025' Google Docs page: https://docs.google.com/document/d/1CUmVPbWMgVdyN08-bxeif6PmfrN-q1tMfVEojrgTRdQ/edit?tab=t.0.

Following this, you could look at the religious arguments surrounding abortion, through application of passages from sources of authority.

Videos

Videos can be really helpful for bringing a controversial issue to life and showing different perspectives. The videos you use in a lesson must be tied to the lesson specifically, supplement explanations you have provided and be pitched at an appropriate level for your students.

Websites such as TrueTube have excellent resources to use when teaching controversial topics: www.truetube.co.uk.

The BBC video series for GCSE religious studies, *Matters of Life and Death*, provides excellent overviews for teaching controversial topics such as the death penalty, war and animal experimentation. Each film provides social science data, testimonies from different perspectives and the responses of individuals from various religious backgrounds. Access the series on the 'Teachers' page of the BBC Bitesize website: www.bbc.co.uk/teach/class-clips-video/articles/zy24bqt.

Maps and timelines

Maps and timeliness can also be useful to provide historical and geographical context. When using maps, controversies become more understandable, as they provide the geographical context for an issue, demonstrating that controversial issues are not just grounded in personal opinion. Moreover, they provide students with a greater understanding of diversity within or across religion, which can influence views on controversial issues.

The use of timelines helps to show that many controversies didn't suddenly appear but developed through centuries of social, cultural and political change. They help students see that these issues are rarely static – they change as societies, beliefs and laws evolve.

Maps or timelines may be useful for topics such as debates about gender roles, interfaith conflicts or diversity of attitudes to ethical issues such as euthanasia.

Guest speakers

Guest speakers are useful when teaching controversial topics because they bring real-life experience, diverse perspectives and authenticity to the lesson. Hearing directly from someone who has personal knowledge or expertise can make complex or sensitive issues more relatable and credible for students. They can challenge stereotypes by sharing viewpoints that students might not encounter otherwise.

Chapter 13 has more information on the use of guest speakers.

Reinforce good practice

Throughout the lesson, look to praise those students who are engaging with the material in the way you want them to. Consider:

- Where has a student acknowledged a different point of view?
- Have students actively listened to the responses of others?
- Have they articulated their view with clarity and a clear chain of reasoning?
- Have they recognised their own positionality?

When they ask you a question but you don't know the answer

This is completely fine – we are not expected to know everything! When this does occur, my advice would be to simply admit you don't know the answer but you will find out for the next lesson. This intellectual honesty does far more to build a relationship with a class than attempting to bluff an answer that you are not confident in.

Share what you believe

When teaching controversial topics, I have often been posed the question, 'Sir, what do you think?' On a fundamental level, we have to remind ourselves that expressing religious and political views inappropriately can breach the Teachers' Standards. Our role is to educate about beliefs, not promote our own.

The Department for Education's guidance on political impartiality in schools (2025b) states that teachers must act carefully when expressing political views. They are not banned from sharing personal opinions, but doing so risks promoting partisan views due to their position of authority. As a rule, they should avoid expressing personal politics or views unless confident this won't be seen as promotion. If they do share their views, they must present them as opinions, not facts, and acknowledge that other perspectives exist.

You can read more about the Department for Education's guidance on political impartiality by searching 'Political impartiality in schools' on the gov.uk homepage: www.gov.uk/government/publications/political-impartiality-in-schools/political-impartiality-in-schools#teaching-about-political-issues.

When a student asks what we believe about a particular topic, we need to answer very carefully. Here are some points to consider when it comes to sharing your own views:

In favour of sharing personal views	Against sharing your personal views
Promotes intellectual honesty: Admitting uncertainty on a topic, e.g. life after death, shows your thinking is ongoing. **Can humanise the learning process:** Thoughtful honesty can build trust and openness in the safe space of the classroom. **May enrich discussion when used selectively:** Helps clarify ideas in complex debates. **Shows emotional complexity:** Sharing struggles, e.g. how you would struggle deciding what to do in a particular moral dilemma, can deepen discussion.	**Not the focus of RE:** Students should learn about religious and non-religious traditions, not teacher beliefs. **Could influence students unfairly:** Teacher authority may shape student views on a range of topics. **Could be used as a distraction:** Students may use the question to avoid engaging with content. **Lacks a consistent rule:** Opens up risk of inconsistency or misunderstanding, e.g. if teacher believes X, do they also believe in Y?

Encourage religious literacy

In case discussion is diverting too far from the planned topic, or students are merely offering opinions, use questioning to tie student thinking back to relevant sacred texts, key terms or beliefs. For example:

- Can you link that to a specific text in the Qur'an?
- How might some Hindus support this position?
- Which teaching from Jesus would challenge this view?

Summarise and reflect on class discussion

A rich classroom discussion will generate a wide range of ideas and perspectives. To help pupils assimilate these ideas into their existing schema, creating a summary of the discussion may be helpful. Here is an example:

> 'Today we explored the question, "Should assisted dying be legalised?" Some of you argued it should be allowed because of quality of life – people in severe pain should have a choice to

end their suffering. Others said life is sacred (sanctity of life) and should be protected, raising concerns about abuse or pressure on vulnerable people. Some focused on the role of doctors, questioning whether they should ever help end a life.'

Case study on the role of intellectual humility in the RE classroom

Karen Steele, senior lecturer for Secondary RE PGCE, University of Worcester

Argument, defeat, opposition. How many of these do you hear on social media? In our political discourse? In your classroom?

As a young RE teacher at the start of the century, I encouraged this kind of language, convinced that in order to make RE engaging, challenging and relevant, I needed to make it hard-edged, critical and edgy; what the wonderful, late Dawn Cox called 'shock-jock RE'. Shock jocks are radio personalities who use controversy to attract, entertain and provoke listeners. I would encourage debate, present dichotomous positions and give airtime to loud voices. In my defence, I was struggling against negative attitudes to RE, the rise of new atheism, and specifications that required this sort of thinking. Many pupils liked it; more of them opted for RE and I was able to say it equipped them for the world they would be living in. On reflection, I'm not sure everyone liked it, or that it was what the world needed.

Of all the topics a secondary teacher has to teach, abortion is the one that has been the most challenging for me. At first, I relished the opportunity for debate and knew my teenage audience would find it 'relatable'. However, over the last 20-ish years, I have found it increasingly difficult; my pupils' starting positions were becoming more entrenched. Girls sometimes refused to engage with dissenting voices, claiming that any opposition to abortion was anti-women and should not be voiced. I knew pupils in the same classroom came from backgrounds that took a different position, but that they would never express it in such a climate. This is just one example.

It's hard to know exactly why, but I suspect the nature of social media and public discourse has encouraged us to listen to fewer voices and to develop an appetite for sound bites. Cognitive science offers some insight into how the mind works and how we learn. We have biases, often hold contradictory beliefs and we have blind spots. Take the Dunning–Kruger effect, a claimed cognitive bias where the least knowledgeable are more likely to overestimate their knowledge and ability. Sound familiar? We are prone to getting things wrong and we have inbuilt biases in our thinking. All of this means we must be vigilant about our beliefs and be more open to questioning them.

My classroom experiences meant I had to think more carefully about how to approach contentious issues and create a climate where students would listen to other views and be willing to shift their thinking as and when necessary. Then I discovered 'intellectual humility'. The term encapsulated exactly what I wanted my classroom to be like and what, in my opinion, we need more of in the world today. I was fortunate to be able to pursue this further as part of my project for the Edge Hill University RE Summer School in 2023.

There are many interpretations of intellectual humility. A simple definition might be 'the willingness to recognise the limits of your knowledge, stay open to new ideas and evidence, and accept that you could be wrong'. The John Templeton Foundation produced a short film, *The Joy of Being Wrong*, which explains it well.

There are many possible characteristics of the intellectually humble person. They tend to display a willingness to reconsider, are not defensive when challenged, strive for accuracy and correct a natural tendency to prioritise their own needs. I really like the 'bend-but-not-break' analogy provided by Hook and Davis (2018): the palm tree might bend almost horizontal in a hurricane and never stand quite the same again, but it rarely breaks.

We have a lot of freedom in who we bring to our classrooms. Often, we do this without much thought. I took pupils to see Richard Dawkins and Richard Swinburne in discussion. We were excited to witness these giants of RE in action, only to be disappointed by their performances. Both men trotted out their well-rehearsed arguments, talking over one another and each failing to listen to the other at all. In contrast, the younger female philosophers on the panel stood out. They tried (in vain) to point out where Swinburne and Dawkins actually had some agreement, and suggested alternative directions for the discussion. This made me question the role models I was presenting in RE, so I asked around: who in the public eye could be described as intellectuality humble? Responses included Brian Cox, Mary Beard, Jon Ronson, Louis Theroux, Robert Beckford, Natalie Haynes, David Olusoga, David Attenborough, Brian May, Rory Stewart, Al Murray and Dan Snow. Many come from scientific or journalistic backgrounds. Indeed, some of what I read made links between the scientific method and intellectual humility. This is interesting for us to consider in RE, given that religion and science are often seen as being in opposition.

Research into the benefits of intellectual humility is tentative, but there are claims that it may help wellbeing as it cultivates a reality-grounded view of oneself within one's culture or tradition that balances the good and bad. It allows us to acknowledge that we cannot have a complete understanding and to be mindful of our blind spots, encouraging us to address them. It seems likely that being intellectually humble encourages dialogue, collaboration and reflection, all of which could have significant personal and societal benefits. From an RE teacher's perspective, it could be a powerful tool to improve learning about and dealing with the controversy and disagreement inherent in our subject.

However, intellectual humility is not without problems. Concerns have been expressed about the extreme anxiety that might result from realising that we know so little. From a philosophical viewpoint, it leads us to questions about relativism and truth claims. Does intellectual humility mean we must all accept other perspectives, even when they appear to be wrong? How does intellectual humility relate to any ultimate reality? Does it require us to give up on ever knowing? What does it mean for those of us who come from communities where there are very strong claims to truth that an intellectually humble disposition would require us to question? Hook and Davis (2018, p. 220) use a Jenga analogy, where belief for many is 'like a load-bearing block' which, if moved, may cause a complete collapse. This is a challenge for RE teachers and does require careful thought when dealing with individual students. But it is not sufficient reason to abandon striving for intellectual humility.

By the time I left the (school) classroom, I'm proud to say intellectual humility was very much in evidence. By thinking carefully about the language, role models and tasks I set, I created an environment in which listening to understand and valuing our ability to change our minds was important. I explicitly discussed intellectual humility with my pupils. I found that giving them the words helped them to operationalise it, to strive for it themselves and to encourage others to develop it (while being mindful that it can be difficult).

I would encourage you to do an intellectual humility audit of your classroom and curriculum. Here are a few questions to consider:

- How do you model intellectual humility?

- What examples and role models do you present in the classroom, and how do they encourage/discourage intellectual humility?

- What dispositions does your use of language and choice of activity in the classroom foster?

- How do your assessments foster/inhibit intellectual humility?
- What can you do to minimise potential barriers to intellectual humility, e.g. creating a safe and secure environment where status is not challenged?
- Can cognitive science help us?
- What is the relationship between intellectual humility and religious belief?
- What is the connection between intellectual humility, science and religion?
- Should you teach intellectual humility explicitly? Can it be learned?
- Can you measure intellectual humility? If so, should you?

Resources to support teaching controversial issues

Here is a list of resources that can support with the teaching of controversial issues:

- NATRE provides resources for 'Together for Humanity', a campaign working to address rising anti-Semitism and anti-Muslim hate. These resources aim to support schools, universities and councils in building bridges within communities.
- RE Hubs provides links to a number of resources and websites that seek to help teachers navigate sensitive issues in the classroom: www.re-hubs.uk/upskill/controversial-issues-in-re.
- In light of political polarisation in recent years, and particularly the UK riots over summer 2024, the Faith & Belief Forum has produced resources and guidelines to help teachers embark on what might be difficult discussions in the classroom: https://faithbeliefforum.org/wp-content/uploads/2024/09/FBF-School-Resources-%E2%80%93-Skills-for-Dialogue-Sensitive-issues-Autumn-2024-1.pdf.
- The RE Matters' 'Challenging religious and worldview stereotypes' toolkit is a resource designed to help schools with practical strategies and approaches for addressing stereotyping. It also offers reflections and suggestions on ways to challenge and overcome such stereotypes: www.rematters.co.uk/challenging-stereotypes.
- REsilience is a project by the REC, focused on helping RE teachers address contentious issues, particularly those linked to extremism, by enhancing their confidence and developing effective teaching strategies: https://religiouseducationcouncil.org.uk/our-work/other-projects/resilience-teaching-controversial-topics.

CHAPTER 13
HOW CAN I PROMOTE RE BEYOND THE CLASSROOM?

RE holds its greatest impact when it is experienced as a living, breathing subject that reaches beyond the classroom. Addressing RE across the wider school community allows students to encounter diverse worldviews, develop deeper cultural and religious literacy, and reflect on their own values and identities. It enriches their understanding through lived experiences, supports spiritual and moral development, and enhances critical thinking by connecting classroom learning to real-world contexts. This broader approach allows students to see the relevance and importance of the subject as part of the fabric of human experience. Moreover, embedding RE into wider school life supports personal growth, contributes to social and emotional learning, and builds the cultural capital necessary for students to thrive as informed, empathetic citizens.

This chapter looks at some of the ways in which you can promote RE outside of the classroom.

Guest speakers and visitors

Inviting guest speakers and visitors to your school is an excellent way of further bringing the subject to life and illustrating the importance of lived experience, as RE is about people. The benefits of inviting a guest speaker are:

- **Brings lived experiences:** Speakers provide first-hand experiences of beliefs, practices and values. They allow students to move beyond textbooks to understand religion as something real, personal and dynamic.

- **Challenges stereotypes and misconceptions:** Seeing people from different faiths and worldviews helps students see diversity within beliefs, not just between them. This can encourage open-mindedness and help reduce prejudice.

- **Promotes dialogue:** Speakers can provide opportunities for students to ask questions and engage in thoughtful discussion. They can

model how to have intellectual and respectful conversations about challenging topics.
- **Supports cultural capital:** Hearing from a guest speaker allows students to understand the real-world impacts of beliefs on careers, communities, culture and daily life.
- **Allows for deeper engagement:** Personal stories and testimonies of guest speakers can spark intellectual curiosity in students and engage them even further with the subject.

A range of resources can help you arrange for this. For example:
- RE Hubs provides a database of available speakers from different religions and non-religious worldviews, as well as experts in social science, philosophy and theology. It also offers free CPD on how to make the most of a guest speaker visit: www.re-hubs.uk/get-involved/school-speakers.
- The Holocaust Educational Trust's Outreach Programme allows schools to arrange an in-person or online survivor testimony event. Hearing from a survivor allows students to personally connect with one of the darkest periods of history: www.het.org.uk/education/outreach-programme.

Trips

Organising a trip – local, abroad or virtual – can be an excellent way of bringing the subject to life outside of the classroom because:
- it allows students to see, hear and experience what they've studied in class
- visiting places of worship, museums or sacred sites helps students to see what abstract ideas look like in reality
- it develops empathy, as students are exposed to different communities and ways of life
- diversity can be experienced at first hand, which allows students to become more open-minded and globally aware
- it encourages intellectual curiosity, as students begin to see how belief shapes identity and culture
- it promotes interdisciplinary learning, as trips combine elements of other subjects such as history, geography and art, which allows students to make cross-curricular links.

If planning a trip, here are some questions you might wish to consider:

- How does the trip link to your curriculum?
- How does the trip build on prior learning and support future learning?
- What should students learn, experience and reflect on during the visit?
- Does the place of visit allow for an authentic insight into the religious tradition?
- Will the place of visit provide a tour guide, speaker or Q&A for the visit?
- Are students clear on the context, beliefs and people they will encounter?
- In what ways will the experiences, insights and knowledge encountered on the trip be revisited in the classroom?

Cumbria Development Education Centre (CDEC) and Cumbria SACRE have worked together to provide a collection of virtual tours of religious sites. They also provide some ways in which you can find places of worship in your local area. Access these via the 'Use our resources' page of the CDEC website: www.cdec.org.uk/use-our-resources/films-and-virtual-tours/virtual-tours.

In addition, you can find live streams of many holy sites, such as the Kab'ah, on YouTube. These can be found by simply searching for the name of the holy site and adding 'live stream' to the end of your search term. When teaching topics such as Hajj, the live stream can be a really powerful way of bringing the topic to life.

Case study on extracurricular opportunities in RE
Rachael Jackson-Royal, King Edward VI High School for Girls

For many years I have tried to extend the learning pupils engage with in the classroom through providing extracurricular opportunities. One of the ways in which I have done this is through looking for trip opportunities that link to the curriculum for each year group. This has included undertaking the truth and reconciliation tour at Coventry Cathedral, and exploring how this links to the unit of work on Religion, Peace and Conflict in Year 9; learning about some aspects and groups within the Sikh and Jewish faiths in Year 7 by visiting various places of worship associated with these religions; then in Year 11 undertaking a tour of Shrewsbury Prison in order to enrich the students' study of Religion, Crime and Punishment for GCSE. These trips are not just for those who are lower down in the school but also continue into A-level. For example, we spend time visiting Cadbury World in order to enrich the unit of work on Business Ethics, and we plan to visit the psychology department at the local university in order to enhance student understanding on materialist views of the mind.

In addition to trips, I also organise a series of talks from a host of guest speakers. For example, I have routinely invited a variety of people who specialise in different areas within philosophy, theology and ethics to speak to students about a particular topic connected to A-level. These tend to be academics from local universities, and the areas they have focused on include Kantian ethics, Wittgenstein and religious language, the Natural Moral Law Theory of Aquinas and the Ontological Argument of Anselm.

We have also had visitors from various faith communities come to speak to the pupils on topics such as women in Islam, the fundamentals of the Sikh faith and how the local church in Christianity plays a role in society. This has been enriched by students and staff from within the school who have also discussed their own faith. In addition, each year previous pupils return to the school to discuss how the study of the subject has been useful and relevant in their further studies and jobs.

In order to enable pupils to become more confident in discussing and engaging with philosophical, ethical and theological ideas, we also run and host our annual Philosothon event. This entails students working together in a community of inquiry to consider issues that arise after considering a piece of stimulus material. Both this and the various talks we have organised have been completely free, making them incredibly accessible for departments on stretched budgets. Finally, we have tried to enrich the curriculum further through providing a departmental library of books, sourced from second-hand book shops, that students can borrow, which encourages them to look at relevant competitions (such as essay and film competitions, as well as spirited arts).

RE in the news

Finding examples of RE in the news is important because it helps students see that religion and belief are not just historical or theoretical – they are active, relevant and influential in today's world. Students will appreciate the relevance of RE if they see how religion and belief are always integral to political, cultural and current affairs.

You can recognise this in various ways:

- Have an 'RE in the News' display board that is regularly updated with articles, big questions relating to current events and student responses.

- Set homework tasks where students read news articles or opinion pieces that are linked to a topic they are currently studying.
- Use news stories that are relevant to topics currently being taught, e.g. media discussion of the Terminally Ill Adults (End of Life) Bill currently being debated in parliament.
- Use online platforms such as Padlet or Google Classroom for students to post and comment on articles.
- Look to integrate news stories into curriculum planning.

Many news websites will have sections dedicated to religion. In addition, the Religion Media Centre website is a great source of religion in the news for teachers: https://religionmediacentre.org.uk/.

Philosophy film and book clubs

These are excellent ways to showcase how religious, philosophical and ethical themes are discussed in the arts. Films and books explore themes like morality, meaning and belief, which are all integral to RE. They can help students connect abstract concepts to real-life situations, characters and dilemmas. A philosophy film or book club allows students to explore big questions at their own pace, outside of the traditional classroom set-up. In addition, they help to grow their cultural capital by discussing classic or contemporary texts or films, as they allow them to access intellectual and cultural experiences they might not otherwise encounter.

Here are some examples of films and books with thematic connections to RE:

Films	Books
• *Life of Pi* (2012) – the nature of faith, understandings of truth, interfaith dialogue	• *Sophie's World* (Jostein Gaarder) – history of philosophy, personal identity, nature of reality
• *The Truman Show* (1998) – free will vs determinism, ethics, personal identity	• *The Sage Train* (Nicky Hansell) – morality, existence of God, justice
• *The Matrix* (1999) – enlightenment, epistemology	• *Animal Farm* (George Orwell) – political philosophy, human nature, free will
• *Inside Out* (2015) – soul, suffering, human nature	• *The Alchemist* (Paulo Coelho) – meaning, the nature of faith, ethics

If you are looking to use non-fiction texts as part of a book club, the following may be helpful:

- A *Little History of Religion* by Richard Holloway (2016) provides a concise overview of the world's major religions, from ancient beliefs to contemporary spiritual movements. Holloway examines how religions have shaped human history and thought.
- A *Little History of Philosophy* by Nigel Warburton (2011) gives an accessible introduction to the major ideas and thinkers in Western philosophy. The book provides an overview of the lives and key concepts of famous thinkers in a clear, straightforward style.

Here are some tips to get the most from running a philosophy film or book club:

- Pick material that is age appropriate and raises big questions that are understandable for your group's age.
- Organise each session around a theme and material that relates to it, e.g. freedom, identity, justice.
- Prepare questions that encourage personal reflection and discussion related to the material, e.g. 'What does this film/book say about human nature?' or 'How would you act in this ethical dilemma?'
- As clubs take place at lunchtime or after school, use extracts from films or short chapters from books to make the most of time together.
- At the end of the session, share the key takeaways and suggest related readings, articles or films for deeper exploration.

If you would like to learn more about running an RE book club, read this blog by Nikki McGee on her 'RE with Mrs McGee' page: https://rewithmrsmcgee.wordpress.com/2023/11/05/running-an-re-book-club/.

Interfaith forum

An interfaith forum is an excellent way of promoting interfaith dialogue, showcasing the lived experience of religion and promoting diversity. An interfaith forum could run in many ways. The text below describes how we used to run it at my schools.

Once a month, we would host an evening interfaith forum that was framed around a big question, such as 'Why do we suffer?' We established links with guest speakers in the local area and invited them to be on the panel. Our keen RE students would attend and we advertised the event locally so that people in the community could attend. We aimed to have representatives from three or four different religious traditions. Each would give an introductory answer to the question before a discussion between the panel and the audience took place. The forum would be chaired by me or one of our confident A-level students, who would pose follow-up questions based on responses from the panel and audience.

While events such as these take a lot of organisation, they provide a safe space for open dialogue where misconceptions can be addressed and empathy built. They allow students to meet and interact with people from different backgrounds, moving beyond abstract ideas or practices they have encountered in the classroom.

There are other ways you could look to run this kind of activity to make it more accessible and practical:

- Run the interfaith forum at a lunchtime or after school.
- Ask members of your school community (staff or students) to serve as members of the panel.
- Link the question for discussion to a topic currently being taught in your curriculum.

Careers in RE

Talking to students about careers related to RE is important because it helps them to see the subject's relevance, broadens their horizons and challenges narrow assumptions about where RE can lead. It is important to show students how RE provides powerful knowledge and transferable skills that apply to many professions. Many students (and adults) assume RE only leads to religious roles, but it connects to a wide range of careers in law, medicine, journalism, politics, education and more.

Here are some of the ways in which you can talk about careers relating to RE:

- Invite guest speakers who use RE-related skills or knowledge in their job and ask them to explain how RE shaped their thinking or career path.
- Explicitly highlight how skills developed in RE lessons, such as empathy and using logical chains of reasoning, are used in the workplace.

- Use case studies of real jobs when discussing philosophical or ethical issues, e.g. the implications of the Hippocratic Oath for a doctor when exploring the rights and wrongs of euthanasia.
- Create a display that features RE-related jobs and quotes from people in those jobs.
- Use a search engine to find free online educational resources, such as My Future. My Career. My RE. (https://www.truetube.co.uk/resource/my-future-my-career-my-re/), which promote the study of the subject and how it links to a variety of different career paths.

Case study on raising the profile of RE in your school
Zainab Ali, Trinity Academy Leeds

Why should we raise the profile of RE?

As a reader of this book, you already have a vested interest in the leadership, quality and outcomes of religious education. Of all subjects that our most inclusive curriculums have to offer, RE is best placed to prepare students for leading a life of tolerance, enabling them to truly become model citizens in their communities.

We are not required to raise the profile of RE in our setting, however we ought to, as we have a responsibility to ensure all students reap the rewards of studying RE.

What are the limitations in raising the profile of RE?

The table lists the key hurdles many schools face in raising the profile of RE, and how we have approached them in our setting:

Limitation	What does the research say?	How have we approached this?
Inadequate curriculum time allocation to delivering RE, leading to lack of recognition	• All schools that are state-funded, including free schools and academies, are legally required to provide RE as part of their curriculum as outlined in the *National Curriculum in England* (2014). • Most locally agreed syllabuses are constructed on the assumption that the amount of curriculum time given to RE is at or above 5%. However, despite the clear legal and contractual obligations schools have to teach RE, the *State of the Nation Report* (REC, 2017) estimated that this was met in only 44% of academies and 62% of schools where the locally agreed syllabus applies.	• We have separated RE from our 'personal development' provision to allow RE to have its own timetabled allocation every week for all KS3 students. • In championing the subject to SLT and stressing the importance of our legal obligation, it was agreed that our RE provision would continue into KS4, so all students are taught non-examined core RE through our form-time routine. • At both KS3 and KS4, the quality of our RE provision has not wavered; every access to RE that students have is purposeful, challenging and meaningful, so that students continue to see the value even through non-examined provision.

Limitation	What does the research say?	How have we approached this?
Increasing number of non-specialists leading and/or delivering RE, resulting in lack of high-quality RE	• According to the 2017 *State of the Nation Report*, only 58% of RE lessons were taught by subject specialists in schools where the locally agreed syllabus applied, and 47% in academies. • The 2024 *Deep and Meaningful?* Ofsted report concluded that the better-quality RE included strong teacher subject knowledge and a well-organised curriculum. Though not impossible, without adequate training or specialism, this remains a difficult task.	• We deliver termly CPD to non-specialists teaching RE on a topical basis. This CPD includes the purpose of the topic, its place within the curriculum, how our 'golden threads' are shown, misconceptions that may arise and further reading. • All topics are supported with teacher answer booklets. These not only include answers to tasks, but also questions to ask, core content students must know, and guidance on adaptation to stretch or support learners.
SLT often undervalue the complexities of teaching diverse worldviews, causing lack of recognition	• The Ofsted *Research Review* of RE (2021) concludes that the limitations in the quality of RE are in part due to the subject being weakly framed, so that it is often considered by school leaders as an afterthought. • The report recommends that senior leaders should recognise that if they invest in a high-quality RE curriculum, well taught by subject specialists, then they will not have to make reactive changes to it in order to incorporate (what should otherwise be) the latest whole-school initiatives.	• To prevent any diminishing of the subject, I have ensured that RE carries the same value and place as history or geography. For example, in matters of formal assessment at KS3, RE exams take place alongside history and geography to give the same value. • Our curriculum is multifaceted and challenging, leading to positive outcomes and strong reputation among students. This in turn supports a strong reputation among SLT.

Limitation	What does the research say?	How have we approached this?
Parental views are often misguided about the nature and importance of RE	• Schools have to teach RE, but parents can withdraw their children for all or part of the lessons (*National Curriculum in England*, 2014). • In 2012, a YouGov poll showed that 14% of Britons say RE should not be taught in schools at all (Gardiner, 2012). • In 2022, almost three-fifths (58%) of British adults said religious studies is 'not very important' (31%) or 'not at all important' (27%) in secondary education. However, Culham St Gabriel's Trust found increasingly positive findings (YouGov, 2022).	• Our curriculum is relevant to our cohort of students. It prompts discussion for students to converse with family members about their attitudes in response. • We invite students of all and no faith to contribute, for example to our school newsletter, so that parents can share in the pride of their children. • During open days, we showcase how RE contributes to our wider school culture, such as quality competition entries, so that parents understand the value RE has at our school.

So, how can we raise the profile of RE?

I view this as a process in three parts, as shown in Figure 13.1.

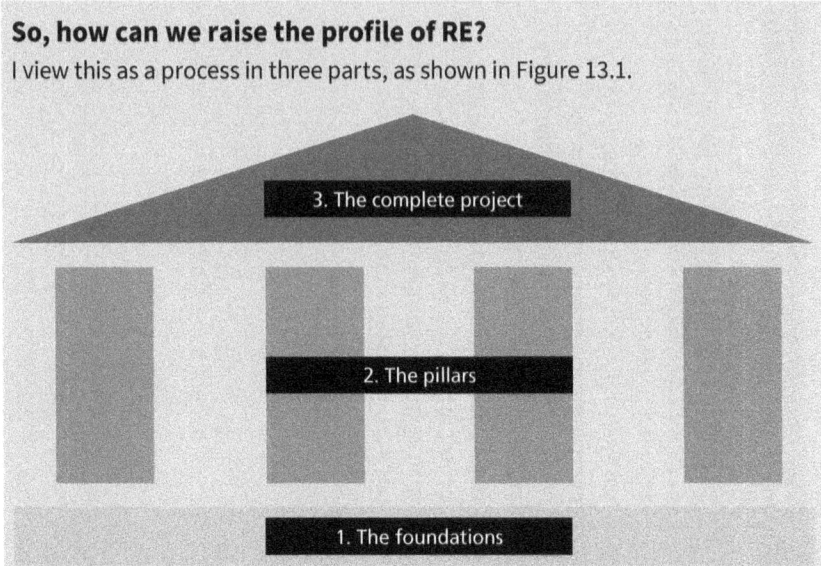

▲ Figure 13.1 The three-part process of raising the profile of RE

1. The foundations
There are several prerequisites to ensure the foundations are laid that raise the profile of RE in a school setting, including, though not limited to, a passionate subject leader, a relevant curriculum and an SLT that sees value in RE.

As a passionate subject leader, I live by the mantra 'Wherever history and geography are, RE will be there too.' Though RE no longer forms part of the English Baccalaureate, unlike its counterparts in humanities, I am adamant that RE be given the same standard of value. For example, in my setting, RE, history and geography all set formal examinations at KS3 in the same time period. All three subjects are assessed rigorously in the same way, though not necessary for RE. A passionate subject leader ought to share that same competitive thirst for representation and success. This involves a willingness to put work into raising the profile of RE in the short term, in order to reap the long-term benefits and inevitable successful outcomes.

The importance of RE within the curriculum has previously been established. However, when taught within one lesson per week, this amounts to less than 40 lessons on average per academic year. This demonstrates how every lesson in the curriculum must be designed carefully and purposefully to ensure powerful knowledge. Our RE curriculum is relevant to our cohort of students in terms of religious demographics. This enables our students to feel seen and therefore engage with the curriculum content in reflecting on their own worldviews.

Finally, the recommendations I outline below would be amiss without an SLT that sees value in RE. Some may not be in such a privileged position, but one ought to remember that this is a journey of raising the profile of RE – not just among students, but among senior leaders too.

2. The pillars
The pillars (such as those presented in the table that follows) are the part of the process where one can now build on the foundations through action. These actions do not need to be extensive or numerous – in fact, I was selective in what brings about the most impact while protecting curriculum time. I simply asked myself, 'What would make my students feel seen, heard and valued?'

While the table does not present an exhaustive list, there are many other ways that RE can have a greater impact on wider school culture, which are outlined in this chapter.

3. The complete project
A cumulation of all of the above leads to what I call 'the complete project': RE being a valued, highly respected and necessary part of the school curriculum and wider school culture. As mentioned, raising the profile of RE is a journey – but a rewarding one. Teachers of RE know best the true value of the subject, and we therefore have a responsibility to ensure that this is recognised by all stakeholders involved in the personal development of our students.

Strategy	What does this involve?	Considerations
Interfaith Week: A week dedicated to celebrating diverse religious traditions	• The timing of Interfaith Week is chosen specifically – in the past, this has been during Ramadan and in the lead-up to Easter/Passover, to raise greater awareness and invite further discussion. • Promotion of Interfaith Week – a purpose-built graphic was created free of charge using Canva. This ensures the week is given status and value, and is viewed professionally. This graphic and colour scheme is used for all Interfaith Week-related resources. • 'Bingo' competition – a low-scale competition where students must seek answers and complete a worksheet. Completed entries are awarded. • Art competition – a larger-scale competition that runs over two weeks, where students are invited to submit entries in the form of poetry or art in response to an interfaith theme (e.g. peace). • Lunchtime discussions – challenging and philosophical questions are printed and shared on refectory tables. Teachers are invited to have lunch with students and discuss questions. • Curriculum-wide questioning – all lessons start with a 'Recall 6' quiz. All subjects make one question relevant to religion for the duration of the week. Curriculum leaders are provided with a bank of interfaith-themed questions and answers to choose from. • Online promotion – during the week, interfaith-themed recipes are shared via our Humanities Twitter page (@TAL_Humanities), as well as quiz (poll) questions around religious traditions.	• Timing to organise – invite a committee of students to support the organisation or delegate within the department. • Timeline of events – our large-scale competition usually begins prior to Interfaith Week, to promote it in advance. • Additional opportunities include promotion of religion in different subject areas, such as language, history, geography, poetry, art, etc.

Strategy	What does this involve?	Considerations
	• Investment in library books – we promote a culture of reading, and during Interfaith Week a specific display is organised that showcases interfaith-themed books.	
Religious celebrations: Recognising celebrations that reflect the cohort of your students	Our student demographic is predominantly Christian and Muslim, so we prioritise celebrating Ramadan and Easter (fewer celebrations, but in more depth). • CPD – in Ramadan, we deliver CPD to all staff, to encourage having open conversations with students. • Staff fast – colleagues are invited to participate in a fast and share their reflections with students. • 30 Acts of Kindness calendar – a recurring calendar during the month of Ramadan that provides a daily act of kindness for students to achieve, as well as weekend challenges, in order to promote the values associated with Ramadan. • Easter competition – a recurring competition of guessing how many Easter eggs are in the jar. This is open to all form groups with a reward for the winning team. • Easter quizzes – a variety of different Easter challenges are shared on refectory tables in the week leading up to Easter. This engages students on their knowledge of Easter in a fun and competitive way.	• Promotion of events – as with Interfaith Week, specific graphics are created on Canva to raise the events' profile. • The 30 Acts of Kindness are promoted daily through form time, heads of year, and form tutors. • Easter quizzes can be created easily via AI technology.

Strategy	What does this involve?	Considerations
External visitors: Speakers of faith are invited to discuss and answer questions	• We have contacted local places of worship to invite speakers of faith to our school, many of whom offer the potential of providing religious artefacts. This also tends to be low cost. RE Hubs also offer a selection of faith speakers categorised by region. • Format of invitation – we have previously invited speakers into our classrooms in a 'hot seat' format, where students are prepared in advance with challenging questions to pose to the speakers. This gives the students more autonomy to lead the discussion, further engaging them in conversation.	• Consider vetting of speakers if sourcing locally. • Involve students in the questioning of speakers and provide notice in advance to build the excitement.
Assemblies: Make relevant to the promotion of RE	• We have a rotation of assemblies that centre around significant people of faith or no faith; these carry important and inspirational life lessons for all students. Previous assemblies have included Guru Nanak (with a focus on equality) and Rumi (with a focus on spirituality). • Inviting guest speakers and external visitors to deliver assemblies – spreading this out over the academic year ensures that RE remains a prominent topic of discussion. • Inviting students to participate in delivering assemblies – this requires more preparation, but it engages students in the study and discussion of RE to confidently lead assemblies on a topic of their interest.	• Consider the topics that are relevant to your cohort of students – what values, stories, religions or people would it benefit them most to hear and learn about?

Strategy	What does this involve?	Considerations
Competitive success: Encouraging healthy competition	• At our school, students take multiple-choice tests as a form of summative assessment. Healthy competition allows them to value RE among other subjects. For example, I show students the comparison of scores between RE and other subjects, and between their form groups, to encourage healthy competition. As a result, RE is consistently one of the highest-scoring subjects. • We encourage students to share their revision and preparation for assessments with us and then nominate these students for awards as their reward. We also showcase this in lessons, assemblies and online to prompt other students to do the same.	• Requires department-wide support to be effective; every teacher should promote healthy competition, to continue to raise the profile of RE.
Extracurricular clubs: Inviting students to enjoy engagement in multiple disciplines in RE.	There are numerous clubs relevant to RE that can be offered, such as book clubs, film clubs, religious art clubs and more. We currently offer these clubs: • Philosophy Club – students discuss a different philosophical question on a weekly basis. The session begins by learning different philosophical views in response to the question, and then students are invited to debate in small groups, before feeding back to the class. Previous debates have included the possibility of an afterlife, free speech, the ethics of veganism, innate goodness and general ethics.	• Consideration of timing required to promote, plan and support the running of clubs.

Strategy	What does this involve?	Considerations
	• Interfaith Club – this club centres around education about minority and new religions. Each week, students learn about a new faith that is not taught within our curriculum. They are invited to learn about, discuss and research the faith. By the end of the 12-week club programme, students present back to the class on one faith they have learned about. • Psychology Club – though less relevant to RE, the club is designed to invite students into psychological and ethical topics of discussion, some of which overlap with our RE curriculum. For example, this can involve the discussion of free will and the functions of the brain in allowing for freedom of thought and action, which complement and reflect the learning of predestination and free will in our RE curriculum. • We celebrate and showcase the work of all clubs to further promote them in the future.	• There are many resources online from colleagues who have shared resources from their clubs, and AI technology can also support with the creation and planning of resources.

Strategy	What does this involve?	Considerations
Newsletter: Promotion of RE accessible to parents/carers	• We have a termly newsletter that is shared to all students, parents and carers. Each term it is dedicated to a different area of our academy. • Our recent RE-themed newsletter invited students from all year-groups to contribute. It included the curriculum journey and current learning of students, celebration of competition winners and entries, exemplary work completed in lessons, highlights of our annual Interfaith Week and culture day, and contributions of students. This newsletter (the 13th edition) is available for viewing via the Trinity Academy Leeds website: https://leeds.trinitymat.org/voice-newsletter-13/.	• A newsletter does not have to be extensive – it could focus on one success of RE in the term. The more students that are involved, celebrated and have contributed, the greater the promotion of RE.

BIBLIOGRAPHY

Armstrong, K. (2001). *Buddha*. Penguin LIVES Series. Viking.

Barton, C. (2023). *Tips for Teachers: 400+ Ideas to Improve Your Teaching*. John Catt Educational.

Bowie, R. A., Panjwani, F., Carswell, M. and Clemmey, K. (2020). *Texts and Teachers: The Practice Guide*. Canterbury Christ Church University. Available at: https://repository.canterbury.ac.uk/item/8vzy1.

Brewer, W. (n.d.). *Learning Theory: Schema Theory*. Available at: https://education.stateuniversity.com/pages/2175/Learning-Theory-SCHEMA-THEORY.html.

Buisst, W. (2024). 'Hinterlands', *Buisst_Teaching*. Available at: https://venividiteachy.wordpress.com/2024/03/27/hinterlands.

Caviglioli, O. (2019). *Dual Coding with Teachers*. John Catt Educational.

Chang, W.-C. and Ku, Y.-M. (2015). 'The effects of note-taking skills instruction on elementary students' reading', *Journal of Educational Research*, 108, pp. 278–291.

Chater, M. (2020). *Reforming RE: Power and Knowledge in a Worldviews Curriculum*. John Catt Educational.

Chiles, M. (2023). *Powerful Questioning: Strategies for Improving Learning and Retention in the Classroom*. Crown House Publishing.

Christodoulou, D. (2017). *Making Good Progress? The Future of Assessment for Learning*. Oxford University Press.

Church, I. M. and Samuelson, P. L. (2017). *Intellectual Humility: An Introduction to the Philosophy and Science*. Bloomsbury Academic.

Claire, H. and Holden, C. (2007). *The Challenge of Teaching Controversial Issues*. Trentham Books.

Clarke, C. (2025). 'Three possible outcomes for RE … a choice to be made', RE:ONLINE, 28 January. Available at: www.reonline.org.uk/2025/01/28/three-possible-outcomes-for-re.

Commission on Religious Education (CoRE) (2018). *Religion and Worldviews: The Way Forward. A National Plan for RE*. Religious Education Council of England and Wales. Available at: https://religiouseducationcouncil.org.uk/rec/wp-content/uploads/2017/05/Final-Report-of-the-Commission-on-RE.pdf.

Cooling, T. (1994). *Concept Cracking: Exploring Christian Beliefs in School*. The Stapleford Centre. Available at: www.natre.co.uk/uploads/Support%20materials%20for%20videos/concept_cracking.pdf.

Cooling, T. (2025). 'Should RE be included in the national curriculum? It's the standard, not the stuff!' *RE:ONLINE*, 29 January. Available at: www.reonline.org.uk/2025/01/29/should-re-be-included-in-the-nc.

Cooling, T., Bowie, B. and Panjwani, F. (2020). *Worldviews in Religious Education*. Theos Think Tank. Available at: www.theosthinktank.co.uk/cmsfiles/Worldview-in-Religious-Education---FINAL-PDF-merged.pdf.

Counsell, C. (2018). 'Senior curriculum leadership 1: The indirect manifestation of knowledge: (A) curriculum as narrative', *The Dignity of the Thing*, 7 April. Available at: https://thedignityofthethingblog.wordpress.com/2018/04/07/senior-curriculum-leadership-1-the-indirect-manifestation-of-knowledge-a-curriculum-as-narrative.

Counsell, C. (2025). 'It's time to finally put RE in the national curriculum where it belongs', *Schools Week*, 30 January. Available at: https://schoolsweek.co.uk/its-time-to-finally-put-re-in-the-national-curriculum-where-it-belongs.

Coventry & Warwickshire Local Authorities (2024). *Coventry & Warwickshire Religion and Worldviews Agreed Syllabus for Religious Education 2024–2029*. Available at: www.churchofengland.org/sites/default/files/2024-12/coventry-and-warwickshire-agreed-syllabus-2024-2029_0.pdf.

Coventry City Council (n.d.). *Standing Advisory Council on Religious Education (SACRE)*. Available at: www.coventry.gov.uk/standing-advisory-council-religious-education-sacre.

Cox, D. (2020). 'The golden threads: substantive concepts in RE', *Miss D Cox Blog*, 18 July. Available at: https://missdcoxblog.wordpress.com/2020/07/18/the-golden-threads-substantive-concepts-in-re.

Cox, D. (2021a). 'Disciplines: a new direction for assessment in RE?' *Miss D Cox Blog*, 27 March. Available at: https://missdcoxblog.wordpress.com/2021/03/27/disciplines-a-new-direction-for-assessment-in-re.

Cox, D. (2021b). 'The Ofsted RE Research Review and Assessment: thoughts & suggestions', *Miss D Cox Blog*, 4 July. Available at: https://missdcoxblog.wordpress.com/2021/07/04/the-ofsted-re-research-review-and-assessment-thoughts-suggestions.

Cox, D. (2023). 'A worldviews approach to RE: what it really means for teachers', *Miss D Cox Blog*, 18 June. Available at: https://missdcoxblog.wordpress.com/2023/06/18/a-worldviews-approach-to-re-what-it-really-means-for-teachers.

Cox, D. (2024). 'Digging deeper: hinterland and core knowledge in RE', *Miss D Cox Blog*, 2 April. Available at: https://missdcoxblog.wordpress.com/2024/04/02/digging-deeper-hinterland-and-core-knowledge-in-re.

Department for Children, Schools and Families (DCSF) (2010). *Religious Education in English Schools: Non-Statutory Guidance 2010*. Available at: https://assets.publishing.service.gov.uk/media/5a7adb3ce5274a34770e7953/DCSF-00114-2010.pdf.

Department for Education (2013a). *National Curriculum in England: Framework for Key Stages 1 to 4*. Available at: www.gov.uk/government/publications/national-curriculum-in-england-framework-for-key-stages-1-to-4/the-national-curriculum-in-england-framework-for-key-stages-1-to-4.

Department for Education (2013b). *Religious Education: Realising the Potential*. Available at: https://assets.publishing.service.gov.uk/government/uploads/system/uploads/attachment_data/file/413157/Religious_education_-_realising_the_potential.pdf.

Department for Education (2025a). *Curriculum and Assessment Review Final Report: Building a World-Class Curriculum for All*. Available at: https://assets.publishing.service.gov.uk/media/690b96bbc22e4ed8b051854d/Curriculum_and_Assessment_Review_final_report_-_Building_a_world-class_curriculum_for_all.pdf.

Department for Education (2025b). *Curriculum and Assessment Review: Interim Report*. Available at: https://assets.publishing.service.gov.uk/media/6821d69eced319d02c9060e3/Curriculum_and_Assessment_Review_interim_report.pdf.

Department for Education (2025c). *Political Impartiality in Schools*. Available at: www.gov.uk/government/publications/political-impartiality-in-schools/political-impartiality-in-schools#teaching-about-political-issues.

Diocese of Lincoln Board of Education (2025). *Assessing Progress in RE*. Available at: www.lincolndiocesaneducation.com/page/?pid=48&title=Assessing+Progress+in+RE.

Education Endowment Foundation (EEF) (2018). *Metacognition and Self-regulated Learning*. Education Endowment Foundation. Available at: https://educationendowmentfoundation.org.uk/education-evidence/guidance-reports/metacognition.

Erricker, C. and Erricker, J. (2000). *Reconstructing Religious, Spiritual and Moral Education*. Routledge.

Faith & Belief Forum (2024). *Sensitive Issues: Supporting: Students with Skills for Dialogue*. Available at: https://faithbeliefforum.org/wp-content/uploads/2024/09/FBF-School-Resources-%E2%80%93-Skills-for-Dialogue-Sensitive-issues-Autumn-2024-1.pdf.

Fraser-Pearce, J. and Stones, A. (2023). 'Knowing well in religious education', RE:ONLINE. Available at: www.reonline.org.uk/wp-content/uploads/2023/06/Knowing-Well.pdf.

Gardiner, B. (2012). 'Religious education in schools', YouGov, 8 March. Available at: https://yougov.co.uk/politics/articles/3066-religious-education-schools.

Georgiou, G. (2024). *Teacher-led Framework: An Exemplification of a Religion and Worldviews Approach in RE*. Available at: https://religiouseducationcouncil.org.uk/rec/wp-content/uploads/2024/04/24-25756-REC-Teacher-Led-Framework-Final-Report-DIGITAL-PAGES.pdf.

Georgiou, G. and Wright, K. (2020). 'Disciplinarity, religion and worldviews: making the case for theology, philosophy and human/social sciences', in Mark Chater (ed.), *Reforming RE: Power and Knowledge in a Worldviews Curriculum*. John Catt Educational.

Grimmitt, M. (ed.) (2000). *Pedagogies of Religious Education: Case Studies in the Research and Development of Good Pedagogic Practice in RE*. McCrimmon Publishing.

Hammond, J. and Hay, D. (1990). *New Methods in RE Teaching: An Experimental Approach*. Oliver & Boyd.

Hannam, P. (2024). 'Teaching religious education as if the world mattered', *British Journal of Religious Education*, 46(3), pp. 245–256.

Henrich, J. P. (2020). *The WEIRDest People in the World: How the West Became Psychologically Peculiar and Particularly Prosperous*. Farrar, Straus and Giroux.

Hochman, J. C. and Wexler, N. (2017). *The Writing Revolution: A Guide to Advancing Thinking Through Writing in All Subjects and Grades*. Wiley.

Holt, J. H. (2022). *Religious Education in the Secondary School: An Introduction to Teaching, Learning and the World Religions*, 2nd edn. Routledge.

Hook, J. N. and Davis, D. E. (2018). 'Intellectual humility and religious belief; Part 1a: Intellectual humility and religion: a psychological perspective', *Journal of Psychology and Theology*, 46(4), pp. 219–242.

Hussain, Z. (2022). 'What is a worldview?' Unit presented at NATRE StrictlyRE Conference [online], 29–30 January.

Hutton, L., Cox, D., Tharby, A. and Allison, S. (2021). *Making Every RE Lesson Count: Six Principles to Support Religious Education Teaching*. Crown House Publishing.

Independent Schools Religious Studies Association (ISRSA) (2022). *ISRSA Report: Religion and Worldviews*. Available at: https://isrsa.co.uk/wp-content/uploads/2022/06/ISRSA-Report-Religion-and-Worldviews-LowRes.pdf.

Jackson, R. (1997). *Religious Education: An Interpretive Approach*. Hodder & Stoughton.

John Templeton Foundation (n.d.). 'Intellectual humility', John Templeton Foundation. Available at: www.templeton.org/discoveries/intellectual-humility.

Kerr, D. and Huddleston, T. (2015). *Teaching Controversial Issues Through Education for Democratic Citizenship and Human Rights*. Available at: https://rm.coe.int/22122020-teaching-controversial-issues-final-web/1680a12735.

Kinnaird, J. (2021a). 'Teach them how to write like … a philosopher', *Reforming RE*, 4 May. Available at: https://reformingre.wordpress.com/2021/05/04/teach-them-how-to-write-like-a-philosopher.

Kinnaird, J. (2021b). 'Teach them how to write like a social scientist', *Reforming RE*, 25 May. Available at: https://reformingre.wordpress.com/2021/05/25/teach-them-how-to-write-like-a-social-scientist.

Kinnaird, J. (2021c). 'Teach them how to write like … a theologian', *Reforming RE*, 23 March. Available at: https://reformingre.wordpress.com/2021/03/23/teach-them-how-to-write-like-a-theologian.

Kueh, R. (2025). 'Things fall apart; the centre cannot hold', RE:ONLINE, 31 January. Available at: www.reonline.org.uk/2025/01/31/things-fall-apart-the-centre-cannot-hold.

Larkin, S., Freathy, R., Doney, J. and Freathy, G. (2020). *Metacognition, Worldviews and Religious Education: A Practical Guide for Teachers*. Routledge.

Leary, M. R. (2020). *The Psychology of Intellectual Humility*. John Templeton Foundation. Available at: www.templeton.org/wp-content/uploads/2020/08/JTF_Intellectual_Humility_final.pdf.

Lemov, D. (2010). *Teach Like a Champion: 49 Techniques That Put Students on the Path to College*. Jossey-Bass.

Lemov, D. (2021). *Teach Like a Champion 3.0: 63 Techniques That Put Students on the Path to College.* Jossey-Bass.

Lewin, D. (2023). 'After religious education: lessons from continental pedagogy', *Journal of Religious Education,* 71, pp. 197–211.

Lewin, D., Orchard, J., Christopher, K. and Brown, A. (2023). 'Reframing curriculum for religious education', *Journal of Curriculum Studies,* 55(4), pp. 369–387.

Lincoln Diocesan Education (2025). *Lincolnshire Locally Agreed Syllabus for Religious Education 2025–30.* Available at: www.lincolndioceseducation.com/_site/data/files/key_documents/CA54AAE1426142B5E48C9F7991EDEA9F.pdf.

McDonald, C. (2024). 'Superpower to see other viewpoints', *Church Times,* 16 August. Available at: www.churchtimes.co.uk/articles/2024/16-august/comment/columnists/chine-mcdonald-superpower-to-see-other-viewpoints.

McGee, N. (2019). 'Planning an interweaved key stage 3 curriculum', *RE with Mrs McGee,* 29 October. Available at: https://rewithmrsmcgee.wordpress.com/2019/10/29/planning-an-interweaved-key-stage-3-curriculum.

McGee, N. (2021). 'RE', in Myatt, M. and Tomsett, J. (eds.) *Huh: Curriculum Conversations Between Subject and Senior Leaders.* John Catt Educational, pp. 235–248.

McGee, N. (2023). 'Running an RE book club', *RE with Mrs McGee,* 5 November. Available at: https://rewithmrsmcgee.wordpress.com/2023/11/05/running-an-re-book-club.

Myatt, M. (2018). *The Curriculum: Gallimaufry to Coherence.* John Catt Educational.

Myatt, M. (2023). 'Are our resources useful and beautiful?', *Mary Myatt,* 8 June. Available at: www.marymyatt.com/blog/are-our-resources-useful-and-beautiful.

National Association of Teachers of Religious Education (NATRE) (2023). *NATRE Secondary Survey 2023.* NATRE.

National Association of Teachers of Religious Education (NATRE) (2024). *Curated List of Resources for Supporting Schools with Contentious Topics.* NATRE.

National Association of Teachers of Religious Education (NATRE) (2025) *The Curriculum Assessment Review: A Summary Report by NATRE.* Available at: https://natre.org.uk/resources/the-curriculum-assessment-review-a-summary-report-by-natre/.

Norfolk County Council (2019). *Norfolk Agreed Syllabus 2019: A Religious Education for the Future.* Available at: www.schools.norfolk.gov.uk/media/13960/download/pdf/norfolk-religious-education-agreed-syllabus-2019.pdf.

Ofsted (2019). *Education Inspection Framework (EIF).* Available at: www.gov.uk/government/publications/education-inspection-framework/education-inspection-framework.

Ofsted (2021). *Research Review Series: Religious Education.* Available at: www.gov.uk/government/publications/research-review-series-religious-education.

Ofsted (2024). *Deep and Meaningful? The Religious Education Subject Report.* Available at: www.gov.uk/government/publications/subject-report-series-religious-education/deep-and-meaningful-the-religious-education-subject-report.

Pett, S. (2022). *Religion and Worldviews in the Classroom: Developing a Worldviews Approach.* Available at: https://religiouseducationcouncil.org.uk/rec/wp-content/uploads/2022/09/REC-Worldviews-Project-double-pages-Revised-cover-v1.2.pdf.

Pett, S. (2024). *Developing a Religion and Worldviews Approach in Religious Education in England: A Handbook for Curriculum Writers.* Religious Education Council of England and Wales. Available at: https://religiouseducationcouncil.org.uk/rec/wp-content/uploads/2024/04/24-25698-REC-Handbook-A4-DIGITAL-PAGES.pdf.

Pinkett, M. and Roberts, M. (2019). *Boys Don't Try? Rethinking Masculinity in Schools.* Routledge.

Platter, P. (2023). 'Personal worldviews: lessons from James Fowler', *Journal of Religious Education,* 71, pp. 213–224.

Plymouth City Council (2024). *Plymouth Agreed Syllabus for RE 2024–2029.* Available at: www.churchofengland.org/sites/default/files/2024-12/plymouth-agreed-syllabus-2024-2029.pdf.

Polanyi, M. (1958). *Personal Knowledge: Towards a Post-Critical Philosophy.* University of Chicago Press.

Polanyi, M. (1966). *The Tacit Dimension.* Doubleday & Company.

Quigley, A. (2018). *Closing the Vocabulary Gap.* Routledge.

Religious Education Council of England and Wales (2023a). *National Content Standard for Religious Education in England.* Religious Education Council of England and Wales. Available at: https://religiouseducationcouncil.

org.uk/rec/wp-content/uploads/2023/09/RE-Council-National-Content-Standard-for-Religious-Education-for-England-July23.pdf.

Religious Education Council of England and Wales (2023b). *Spread the Word – Parents Value an Education in Religion and Worldviews!* Religious Education Council of England and Wales. Available at: https://religiouseducationcouncil.org.uk/2023/01/spread-the-word-parents-value-an-education-in-religion-and-worldviews.

Religious Education Council of England and Wales and National Association of Teachers of Religious Education (2017). *State of the Nation Report on RE Provision at Secondary Schools in England.* Available at: https://religiouseducationcouncil.org.uk/resource/state-of-the-nation-report-on-re-provision.

Religious Education Policy Unit (2023). *Addressing the Crisis: Revitalising Religious Education Teacher Recruitment.* Available at: www.cstg.org.uk/wp-content/uploads/sites/4/2024/03/Addressing-the-Crisis.pdf.

Rosenshine, B. (2012). 'Principles of instruction: research-based strategies that all teachers should know', *American Educator*, Spring. Available at: www.aft.org/sites/default/files/Rosenshine.pdf.

Saunders, A. (2024). 'Teaching personal knowledge: why we must help learners navigate their (changing) positionality in the classroom', *Education Matters*, 18 June. Available at: https://missavecarter.wordpress.com/2024/06/18/teaching-personal-knowledge-why-we-must-help-learners-navigate-their-changing-positionality-in-the-classroom.

Sealy, C. (ed.) (2020). *The researchED Guide to The Curriculum: An Evidence-Informed Guide for Teachers.* John Catt Educational.

Sherrington, T. and Caviglioli, O. (2020). *Teaching WalkThrus: Five-Step Guides to Instructional Coaching.* John Catt Educational.

Smart, N. (1984). *The Religious Experience of Mankind.* Fount.

Steele, K. (2023). 'Using mini whiteboards in religious education', *Miss Eva RE Teacher*, 19 June. Available at: https://missevareteacher.wordpress.com/2023/06/19/using-mini-whiteboards-in-religious-education.

Tharani, A. (2020). *The Worldview Project: Discussion Papers.* Religious Education Council of England and Wales. Available at: https://religiouseducationcouncil.org.uk/rec/wp-content/uploads/2021/01/The-Worldview-Project.pdf.

Theos Think Tank (2025). *Why RE Matters.* Available at: www.theosthinktank.co.uk/cmsfiles/RE-Pamphlet_V3.pdf.

Warner-Meanwell, D. (n.d.). *Story, Source, Scholarship: A Collaborative Resource for History Teachers.* Available at: https://storysourcescholarship.wordpress.com.

Wiliam, D. (2011). *Embedded Formative Assessment.* Learning Sciences International.

Williams, D. (1993). *Sisters in the Wilderness: The Challenge of Womanist God.* Orbis.

Willingham, D. T. (2009). *Why Don't Students Like School? A Cognitive Scientist Answers Questions About How the Mind Works and What It Means for the Classroom.* Jossey-Bass.

Wright, A. (1993). *Religious Education in the Secondary School: Prospects for Religious Literacy.* David Fulton.

YouGov (2022). 'Political tracker survey'. Available at: https://docs.cdn.yougov.com/fpyiw3xdad/P_Main_Political_Tracker_Survey_Rotation8_sr_2.pdf.

Photo credits

Photos reproduced by permission of: **p.50** tl © Peter/stock.adobe.com, t © William/stock.adobe.com, c © Mathew/stock.adobe.com; **p.167** Robert A. Waller Memorial Fund. CC0 Public Domain Designation, https://www.artic.edu/artworks/80084/the-crucifixion; **p.172** © Pictorial Press Ltd/Alamy Stock Photo; **p.174** © GRANGER Historical Picture Archive/Alamy Stock Photo.